THE COMPLETE
SALES
LETTER BOOK

THE COMPLETE SALES LETTER BOOK

Model Letters for Every Selling Situation

Rhonda Harris
Ann McIntyre

SHARPE PROFESSIONAL

An imprint of M.E. Sharpe, INC.

This publication is designed to provide accurate information in regard to the subject matter
covered. It is sold with the understanding that the publisher is not engaged in rendering legal,
accounting, or other professional service. If legal advice or other expert assistance is required,
the services of a competent professional person should be sought.

—From the Declaration of Principles adopted by
a Committee of the American Bar Association and
a Committee of Publishers and Associations

Library of Congress Cataloging-in-Publication Data

Harris, Rhonda
The complete sales letter book : model letters for
every selling situation / by Rhonda Harris and Ann McIntyre.
p. cm.
Includes index.
ISBN 0-7656-0083-8 (alk. paper)
1. Sales letters—Handbooks, manuals, etc.   2. Commercial
correspondence—Handbooks, manuals, etc.
I. McIntyre, Ann.   II. Title.
HF5730.H37   1997
658.8′1—dc21   97-33176
CIP
Printed in the United States of America

The paper used in this publication meets the minimum requirements of
American National Standard for Information Sciences—
Permanence of Paper for Printed Library Materials,
ANSI Z 39.48-1984.

BM (c)   10   9   8   7   6   5   4   3   2   1

About the Authors

Rhonda Harris has more than twenty years of publishing experience, as both a writer and an editor. As an advertising copywriter, she wrote direct-mail letters to market trade books on a variety of topics. She has edited more than forty books for general and college markets on subjects that range from freestyle skiing to international business. For more than seven years, she was managing editor at the Federal Reserve Bank of Dallas, and she is currently a communications consultant in Dallas, Texas. She is a graduate of Southern Methodist University.

Ann McIntyre is a fifteen-year sales veteran. She is Senior Marketing Representative for Storage Technology Corporation, located in Dallas, Texas, where for the past twelve years she has managed key accounts. Dealing with a multiyear sales cycle, her representation of Storage Tek to customers includes managing the account teams that support her customers, developing solutions to customer challenges, cost justifying, and implementing those solutions. She is a member of Storage Tek's Summit Club and is a graduate of Southern Methodist University.

Acknowledgments

This book would not have been possible without the effort and cooperation of many people. We are particularly indebted to Olivia Lane, our editor. Many individuals from all types of organizations were generous with their contributions of model letters. We are especially appreciative to these contributors:

Annie Adams	Frank McIntyre
Bob Campbell	Lynn Morrison
Ron Campbell	Mary L. Piper
Steve Case	Blake Reed
Stephanie Chisholm	Michelle Robinson
Leslie Diers	Pat Romboletti, The Write Sales System™
Brian Duffy	Margie Sullivan
Derrick Gamradt	Susan Wagner
Ralph Greenlee	Tom Wenkstern
William C. Hubbard	John Williams
Ed Keith	Sabrina Zambaradino

Special thanks to Gail Whelan for many hours of help.

What This Book Will Do for You

The Complete Sales Letter Book: Model Letters for Every Selling Situation is for any sales professional who's ever needed inspiration to cope with tough selling circumstances, been too busy to compose original letters for important but routine messages, or felt unsure of how to talk to customers about sticky situations. Authors Rhonda Harris and Ann McIntyre draw from their experience in sales and publishing to show you step-by-step, from introductions to reorders, how effective, well-written letters fit into the sales process.

The authors combine original letters with examples from other successful professionals. The result is a compendium of effective correspondence that will enhance the user's productivity. Sales representatives and managers alike will find time-saving techniques that result in better communication with customers and staff, with fewer misunderstandings about who ordered what, in what quantity, for delivery when.

Letters Throughout the Sales Cycle

The book's table of contents mirrors the progression of the sales cycle. Part 1, "Letters to Get the Sales Cycle Started," inspires and motivates users to continue prospecting even in daunting circumstances. Chapter 1, "Introductions," offers advice on challenging situations: when they don't know you and you don't know them; when the decision maker changes in mid-sale; and after a customer has had a bad experience with your company. Chapter 2, "Getting Started Through Direct Mail," suggests direct-mail techniques for getting started in finance, insurance, and other fields. Letters in chapter 3, "Letters That Get Appointments and Build Goodwill," will help persuade prospects to see you. The chapter concludes with a section on model "thank yous" that express how much you value the customer's time and business. The letters in chapter 4, "Cover Letters," are designed to give you the competitive edge when customers are deciding whose contract to accept, which proposal makes the most sense, or whether your proposed solution is worth the cost. Part 2, "Letters for Overcoming Obstacles, Keeping the Sale Going, and Closing and Confirming the Sale," demonstrates how to get beyond obstacles to close the sale and confirm the order. Letters in chapter 5, "Persuading the Customer to Move Forward," tell prospects why your firm is worth a second look, with examples for product news, market updates, and references for you and your company. Letters in chapter 6, "Letters to Help You Recover When Things Go Wrong," are written to help get past potentially disastrous situations: product delays, bad publicity, one party's Chapter 11 bankruptcy, poor service, and more. Chapter 7, "Letters to Help Disappointed Customers," shows how to maintain goodwill and work toward solutions with customers: finding a fair compromise, showing respect despite differing views of a situation, reassuring the customer after your company falters.

In chapter 8, "Presenting Pricing," the focus is on how to explain the terms you offer while eliminating confusion and conveying your flexibility. Chapter 9, "Letters to Close the Sale and Confirm the Order," moves past problem solving to proven techniques to help close the sale, such as establishing a time limit on the offer, explaining the limited availability of the product, and confirming details and processes after the sale.

The theme of Part 3, "Letters That Sustain Lifetime Relationships with Customers," is how to sustain relationships with customers through timely written communication. Chapter 10, "Keeping the Customer Informed About Your Company," suggests occasions to write customers with updates about your company: what to say when the company is the subject of good or bad financial announcements, when changes in management or ownership occur, when the company releases new products, or when you expand services. Chapter 11, "Showing Continued Interest in the Customer," continues the theme of ongoing interest in the customer on a more personal note. The chapter provides examples of congratulatory messages, acknowledgments of changes in the customer's company, personal greetings for many occasions, and expressions of appreciation for the customer's continued business. Special events, such as a golf tournament, dinner with company executives, open house, and preview of your new product, are the focus of chapter 12, "Special Events and Customer Appreciation." Chapter 13, "References and Recognition," demonstrates how to recognize milestones in the customer's career or organization and ways to request that the customer serve as a reference for you.

In Part 4, "Letters in Cyberspace," the book concludes with a look at online communication. Sample letters from online correspondence illustrate how companies are adapting to the new media and why e-mail is becoming an increasingly important means of communicating information about products, selling strategies, promotions, and productivity inside and outside the organization. Chapter 14, "Customers Are Just An E-mail Away," provides techniques for using electronic mail over the Internet to enhance sales to home-page visitors. Chapter 15, "Improving Internal Communication with the New Media," suggests ways to keep in touch with associates and solve problems at the home office. "Letters" in the chapter are e-mail messages that recognize excellent performance, track service problems, and encourage effective teamwork.

Selling Outlook

"Selling Outlook," a special feature at the end of each chapter, provides practical and philosophical insight into sales and relates the chapter topic to sales correspondence. Among the advice offered: why "in writing" is so important in problem situations, when to type versus handwrite thank yous, tips for writing about competitors, and the power of your sincere interest in customers.

Words That Sell

"Words That Sell," a feature at the end of each part, can boost your confidence as a writer and help prevent common mistakes. The feature provides answers to frequently asked questions about grammar and usage and advice about sometimes confusing words.

How to Use This Book

With more than 450 letters, the book guides you through specific sales situations— prospecting, problem resolution, proposal cover letters, customer appreciation notes and invitations, interoffice correspondence, and much more. By skimming the table of contents, you will become familiar with the topics covered and can then refer to the appropriate chapter and examples as situations arise. The letters can be used "as is" or can be quickly tailored with just a few words. The book is not intended to provide single, pat answers for all occasions. Instead, authors' comments precede examples to explain relevant sales strategies and contingencies.

Contents

Part 2. Letters for Overcoming Obstacles, Keeping the Sale Going, and Closing and Confirming the Sale

Chapter 6. Letters to Help You Recover When Things Go Wrong **225**

Part 3. Letters That Sustain Lifetime Relationships with Customers

Chapter 10. Keeping the Customer Informed About Your Company   353

Letting Customers Know about Corporate Changes

Part 4. Letters in Cyberspace

Chapter 15. Improving Internal Communication with the New Media   515

Messages to Support Teamwork

Reminders for Sales Support Departments

PART 1
Letters to Get the Sales Cycle Started

CHAPTER 1

Introductions

"Say the magic words." It's a phrase you learned in childhood, a promise that what you say can make wishes reality. Words really can work magic. They can make people interested in you, your company, your product. Well-chosen words can initiate the sales cycle and, ultimately, mean the difference between a banner year or a missed quota.

This chapter presents letters of introduction designed to open a dialogue and move the sales process to the next phase. By following the models in this chapter, you can write persuasive letters that work for you. You'll tell prospects who you are, what you are selling, and, most important, why they should see you. Show them you want to learn more about their requirements, and suggest the next move—a phone call, an appointment when you're in town. They will be delighted to hear from you.

CHAPTER 1. CONTENTS

They Don't Know You and You Don't Know Them

MODEL LETTER 1.1

"I Think You'll Be Interested Because . . ."

The letters that follow illustrate first steps in what could be long, productive client–vendor relationships. These examples are easily adaptable to other situations; decide what is unique about the situation, then address that issue in terms of the benefits you and your firm offer.

Dear Ms. Moore:

I am writing to introduce myself to you. My name is Dave Mura, and I am the new sales representative for OneCo Pharmaceuticals. I have been with the firm since April and in the pharmaceutical industry for five years.

Although I will be calling on your company for the first time, the reputation of Standard Drug Stores is second to none. Your company is known for providing top-quality products at a great value, which is why I think you will be interested in OneCo's promotional co-op opportunities for the new skin-care products we are introducing this month.

I would like to discuss the new line, along with all the OneCo products, in a personal meeting. I will call you next week to discuss when you might be available. If you need assistance with anything in the meantime, please do not hesitate to let me know at 888-555-4141.

Sincerely,

Dave Mura

MODEL LETTER 1.2

Introducing Yourself to Your Competitor's Customer

An approach that frequently succeeds is to show respect for the prospect's current vendor choice and initially ask only for orders the main vendor cannot handle.

Dear Mr. Martin:

My name is Ellen Bernard. I am writing to introduce Silicon Technologies Inc., and myself to you. STI has specialized in manufacturing memory chips for the microprocessor industry for the past ten years. I have been with STI for three years, handling large accounts in the Southwest. Recently, STI gave me responsibility for your account, and I am pleased and honored to accept that responsibility.

STI originally made a name for itself with the introduction of the first 4MB memory chip. STI reached the marketplace with reliable technology a full year before any other manufacturer. Since then, we have consistently led the industry with new technology, as well as production capacity and service. Our customer list includes most of the major companies in the industry.

I understand XYZ currently orders most of its chip requirements from ABC Company. Consistently working with a single vendor, especially a quality vendor such as ABC, has its benefits. Nevertheless, there will be times when ABC cannot deliver the product you need, when you need it. Let me remind you that STI will be here when you need us.

It will benefit us both to familiarize ourselves with each other's organization and products. I look forward to meeting you as soon as possible to suggest some ways that purchasing at least part of your requirements from STI could result in a higher-quality product and faster manufacturing process for XYZ.

I will call next week to arrange an initial meeting. Thank you for your time and your consideration.

Sincerely,

Ellen Bernard

Introducing Your Company to an Account That Has Never Let You In

When you have tried but failed to get into an account, one of the best ways to get reconsideration is to give the prospect a new reason to see you.

Dear Mr. Kennedy:

In light of XYZ's rigorous vendor selection criteria, I would like to point out new ways XYZ will benefit from a working knowledge of Silicon Technologies' product design, manufacturing, and support capabilities. This year Silicon Technologies earned a five-star rating from the independent market watch firm, the Howard Group. After ten years of designing, manufacturing, and supporting quality custom chips, the Howard Group has recognized Silicon's long-standing dedication to product excellence. Knowing that XYZ buys only from companies with a five-star Howard rating, I want to bring this award to your attention to let you know that your choice of vendors and product solutions has now been expanded to include Silicon Technologies.

I have long-standing respect for your organization and its accomplishments, both in the marketplace and as a civic leader. I hope you will allow me to show you how Silicon Technologies can help XYZ maintain and enhance its well-deserved reputation. Silicon Technologies is eager to demonstrate our ability to perform as one of your top-quality vendors.

Thank you for your attention and your consideration. I look forward to a long and productive relationship with XYZ.

Sincerely,

Jason Jones

MODEL LETTER 1.4

What to Say When the Customer Was Especially Close to the Previous Rep

Letters can help break the ice in just about any situation, such as when the client adored the previous rep and may not be enthused about meeting someone new.

Dear Dr. Phillips:

I am Medical Products' new representative in your area. My name is Mike Smith, and I have been with Medical Products for two years, primarily in an out-of-state territory.

I am sure you were as disappointed as I was to learn that your previous representative, Tanya Jamison, left Medical Products to pursue an opportunity with another company. Tanya spoke highly of you and your colleagues. I know it will not be easy to take her place, as she had been calling on you for more than five years.

I will miss Tanya very much myself—she was my mentor when I was getting started in this industry. Nevertheless, I am thrilled to have the opportunity to work with Tanya's customers and look forward to getting to know everyone at your practice.

I will call next week to discuss when we might meet.

Sincerely,

Mike Smith

When You Know the Customer Mistrusted the Previous Rep

Reestablishing trust takes time and new opportunities to prove yourself. A phone call might get you a prompt refusal, but a letter can serve as a more subtle, lasting persuader to give your company another chance.

Dear Dr. Moore:

My name is Susan Richards, and I have been an account executive with Medical Products, Inc., for three years. Medical Products assigned me to cover your account when your former representative left our company.

The opportunity to handle your account is a significant one for me, and I want you to know that I will do everything possible to establish a trusting, accountable business relationship with everyone at your practice.

I will call next week to see when it would be convenient for me to stop by. I look forward to meeting you soon.

Sincerely,

Susan Richards

Model Letter 1.6

What to Say About Your Career Change

Sometimes the very subject that makes you hesitant about taking that first step is the subject you should address directly, as this career-changer's example illustrates.

Dear Maggie:

I am writing to you to introduce myself. My name is Margaret Brown, and I have just begun a new career as an Allied Software sales rep. I decided to join Allied after gaining firsthand experience with their software, when I was managing a family business and needed an easy-to-use accounting package. I found the product very user-friendly, and when my youngest child entered school this year, I approached Allied for a sales position. This will be my first selling experience, although I managed an office for five years.

I am very excited about this opportunity at Allied, and am looking forward to getting to know you and everyone in your office.

Sincerely,

Margaret Brown

Introducing the New Sales Manager Who Asked to Meet This Customer

Customers like to stay informed about vendors' companies. Most customers will find your request to introduce them to your manager flattering.

Dear Mitchell:

I am writing this letter to tell you that we have a new sales manager for our state, David Webb. David has been with Allied for five years as an account manager and was recently promoted to area sales manager for our state. David wanted me to tell you that he hopes to meet all the key players at your company and will be calling next week to arrange a time, at your convenience, for such a meeting.

I am delighted to be working for David and am confident that you will enjoy meeting him.

Sincerely,

Debbie Black

MODEL LETTER 1.8

Introducing Yourself to a New Executive

Get right to the point in telling new executives what your company does for theirs and how much you appreciate the business.

Dear Mr. Schmidt:

Congratulations on your new position of executive vice president of Merk Oil and Gas Products. My name is David Jones, and I am senior account manager for Tiger Pipeline, your primary supplier of oil pipelines for use by your subsidiary companies.

I have been calling on Tiger for three years and have appreciated the rapid growth in business between your company and mine during that time. Merk is now our largest customer in this state, which makes me both proud and grateful.

I am confident that my company will continue to satisfy the needs of Merk Oil and Gas Products and to earn your business. I look forward to meeting you personally and will contact you next week to arrange an appointment. Should you have questions before that, please call me at 212-555-1000.

Sincerely,

David Jones

MODEL LETTER 1.9

Following Up on a Lead from a Previous Customer's Colleague

Make sure your sources have no objection to your mentioning their names to a prospect.

Dear Ms. Goode:

Robin Neville called me last week and mentioned that your division of MegaDisk is considering producing a brochure to catalog your consulting services. Robin also said you probably would not begin the project right away. However, I want to introduce myself and show you samples of my work.

I have included in this package two samples of work I produced for Mitchell Brown of MegaDisk. The larger brochure was produced in 19XX and was targeted to CEOs and other nontechnical corporate leaders. The smaller brochure is a product quick reference guide that is in its third printing and will soon be introduced systemwide at MegaDisk.

As you know, there are many factors to consider when you produce a marketing tool. For example, will your group seek to match existing pieces from your corporation or create a different identity? Either way, I can help you take your brochure idea through development, production, and distribution in an effective, cost-efficient manner.

I will call your secretary next week in hopes of arranging an appointment.

Sincerely,

Annie Adams

(Courtesy of Annie Adams, Dallas, Texas.)

"I Hope to Discuss the Possibilities with You in Person"

Phones may go unanswered, but letters have staying power.

Dear Mr. Wagner:

The media supervisor at your advertising agency suggested that I call you, but I have been unable to reach you by phone.

Air-Time TV, with more than 150 U.S. television stations under contract, is one of the largest television station representative firms in the country. One of our stations may be of particular interest to you. KTEX in Austin, Texas, is planning a direct-mail/television synergy campaign for fourth-quarter 20XX. Because your firm uses this media mix, you might consider participating in the KTEX program.

The direct-mail portion will consist of three phases, one a week for three weeks, beginning November 12 and continuing through December 3. This promotion ties into the post-Thanksgiving, pre-Christmas season.

The total value of the television schedule should be $32,000. Each sponsor in the mailer will appear on a portion of the promotional spots the station airs.

All KTEX requires for participation are small incremental dollars over last year's billing on the station. I hope to have the opportunity to discuss the possibilities with you in person. I will call again in a few days to set up an appointment.

Please call me with any questions in the meantime.

Regards,

Sally Lombard

MODEL LETTER 1.11

Why This Prospect May Be Interested in Your Services

Letters, like many other aspects of sales, are more appealing when you begin them with statements about how your product benefits the customer.

Dear Mr. Michaels:

Accurate tracking of material and labor costs can mean the difference between cost overruns and a job finished on time and within budget. That is why I am writing to introduce myself and my firm, IMSS, which provides accounting and job cost systems and support services to commercial builders and subcontractors. Although we have never met, I saw your firm's listing in the National Contractors directory and thought IMSS products and services would be beneficial to you.

The brochure I have enclosed, "Sample Files and Reports," illustrates the accounting information our system captures and the reports it generates. The brochure provides a good overview of the system's input and output features, but a hands-on demonstration of the system will show you how easy it is to learn and to use.

I will call you next week to answer any questions you may have and to offer a demonstration of the IMSS system.

Sincerely,

Frank McIntyre

(Courtesy of Frank McIntyre, Dallas, Texas.)

Model Letter 1.12

"A Mutual Acquaintance Thought
You'd Be Interested. . . . "

Concrete benefits, such as knowing at a glance if you are on budget or headed for disaster, give the customer a reason to see you.

Dear J. B.:

Over the past twelve years, most of my new business has come from referrals by satisfied customers. My customers appreciate the accurate cost tracking the IMSS system provides, and they tell me IMSS reports let them see at a glance whether projects are on budget or having cost overruns.

Randy Porter of PRT Inc. suggested that I write you and describe the IMSS system, which provides accounting and job cost systems and support services to commercial builders and subcontractors.

The brochure I have enclosed, "Sample Files and Reports," illustrates the accounting information our system captures and the reports it generates. The brochure provides a good overview of the system's input and output features, but a hands-on demonstration of the system will show you how easy it is to learn and to use.

I will call you next week to answer any questions you may have and to offer a demonstration of the IMSS system.

Sincerely,

Frank McIntyre

(Courtesy of Frank McIntyre, Dallas, Texas.)

Introducing Yourself
When the Situation Changes

Model Letter 1.13

You've Taken Over a New Territory

Send a letter promptly when your job assignment changes. You want customers to know how to reach you with minimal hassles.

Dear Jeanne:

As you know, I have joined Media International as Mary Thomas' replacement. The past couple of weeks have been a whirlwind. I want to advise you of my marketing assignments and express to you my sincere desire to assist you and your department and to continue the excellent service I am sure your buyers are accustomed used to receiving.

My current assignments are

- KAGR—Beaumont, Linda Goldman
- KWIG—Memphis, Linda Goldman
- KWWI—Knoxville, Linda Goldman
- KXSR—Idaho Falls, Bob Olds
- KVBV—Tri Cities, Bill Brown

I am very excited about my new responsibilities and look forward to continuing my relationships with all the great people in your department.

Sincerely,

Susan C. Wagner

(Courtesy of Susan Wagner, Dallas, Texas.)

MODEL LETTER 1.14

Your Contact Moves to
Another One of Your Accounts

Stay in touch with customers as they make career changes, and you'll strengthen your ties to the industry.

Dear Martha:

Congratulations on your recent move to Nova Fastening Systems. Nova has been a valued customer of mine since I began working at ABC Company. I enjoyed calling on you while you were at Sharp Fastening Systems and hope to continue that same relationship with you at Nova.

Please let me know how I can assist you in this transition phase to a new position and new company. I look forward to working with you again.

Sincerely,

Peter McDaniels

MODEL LETTER 1.15

When the Decision Maker Changes Mid-Sale

Your diligence can save a sale when your primary contact leaves the customer's firm.

Dear Frank:

I am writing to introduce myself and my company to you, and to tell you about an opportunity I have been working on with your predecessor.

My name is Linda Morgan, and I work for the ABC Company, which supplies complete office furniture systems for technology-oriented companies like yours. For the past six months, I have worked very closely with your predecessor, Nancy Goode, in the furnishing plans for your new offices in Walnut Creek. We had agreed on a basic plan, and Nancy told me she intended to process a purchase order within the next ten days. Based on that agreement, I am holding furniture for you at our warehouse while awaiting your purchase order. I hope we can complete this transaction; I look forward to discussing these arrangements with you.

The selections made were an excellent value. They will give your Walnut Creek office the combination of functionality, comfort, and image that I know your firm desires. I will call you on Friday.

Best regards,

Linda Morgan

MODEL LETTER 1.16

Contacting the Decision Maker
After You've Done a Needs/Benefit Analysis

Decision makers will be impressed with the research you do to help them benefit from your products.

Dear Mr. Miles:

My name is Susan Henry, and I am the regional representative for the Original Gizmo Company. OGC provides quality carbon gizmos to manufacturing concerns such as yours.

I have been working with your staff to determine the benefits our carbon gizmo could bring to your manufacturing process. Your staff has been most helpful, which I appreciate.

I think a meeting between us would be productive for several reasons:

- To help us clarify your challenges and requirements
- To update you about the Original Gizmo Company
- To give me your perspective about how my firm might earn your business

I will follow up with your assistant next week to arrange a meeting at your convenience. I look forward to getting together with you and to meeting you.

Yours truly,

Susan Henry

Model Letter 1.17

Explaining the Results of Your Cost/Benefit Analysis

The groundwork you lay will pay off when you use your findings to persuade a decision maker to meet with you and consider your proposal.

Dear Mr. Wells:

I am the senior account representative from Better Circuitry Company assigned to your account. I have been with BCC more than nine years and began calling on your company early this year.

As you may know, BCC is the leader in carbon devices, which we pioneered in 19XX. Since that time, we have sold 500,000 units worldwide, with over 500 in your area. The carbon device is the most effective product of its type on the market today. Additionally, planned enhancements to the product ensure a continued, viable life cycle into the next decade.

Since early spring, I have been working with members of your purchasing staff to understand the challenges they face and the benefits our product will bring your firm. My technical staff and I have identified several possibilities that I believe will be of interest to you. We would appreciate the opportunity to meet you and discuss our findings.

I will call you during the week of September 20 to discuss our findings and to request a meeting, which will enable me to present the results of our analysis in greater detail. I look forward to speaking to you soon.

Sincerely,

Pamela Duke

Introducing Yourself to a New Contact

When your contact at an organization changes, your competitors will be just as eager as you to meet the new client. Distinguish yourself with a well-written letter of introduction.

Dear John:

My name is Lauren Beach, and I am writing to introduce myself to you. I have been your firm's account representative from Swan Laboratories for five years.

During the five years I have been working with Liaison, Inc., your organization has evolved into one of our largest, most esteemed customers. We appreciate your firm's past business and hope to earn your continued loyalty in the future.

As soon as you have relocated to Motor City, I hope to meet you. In the meantime, please do not hesitate to call if I can be of assistance to you in any way. I can be reached at 280-555-9000.

Very truly yours,

Lauren Beach

Introducing Your Company and Your Management

MODEL LETTER 1.19

When Your Company Is New

Some industries are more receptive to newcomers than others. Whether your industry has new entrants each week or has been stable for years, a professional letter of introduction can get you in the front door.

Dear John Thompson:

I am writing to introduce myself and my company to you. My name is Teresa Brown, and I have recently incorporated a manufacturers' representative organization, the Wireless Ones. This organization will represent manufacturers that make products used in the manufacture of wireless communication devices.

Before starting this company, I spent ten years with Moshelle Inc., which represented various manufacturers in the communications industry. During that time, I saw the need for a specialized group of representatives that focuses on the wireless market to help organizations like yours. We add value by helping you stay focused in this rapidly changing field.

I hope you will let my organization show you how our services can benefit you. I will call you next week to explore the requirements you have now and solutions the Wireless Ones can offer.

Thank you for this opportunity to introduce myself and my company to you. I look forward to talking with you in the near future.

Sincerely,

Teresa Brown

MODEL LETTER 1.20

Using a Referral to Introduce Yourself

Following up on a lead from a mutual acquaintance is an ideal way to begin the sales process.

Dear Mr. Phillips:

I am writing to introduce myself on the recommendation of Joyce Jones, of International Products. I know Joyce through my neighborhood homeowners association, and she told me of your interest in acquiring property on the Gulf Coast.

I represent BYC Builders, Inc., which owns 25 percent of the property available for development in the gulf area. BYC designs and builds custom homes suitable for either vacation or full-time use. Model homes may be viewed in several locations along the coast.

I would like to discuss your interest in the gulf area in person at a time convenient to you. I will call next week.

Sincerely,

Miles Jones

Model Letter 1.21

You've Heard About a Prospect's Successful Business

Begin by complimenting the prospect, if congratulations are in order.

Dear Mr. Moran:

I have been following the success of your new venture, Norwich Communications, and want to congratulate you on your rapid growth and profitability.

It would be a privilege for me if you would take a few moments to hear about my organization, Brown Personnel. Brown provides personnel consulting and resources specifically for the communications industry. Brown—in business for more than ten years—prides itself on helping companies achieve maximum profitability by alleviating the hassles and expenses associated with personnel recruitment.

Mr. Moran, as president of Norwich, you must be concerned with efficiency in staffing. I hope you will be available for a few moments when I call next week because I am confident my firm could be a great asset to you. I look forward to speaking with you soon.

Best wishes for continued success with Norwich Communications.

Sincerely,

Mona Campbell

MODEL LETTER 1.22

The Prospect Had a Bad Experience with Your Company

Asking for a second chance can be a humbling experience. Use concrete evidence to convince a past customer that your company has made real improvements.

Dear Ed:

As the new account manager for Perfect Printing, I'm responsible for calling on ABC Company. I know that ABC has had some unfortunate experiences with my firm in the past. I regret that several quality and delivery problems occurred and am empathetic to you and the situation you must have been in when we did not perform as required.

Over the past eighteen months, however, my company has made great strides in not only eliminating problems such as you experienced, but also in establishing an exemplary quality record. Perfect Printing has updated our equipment and provided additional training to personnel throughout the production cycle. Our quality and delivery records verify our progress, and I could suggest several customers who would be happy to speak with you about their experiences with us.

At your convenience, I would like to tell you about the process improvements that my company has made. We have done a great deal to ensure that Perfect Printing meets or exceeds customers' quality and scheduling needs. I feel that a face-to-face meeting will be worthwhile, as you have an ongoing need for a reliable supplier.

Congratulations on the continued growth at ABC Company. I look forward to meeting soon. Thank you for your consideration of Perfect Printing.

Sincerely,

Jack Newby

MODEL LETTER 1.23

Networking for Referrals

This example of Pat Romboletti's winning approach to writing and sales is one of many sample letters she agreed to share with our readers. After a career in sales management, Pat launched the Write Sales System™, a Dallas-based company that develops complete portfolios of sales letters for clients. Now her customers know the secret she learned long ago: letters extend your reach and help you win more business than you ever thought possible.

Dear Tommie:

I enjoyed meeting you to talk about how we can provide referrals to one another. The information you shared was very helpful, and I will be certain to introduce you to appropriate companies.

I also thought it might be helpful to give you a summary of how we distinguish ourselves in the area of real estate appraisal. We provide appraisals for financial institutions, tax consultants, and major corporations. They select HMC Appraisals because

- We provide dependable, on-time service and offer flexible fee schedules.
- We make it our business to understand their businesses so we can match our services to their specific needs.
- We are experienced in both domestic and international appraisal services.
- We provide customized reports that conform to all industry guidelines.
- We serve as a resource for our clients by providing vital market overviews, preliminary property analysis, and information on real estate market trends.

Our clients retain our services when obtaining business loans, buying or selling a business, and for tax appeals, insurance valuations, and bankruptcy proceedings.

Tommie, I am looking forward to talking with you again soon, and I wish you great success with your business.

Sincerely,

Pat Romboletti

(Courtesy of Pat Romboletti, The Write Sales System™, Dallas, Texas.)

MODEL LETTER 1.24

Your Company Was Just Acquired
by Another Company

Uncertainty about your firm's future can undermine your best sales efforts. By addressing possible concerns in a letter, you give the customer written assurance that your company and you deserve the business.

Dear Sam:

After competing successfully in the networking marketplace for ten years, Network Solutions has been acquired by Open Systems Solutions. OSS, as you may know, is a $5 billion company that provides products and services for the networking world and is the leader is software solutions for the Unix area.

We at Network Solutions believe this is a win–win acquisition for everyone. From a product development perspective, we will now have access to a substantially greater pool of resources, which will help us bring competitive new solutions to the marketplace with even greater speed than before. As a customer, you will reap the benefits of not only a larger product selection but also a mature service organization, with manpower and coverage in all parts of the globe.

After November 1, our name will be Network Solutions, an Open Systems Solutions Corp. At this time, telephone numbers and addresses remain the same, as do the people who support your site. I will continue to be your sales representative, which pleases me very much.

Let me know if you have any questions or concerns regarding this acquisition. I will contact you soon to pass along any new information I learn.

Thank you for your continued support.

Sincerely,

Pat Meyers

Explaining How Your Company Will Benefit the Prospect

Customers who are trying to solve problems in their businesses will be interested in details about what your product does.

Dear Jack:

I am writing to introduce myself and my company to you, and to tell you about a product that I believe could impact the profitability of XYZ Corp. My name is Tim Rogers, and I represent the ABC Company, which manufactures automation tools for manufacturing concerns such as yours. Our automation tools have enabled manufacturers to eliminate the errors and excessive costs related to manual assembly line work, which can really hurt the bottom line, as you well know.

I would appreciate the opportunity to talk to you, either in person or on the phone, so that I may explain in more detail how my product will benefit your business. These tools have produced significant positive effects for other clients, and I think you will find your time with me well spent.

I will follow up with a phone call next week when I am in town. I hope we can get together then.

Very truly yours,

Tim Rogers

Introducing Your Product or Service

There is no need to reinvent the wheel. Write your sales story in a compelling, thorough way, and use that letter as a model for many prospects.

MODEL LETTER 1.26

Introducing Your Product as Something the Customer Needs to Think About

When the customer has not already identified his or her need for the product, a letter enclosing an article on the problem can help the prospect recognize an important need.

Dear Mr. Jacques:

I enclosed this article from the *Wall Street Journal* describing how some hackers managed to get through to the client database of a major New York bank. The hackers stole $100,000 before they were discovered. In the process they severely embarrassed the bank's security personnel. Prior to the break-in, the bank involved was quoted as saying it had a world-class security system.

The good news is that we developed Fortress™ after consulting for two years with these same hackers to identify and remedy the weaknesses they typically exploit. As a first step, we have developed a security audit to identify the strengths and weaknesses of your existing system. We then show you how Fortress™ augments your strengths and remedies your weaknesses.

I hope this letter kindles some thoughts about your protection and what you can do about it. I will call next week to discuss the issue.

Thank you for your time.

Sincerely,

Greg Greene

MODEL LETTER 1.27

Describing Your Major Projects to a Prospect Who's Issuing an RFP

Prepare an informative introductory letter long before you need it. You can quickly customize it to follow up on leads.

Dear Noelle Fischer:

I understand that CompuCon may issue a Request for Proposal for hiring a consultant to review your firm's approach to management of its San Diego headquarters and other corporate facilities. If so, you may be interested in knowing more about XYZ's consulting expertise in corporate real estate and facilities management.

As you know, XYZ worked with CompuCon in 19XX to address the issues relating to CompuCon's various real estate investments. For many years, XYZ has been advising major corporations about the use of real estate to support core business operations. In the past 18 months, however, we have developed cutting-edge expertise in the management of corporate facilities.

Corporations today are focusing on cost reductions, service improvement, and allocation of resources to core business activities and are reevaluating support services such as corporate real estate and facilities management, food service, security, document reproduction, messenger and delivery services, and travel. XYZ has become the industry leader, advising corporations on the reengineering and outsourcing of these functions. Summarized below are several representative engagements that reflect XYZ's experience.

Blake Bank XYZ helped this financial institution plan and coordinate the outsourcing of management of more than 30 million square feet of space used for offices, retail branches, and other purposes. Functions outsourced included property management, leasing and lease administration, and design and construction management. XYZ's responsibilities included designing implementing the evaluation and selection process, advising the institution of the transition process, and evaluating the information technology issues related to outsourcing.

Manufacturing Inc.   This Fortune 200 corporation is moving from a leased corporate headquarters where the landlord provides property management services to a new 400,000-square-foot facility. MI will be responsible for more than thirty different property and management functions in this new facility. XYZ is advising MI on outsourcing these services to a third party. Our responsibilities include designing and implementing the evaluation and selection process, working with management to determine the proper decision, participating in drafting the legal agreement for management services, and assisting in negotiations with firms competing for the outsourcing contract.

Major Publishing Company   XYZ is advising this firm on the reengineering and potential outsourcing of numerous support functions for its U.S. operations. Candidates for outsourcing include property and facility management, food services, security, document reproduction, and mail services. XYZ's role is to assist management in determining the appropriate mix of reengineering or outsourcing of these internal functions. The primary drivers for this initiative are cost reduction, streamlining processes, and adjustment of service levels.

International Facility Management Company   XYZ is providing this client strategic advice about its service offerings for facility management. The company has a preeminent reputation but is exploring the mix of services needed to maintain its competitive position in the future.

I am interested in arranging a meeting with you to reintroduce you to the XYZ consultant who is leading the firm's initiatives in corporate real estate and facilities management. Her name is Lucinda Rogers. Lucinda, a senior manager in the Tulsa office, was responsible for the real estate consulting assignments XYZ did for your firm in 19XX. You may remember meeting her at the March 19XX status review meeting.

I have enclosed copies of two presentations Lucinda delivers to industry groups interested in how outsourcing and reengineering relate to real estate and facilities management. I think you will find both discussions interesting because they focus on the issues your firm wants to evaluate.

I look forward to speaking with you in several days to discuss my request for a meeting.

Sincerely,

Tom Wenkstern

(Courtesy of Tom Wenkstern, Plano, Texas.)

MODEL LETTER 1.28

"I May Have a Buyer for Your Property"

Even a brief note can yield dividends when you pique a prospect's interest.

Re: Vacant Land on Bluebonnet Road in Lakeside, Arkansas

Dear Dr. McAdams:

The City of Lakeside is interested in acquiring some land for a specific use. Our firm is assisting the city in identifying parcels of land that will fulfill the need.

I have been unable to reach you, but I would like to discuss your tracts of land on Bluebonnet Road. Will you please call to advise me of your plans for this property?

Sincerely,

Blake M. Reed

(Courtesy of Blake M. Reed, Dallas, Texas.)

MODEL LETTER 1.29

"I Have Been Unable to Reach You"

A brief note can help break the ice with an elusive prospect.

Re: Approximately 50 acres located in Pleasantville, Texas

Dear Mrs. McDonald:

I have been unable to reach you regarding your property in West Texas. Will you please call me to discuss your plans for this acreage?

Sincerely,

Blake M. Reed

(Courtesy of Blake M. Reed, Dallas, Texas.)

Model Letter 1.30

A Request to Meet a Prospective Seller

Your well-crafted letter tells prospects you are articulate, professional, and effective—before you ever meet.

Re: Future automobile dealership site, northeast Roberts County

Dear James Robb:

Thank you for visiting on the phone with me this week about your preliminary interest in acquiring land near the intersection of State Highways 303 and 118 in northeast Roberts County.

This letter is to encourage you to engage Reed and Reed Realty Company to represent you exclusively in your search for a suitable site. My partner, Roger Reed, and I have more than forty years of combined experience in the commercial land business in the metropolitan area. We are well equipped to identify all the alternatives and represent your interests as well.

Reed and Reed Realty is currently representing the Roberts Independent School District in its search for one middle school site and two elementary school sites. We are also helping the City of Lakeside in its search for a thirty- to forty-acre sports-related site and a ten- to twenty-acre neighborhood park site. The school work began with our identification of more than thirty alternative sites, and the city work began with sixty-five alternative sites. These institutional users chose Best Ones because of our knowledge of the local market, our thoroughness, and our straightforward approach to doing business. We can lend the same expertise to your business as well.

I would like the chance to meet you personally to discuss this idea in greater detail. Perhaps you would let me buy you lunch in a town halfway between your home and mine, say Lincoln or Waters?

Thank you.

Sincerely,

Blake M. Reed

(Courtesy of Blake M. Reed, Dallas, Texas.)

A Letter to a Prospect
Who Has Inquired About Your Products

Letters 1.31 and 1.32 illustrate how one salesperson prepared letters for different purposes by changing the opening paragraph of a basic descriptive letter.

Dear Ms. Rogers:

Thank you for your recent inquiry regarding SCH Technologies' storage management product line. I have enclosed product literature for your review.

The robust storage management product family offered by SCH is the only complete tape management and backup/restore software available for heterogeneous Unix networks. These products save time, ensure data integrity, protect against human error, and provide superior performance. The REELproducts, the basic components in this line, are developed by Storage Tek and are exclusively represented by SCH. In addition, SCH has developed products that integrate with and further the capacity of the products to provide a complete solution for data centers.

The SCH line of storage management solutions includes

REELlibrarian—complete tape management system for heterogeneous Unix network.
REELbackup—high-performance backup/restore solution for Unix data center environments.
REELexchange—conversion/translation products for proprietary IBM- and ANSI-labeled tapes.
REELaccess—enables REELlibrarian and REELbackup to access Storage Tek automated robotic tape libraries.
SCH:HotBackup—extends the functionality of REELbackup to accommodate hot backups for the most popular commercial databases.
SCH:Robot—connection for REELbackup and REELlibrarian to a variety of automated tape robotics.

In addition to our storage management line, SCH represents other superior Unix software products, including solutions for distributed systems management, security, user interface tools, connectivity, fax management, integrated office, and mainframe connectivity. We also provide an extensive array of professional services to facilitate your implementation.

As you review the enclosed information, please do not hesitate to call if you have any questions or would like to discuss a demonstration or technical review of these products. You can reach me at 888-555-0000 or by e-mail at @not.really.

Cordially,

Mary L. Piper

(Courtesy of Mary L. Piper, SCH Technologies, Inc., Cincinnati, Ohio.)

Model Letter 1.32

Introducing Your Products to the Customer of a Company Affiliated with Your Firm

What may look like a list to you can provide the prospect with a quick reference to your products and their functions.

Dear Ms. Michaels:

As a customer of Storage Tek, you may be interested in one of SCH's ways to utilize your current hardware investment as you move to open systems in a shared or stand-alone environment. To that end, I have enclosed product literature for your review.

The robust storage management product family offered by SCH is the only complete tape management and backup/restore software available for heterogeneous Unix networks. These products save time, ensure data integrity, protect against human error, and provide superior performance. The REELproducts, the basic components in this line, are developed by Storage Tek and are exclusively represented by SCH. In addition, SCH has developed additional products that integrate with and further the capacity of the products to provide a complete solution for data centers.

The SCH line of storage management solutions includes

> REELlibrarian—complete tape management system for heterogeneous Unix network.
> REELbackup—high-performance backup/restore solution for Unix data center environments.
> REELexchange—conversion/translation products for proprietary IBM- and ANSI-labeled tapes.
> REELaccess—enables REELlibrarian and REELbackup to access Storage Tek automated robotic tape libraries.
> SCH:HotBackup—extends the functionality of REELbackup to accommodate hot backups for the most popular commercial databases.
> SCH:Robot—connection for REELbackup and REELlibrarian to a variety of automated tape robotics.

In addition to our storage management line, SCH represents other superior Unix software products, including solutions for distributed systems management, security, user interface tools, connectivity, fax management, integrated office, and mainframe connectivity. We also provide an extensive array of professional services to facilitate your implementation.

As you review the enclosed information, please do not hesitate to call if you have any questions or would like to discuss a demonstration or technical review of these products. You can reach me at 888-555-000 or by e-mail at @not.really.

Cordially,

Mary L. Piper

(Courtesy of Mary L. Piper, SCH Technologies, Inc., Cincinnati, Ohio.)

MODEL LETTER 1.33

Introducing Yourself and Your Products

The list that opens this letter can help prospects find a topic of interest immediately.

Dear Mr. Hatfield:

SCH offers a full range of Unix-based products for

- Storage management
- Distributed systems mangement
- Security
- User interface tool
- Connectivity
- Fax management
- Integrated office
- Mainframe connectivity
- Professional services

I am your account manager with SCH Technologies, Inc. Our focus at SCH, in addition to our extensive product offerings, is on customer support and service. Our relationship with your company is very important to us. This relationship has been critical to our success over the years. SCH will continue to work with you and other representatives of your company in both presale and postsale activities.

I am enclosing some basic information about our products for your review. Please let me know how I can be of assistance to you now and as opportunities arise in the future. You can reach me at 888-555-0000 or by e-mail at @not.really. I have also enclosed a business card for your files.

I look forward to working with you.

Cordially,

Mary L. Piper

(Courtesy of Mary L. Piper, SCH Technologies, Inc., Cincinnati, Ohio.)

Model Letter 1.34

Introducing New Products to a Former Customer

The approach illustrated in letter 1.33 is easily adapted for other situations.

Dear Ms. Williams:

SCH offers a full range of Unix-based products for

- Storage management
- Distributed systems mangement
- Security
- User interface tool
- Connectivity
- Fax management
- Integrated office
- Mainframe connectivity
- Professional services

If I still have your attention, that means at least one of these products is of interest to you, and we should get together. Our focus at SCH, in addition to our extensive system support product offerings, is on customer support and service. We would like to extend our problem-solving abilities to you. We offer a wide variety of solutions for all your Unix needs—100-plus products from 45-plus development teams, in addition to full professional services offerings to custom-tailor a solution for your environment.

I would attempt to reach you by phone, but I have been unable to locate a correct listing. I understand how hectic your schedule may be and thought that by sending this introductory note and the attached product overview, I might determine whether you would like to receive additional information or a phone call from me.

Please feel free to call me at 888-555-0000 or contact me by e-mail at @not.really. I have also enclosed a business card for your files.

I look forward to working with you.

Cordially,

Mary L. Piper

(Courtesy of Mary L. Piper, SCH Technologies, Inc., Cincinnati, Ohio.)

Selling Outlook
Introductions: The Foundation of Your Selling Style

You Never Have A Second Chance To Make A First Impression

The old adage is so true: An impression formed by any initial contact—whether by letter, in a meeting, or during a telephone conversation—becomes an influential memory. And the discouraging truth is that, somehow, negative impressions tend to linger longer than good ones.

In today's competitive world, a good first impression does not win the business, it merely gets or keeps you in the running. A negative first impression, however, may mean you do not even get to compete. Dealing with busy decision makers, we often work very hard to have any contact at the appropriate level. We may first need to spend a long time working with staff members who feed information to the decision maker.

The fact is, as everyone gets busier and busier, time becomes our most precious commodity. For the sales representative, this means that every move you make matters.

The good news is that if you send an excellent introductory letter to the appropriate person, chances are it will get the results you want. Remember these five guidelines when developing your message:

1. The recipient is probably extremely busy.
2. Keep the message succinct.
3. Explain how your product or service will help meet the recipient's goals (provided you have enough information to know); explain why seeing you could enhance the other person's profitability.
4. Be courteous: explain how much you appreciate the other person's consideration.
5. Be clear about what you intend your next step to be (such as a follow-up phone call or an offer to send additional information).

A courteous, well-executed introductory letter can be the first step in a profitable venture. The introductory letter is your first opportunity to express your personal, tasteful selling style. Use it with confidence, and you will make the valuable first impression that will attract buyers and make them want to do business with you.

CHAPTER 2

Getting Started Through Direct Mail

Most letters in this book are intended for one-on-one selling situations. Sometimes, however, it's productive to target groups of potential customers and use direct-mail marketing to acquaint prospects with your company, products, and services. The letters in this chapter were written for new prospects who may not know your company and who definitely do not know you.

Prospects' names may appear in a list you purchase from a list broker, a membership roster you have permission to use, or convention contacts who gave you business cards and requested a response.

To the extent possible, these letters should be personalized with the recipient's name. The content, however, can be the same for one person or thousands.

CHAPTER 2. CONTENTS

Marketing Business-to-Business Services

Model Letter 2.1

Reasons to Outsource IS Support

Who decides whether to buy your product or service? Chief operating officers? Production managers? Purchasing agents? When you can answer this question, you can develop a mailing for a target group. If phone numbers are available, you can follow up by phone within ten days.

Dear Ms. Loden:

Every passing quarter brings new software and systems installations, upgrades, maintenance issues. Employees complain that they don't get the support they need for the applications that drive your operating systems. Meanwhile, you have forecasts to meet, budgets to plan, R&D setbacks to overcome—plus a litany of other responsibilities. Occasionally you may pause to wonder: *since when did running a business mean becoming a computer expert?*

With Help Online, Inc., the answer is "Not ever." Help Online works with our clients to assess information systems needs, training issues, and maintenance requirements. Together we tailor an IS system that suits your company and your expansion goals. While you stay focused on your primary business, we keep your information systems operating effectively, support your staff with twenty-four-hour dial-up help, and provide complete IS maintenance service.

Help Online, Inc., employs specialists in multiplatform networks and twenty-five of the most frequently used business applications. These resources are available to you around the clock, typically at a cost far below previous IS overhead expenses.

So before you have another system outage, before you evaluate another IS budget increase, consider to Help Online. We can reduce your IS worries and help you get back to your primary business.

I have enclosed a brochure that explains more about Help Online services. I will call you in the next few days to answer any questions and offer an on-site presentation.

Sincerely,

Teresa Yarbrough

MODEL LETTER 2.2

"When Your Account Executive Calls . . ."

Always get clients' written permission before using their names, quotations, or other identifying information in promotional material.

Dear Promotions Manager:

The list of IBS clients keeps growing, and so does the number of awards we've helped them win. But the real IBS success story isn't our high-profile clients or NTC design awards; it is the difference our promotions make in sales and market share:

- HTC's 12 percent gain in a single quarter
- The McPherson turnaround within six months
- Hi-Co's record earnings in the two quarters after our product-launch promotion

The brochure I have enclosed lists more of our clients and the details of our awards and market accomplishments.

This letter is your invitation to join IBS and become our next success story. Whatever your goals, we help you design promotions that blow past quotas and exceed the most optimistic sales forecasts.

IBS, founded in 19XX, is a full-service image management agency that develops promotional campaigns for delivery in all media—online, television, radio, print, and more. In a few days, an account executive will call you to follow up on this invitation. Please take a few moments to discuss your current needs and long-range goals.

Sincerely,

Adam Michaels

Temporary Employees Who Make the Difference

Direct-mail marketers follow well-researched rules to increase the response to their mailings: make letters look personal and important, and include a P.S. that restates the essence of your message and urges the recipient to act. (In other types of business letters, however, the P.S. is less acceptable, and some people interpret it as a lack of organization.)

Ringing phones, complaining customers, empty desks . . . Is that how you remember last summer's peak vacation weeks?

Dear Personnel Manager:

Reliable Temporaries can turn your summertime nightmare into twelve carefree weeks of business as usual. Whether you need accounting specialists, computer support technicians, or office staff, Reliable can provide you with dependable professionals who adapt quickly to your work requirements and schedules.

Reliable offers specialists for dozens of jobs specifications. We carefully screen applicants and select only those with outstanding computer, organizational, and people skills. Once hired, our contractors receive continuous training to ensure they are well versed in the latest computing applications—word processing, spreadsheet, presentation, database, and more.

This summer, put an end to staffing problems with one phone call, your call to Reliable Temporaries at 555-2544. Your customers, your full-time employees, and you will be happy you did.

Sincerely,

Mac Truman

P.S. Summer is almost here. Who'll be answering the phones, routing mail, and keeping your office organized when vacation season begins? Call Reliable Temporaries at 555-2544 to eliminate your vacation worries.

MODEL LETTER 2.4

Is a Language Barrier Limiting Your Business in Spanish-Speaking Countries?

One way direct-mail letters differ from other business correspondence is in the use of headlines to draw readers into the letter and remind them of your selling message.

¿Acaso es la barrera del lenguage quién le impide expandir su negocio a paises de habla hispana?

Translation: *Is a language barrier stopping you from expanding into Spanish-speaking countries?*

Dear CEO:

Every day new business opportunities are developing in the Spanish-speaking world. Are you participating, or are language limitations stifling the growth of your business?

Since 19XX, El Mondo Language Services has focused on helping clients develop the skills they need to conduct business in Spanish. Many executives in our programs have gone from speaking no Spanish to conducting Spanish-only contract negotiations within six months—even less time in some cases. El Mondo also offers training programs to help employees conduct telephone business with customers.

Here is an overview of the services we provide companies like yours:

> **Translation services.** Native speakers provide simultaneous translation for meetings and conferences, as well as document translation.
> **One-on-one tutoring.** Most executives learning Spanish prefer semiweekly one-on-one tutoring sessions. We provide computer-based training CDs to help you study between sessions.
> **Classroom instruction.** El Mondo trainers conduct classes each weeknight in our Central St. language labs. We also customize on-site instruction for corporate clients.

Immersion programs. Live with a Spanish-speaking family in the United States, Mexico, or one of twelve other countries for one or more weeks. Whereas most immersion programs last six weeks or longer, El Mondo's customized programs augment our tutoring and classroom instruction. That means you can benefit from an immersion experience in as little as one week.

Tapes, videos, and books. We support our teaching efforts with a full line of El Mondo tapes, videos, and books.

Whether you are interested in Spanish-language instruction for yourself or for your employees, El Mondo's veteran instructors can help you develop the skills you need to speak confidently, grammatically, and fluently. Call us today, and start expanding your business opportunities.

Sincerely,

Raul Ramirez

MODEL LETTER 2.5

What Do Competitors Know That You Don't?

Testing is a key component of direct-mail marketing. Companies test just about every aspect of marketing campaigns—mailing lists, sales offers, and especially letters. For instance, would letter 2.5 pull a better response if it began, "We believe in educated decisions, not educated guesswork." Direct-mail marketers let the market answer.

Dear Mr. Thomas:

As the CEO of a new high-growth company, you know to never take your eye off the competition. But who are they watching?

If your competitors seem to be following a playbook you haven't seen, chances are they have been reading white papers, listening to focus groups, and using market research like the type Brown & Associates provides each of our clients. Brown & Associates specializes in market research for consumer goods manufacturers, and we know that when it comes to rapidly changing consumer markets, what you don't know can kill your business.

For instance, while you make decisions about your business during this high-growth phase, wouldn't it be helpful to know which hour of the weekend most 27- to 38-year-old men are most likely to make beverage purchases? Whether women in the $250,000-to-$300,000 income range are more likely to choose your products for themselves or buy them for other household members? Or whether customers are more likely to remember a billboard they read going to or returning from work?

Customized studies from Brown & Associates help you get maximum market impact from each decision you make. Our studies help you do more than understand the competition's game plan; they help you build strategies to win.

I would like to schedule a meeting with you to talk about ideas for using market research to your company's advantage. I will call you on Friday.

Sincerely,

Brenda Mann

Marketing Financial Services

MODEL LETTER 2.6

"Your Taxes Need Not Grow Along with Your Practice"

Research has convinced most direct-mail marketers to close letters with handwritten signatures in blue ink—or at least what looks like a handwritten signature in blue ink. Tests also show that letters pull better responses when they are posted with hand-applied stamps rather than metered postage or mailing permits.

Mailings can be very effective when these two aspects of the direct-mail formula carried out in a relatively small mailing to a select list, such as medical doctors in a specific town or zip code.

Dear Dr. Briggs:

The taxes you pay need not grow along with expanding your medical practice.

For the past fifteen years, my associates at BGQH CPAs and I have specialized in providing accounting services to physicians across the state. We are experts in both state and federal tax law as it applies to medical services. We understand that without reliable, up-to-date accounting advice, your expansion through new service offerings and additional associates is curtailed.

I think you would find a consultation with me or another BGQH associate most beneficial. With no obligation to you, we will assess your current status. If you decide to engage our services, we will work with you to develop tax strategies and business plans for the next six months, the next two years, and beyond.

BGQH values the opportunity to do business with medical professionals, and we strive to be partners in your success. I will call you next week to follow up.

Sincerely,

Thelma Lewis

MODEL LETTER 2.7

How $15 a Week
Can Pay for a College Education

It is always more appealing to receive a personalized letter than one that looks like bulk mail. Sometimes, however, costs or mailing list limitations may convince you to use a general salutation, such as "Dear Parent."

Dear Parent:

It may sound like allowance money, but $15 a week invested early and regularly can add up to a college education for your son or daughter. My customers have learned that for the price of a few video rentals they can have the peace of mind that comes with knowing they are investing in their child's future.

Whatever your financial goal—early retirement, a second home, your child's education—I can help you devise a strategy to make it happen. We'll look at your spending patterns and find ways to buy more value for your dollar. We'll analyze your goals, the level of risk you want to take, and the assets you can afford to invest today.

Call me today, and start making your financial goals reality.

Sincerely,

Beth Taylor

MODEL LETTER 2.8

Pension, 401K, Social Security—Three Reasons to Ask Us about Retirement Planning

Mailings may involve assumptions about the people on the mailing list. Perhaps you have assumed that because a family lives in a certain zip code, its income fits into the area's demographic pattern, or because a man belongs to a certain organization, he must be near retirement. The accuracy of these assumptions may determine the success of your mailing.

Dear Mr. Hatfield:

Day after day, we hear news about stock market ups and downs, the threat to Social Security, underfunding of some pensions. The closer you get to retirement, the more worrisome the headlines become. They needn't be.

Simon and Associates has helped families and corporate clients plan their financial futures for more than twenty-five years. Our expert advice helps you ride out the market's highs and lows, take full advantage of 401K benefits, and be confident of your financial future.

You may be considering retirement in five years or three decades. Either way, Simon and Associates can set you on course to meet your goals. Take the first step today. Call us at 555-4433.

Yours truly,

Robert Jones

MODEL LETTER 2.9

Why IRAs Are Worth the Effort

Often, one mailing doesn't get the business. A follow-up mailing reinforces your original message and can provide additional information, as in this example.

Dear Mr. Hatfield:

As a successful professional, your earnings have been well beyond the cutoff level for IRA deductions for many years. But tax code changes have made IRAs more attractive than ever.

Although your earnings may make you ineligible for an IRA deduction, IRAs provide tax-free earnings that accumulate over time, building financial equity and future security. Consistent IRA investments made year after year in the instrument best suited to your goals amount to a gift from Uncle Sam—sheltered income that puts you one sizable step closer to your financial goals.

Simon and Associates can suggest many more ways to finance your retirement. Whether you are considering retirement in five years or three decades, Simon and Associates can help you meet your goals. Take the first step today. Call us at 555-4433.

Yours truly,

Robert Jones

Announcing Town Bank's New Division

List brokers and business organizations can provide mailing addresses for large categories of professionals, such as chief financial officers or production managers in the regions you specify.

Dear Mr. Turner:

Town Bank is pleased to announce that Capital Finance Division, another new financial service from Town Bank, has begun operations in the mid-city.

Capital Finance specializes in loans of $100,000 or more to small and mid-sized companies for the purchase of capital assets. Town Bank established the new division to offer attractive terms on loans to the growing number of mid-city industrial customers.

Blair Daniels, divisional vice president, explains: "Our research has shown the single biggest obstacle to business development is the timely purchase of equipment needed for expansion. Whether a company is expanding product lines or adding capacity, capital limitations are limitations on growth."

Capital Finance helps companies overcome limitations and take advantage of development opportunities. When it is time to consider the purchase of your next capital asset, don't be limited by financial uncertainties. Call Capital Finance division, and let your business grow.

Sincerely,

J. M. Argent

Six Examples from the Insurance Industry

MODEL LETTER 2.11

Why It Makes Sense to
Outsource Employee Benefit Services

Your company may already survey customers to learn what they save in a year using your services, what they find most valuable, and why they would recommend you to others. Such information can be compelling documentation in prospect letters.

**What could your company do with
three more engineers, five more support technicians,
or seven more administrative assistants?**

Dear Ms. Overtown:

In today's business environment, managers are fortunate to retain their level of staffing, much less get approval for new positions. That's why clients rely on Myers Livingston to handle employee benefit services, something we have done for dozens of mid-sized to large companies since 1985.

Myers Livingston frees valuable resources that you can utilize to your best advantage—by adding staff in growing departments, making a much-needed capital purchase sooner than budgeted, or enjoying greater profits. Freeing funds for strategic use is one of many benefits our clients report. Some of the others may also appeal to you.

Benefits of Outsourcing

Lower overhead. Depending on the size of your company, outsourcing employee benefit services can trim 2.5 percent or more off overhead expenses. That's money you can shift directly to profit centers.
Focusing on what your company does best. Our clients are experts—in engineering, telecommunications, manufacturing, and

more than twenty-five other fields. What they don't have to be
are experts in employee benefits because Myers Livingston specialists keep them apprised of trends, legislation, and more than
fifteen reporting categories about plan usage among employees.
Offering employees a wider range of options. Many companies have difficulty offering the range of services their employees desire. At Myers Livingston, we are experienced in
administering more than fifty-five benefit options—and we can
make all of them available to your employees.

What We Provide

Plan Administration. 401Ks; medical, dental, and life insurance; cafeteria benefit plans; pensions—more than fifty-five benefit options.
Expert consulting services. Depending on the size of your firm,
one or more account executives will be assigned to help senior
management design and maintain your benefits program, and account executives continue to work directly with employees.
Handling employee queries and claims processing. The
Myers Livingston staff offers a level of specialization and expertise typically available to only the largest firms. Your employees
won't get "I don't know" or "I'll have to check" for answers to
questions about plan coverage.
Twenty-four-hour access. Myers Livingston professional fees
cover the cost of unlimited access to a twenty-four-hour benefits
line customized for your plan. Account executives also work
with employees to process claims and troubleshoot problems.
Extensive reporting. Monthly and quarterly reports keep you informed of associated costs and employee usage of each component of your benefits package.

In short, Ms. Overtown, your employees miss nothing, but your
firm gains a great deal when you utilize Myers Livingston services.
Would you give me the opportunity to explore your needs further
in an interview next week? I will call you on Monday to answer
any questions and, if you desire, to arrange a meeting.

Sincerely,

Dana Westgate

Model Letter 2.12

"Now That Your Teenager Can Drive . . ."

Direct-mail marketers use demographics, such as age, and psychographics, such as enrollment in a driver training course, to derive mailing lists.

Dear Parent:

It's a moment of mixed emotions—relief that you're permanently free of car-pool duty and anxiety about the safety of your son or daughter. Now that your teenager can drive, you may need to re-evaluate your automobile insurance coverage needs.

Insurance Associates has programs to reward your teenager for good driving and for participation education programs:

- **Good driving records**. A year with no traffic violations qualifies your teenager for lower insurance premiums.
- **New driver course**. When new drivers between the ages of sixteen and twenty-five complete a state-approved new driver course, they qualify for additional money-saving programs.

Good driving habits begin early. We encourage your son or daughter to complete qualifying driver training now, and enjoy better rates and safer driving. Call me at Insurance Associates to take advantage of these programs and learn more about other insurance options.

Sincerely,

Libby Sanders

MODEL LETTER 2.13

"Call Me and Save 10% Off Your Car Insurance Bill"

This letter is aimed at consumers who are not current customers; with slight modifications, it could be targeted at current customers.

Dear Good Driver:

Does your insurance company give your family credit where credit is due? My customers receive substantial discounts for their good records and driver training:

- **Better driver training credit**. Take a state-approved driving improvement course and receive a 10 percent discount.
- **Good driving records.** Your good driving record qualifies you for our preferred premium class—you pay the most attractive rates.
- **New driver course.** Your family members between the ages of sixteen and twenty-five qualify for additional discounts with proof of completion of the state-approved new driver course.

Call me at Insurance Associates to learn more about our automobile and homeowners insurance programs.

Sincerely,

Libby Sanders

MODEL LETTER 2.14

How a New Alarm System Can Pay for Itself

Consumers may be unaware of incentives their insurance company offers. By pointing out the benefits of some popular programs, you may convince prospects to call your office and let you write their new policy.

Dear Homeowner:

We all want the comfort of knowing our homes and belongings are safe and secure when we are away. Too often, though, homeowners return to crime scenes and find that they have become the latest burglary statistic.

But there is another kind of burglary statistic, and that's the resounding evidence that monitored home security systems deter crime. For a relatively low monthly fee, your home alarm system can be monitored around the clock—giving you twenty-four-hour peace of mind.

Insurance Associates is so convinced of the value of monitored home security systems that we give our customers a sizable discount starting the day the system is installed. You save three ways: lower insurance premiums, much lower risk of burglary, and much greater peace of mind.

Call our office today for details about the program, and learn how a monitored security system can pay off for you.

Sincerely,

Libby Sanders

MODEL LETTER 2.15

How Much Homeowners Insurance Is Enough?

Market trends can dictate direct-mail messages. For example, rising home prices can be a reason for insurance agents to remind homeowners to increase their insurance coverage. By the same token, an economic downturn may bring higher crime, and homeowners need more insurance for that, too.

Dear Neighbor:

What's your home really worth? The first answer that comes to many homeowners' minds is, "Much less than the tax assessor claims."

But the value of our homes and possessions does increase, especially when you consider the cost of replacing them. Too often, though, homeowners fail to protect what they've gained with adequate insurance—an unfortunate mistake, given the surprisingly low price of several more thousands of dollars worth of insurance.

Insurance Associates encourages you to protect your investment. Don't find out the real value of your home *after* you've suffered a loss. Call our office today for a no-strings consultation. We'll help you assess your home's appreciation and evaluate your insurance needs.

Sincerely,

Libby Sanders

MODEL LETTER 2.16

A Second Opinion on Your Health Insurance

A compelling headline can lead prospects into your sales literature.

Dear Ms. Ruth:

You Wouldn't Have Surgery without a Second Opinion, Would You? We can provide you with a "second opinion" on your health insurance.

We are employee benefits specialists. The QRS Group is dedicated to providing cost-effective and design-sensitive employee benefits for any-size employer.

We can help you decide whether managed care will work for you and teach you the ins and outs of HMOs and PPOs. We can teach you how to offer as many as four different health plans to your employees, which will allow you to solve the wide range of needs of a diverse group.

We can provide you with a full range of "Cafeteria or 125 Plans." They include the premium-only at no cost, where only the insurance premiums are tax sheltered; full reimbursement of unreimbursed medical expenses; and adding child-care reimbursement. We can protect business owners from any expense exposure on the "Cafeteria or 125 Plans" for employees who might leave or be terminated before the full funding of medical accounts.

Enclosed is a copy of a very brief overview of some of the programs we have done in the past. I will be in touch with you next week to see when we can discuss providing you with that "second opinion."

Sincerely,

Brian F. Duffy

(Courtesy of Brian Duffy, Irving, Texas.)

Four Approaches to Finding Real Estate Prospects

MODEL LETTER 2.17

Your Firm Is Moving to Our City. . . . We'd Like to Work with You

Facts vary from place to place. The idea is to explain the advantages of your area in a way that arouses prospects' curiosity.

Dear Ms. Byrd:

My associates and I want to be among the first to welcome the HiCo Corp. to the Tri-Cities area and to congratulate you on your decision to relocate your corporate offices here. Ours is a dynamic community with tremendous business, educational, and cultural opportunities.

The employees who relocate here will be buying homes at an especially opportune time. Recent selling prices have been very favorable for buyers, and our current listings include many excellent values. The selection of new and existing homes is very good right now, and choice lots are available for custom homes in subdivisions close to your new headquarters.

With this letter I am sending you several packets of brochures and business cards, and I ask that you make them available to employees who plan to relocate to the Tri-Cities. I also invite you to call me for more information about the area and the homes we offer. My associates and I look forward to serving you and all the employees of HiCo.

Sincerely,

Kevin James

Model Letter 2.18

Fast Facts About Our City

Companies may be much more likely to distribute your letter in their information packets than to release a mailing list of employee names.

Dear HiCo Employee:

If you are considering making the move to the Tri-Cities, consider these reasons to choose a home in Littleton:

Schools. We grow National Merit Scholars, winning athletes, successful youth. State and national tests consistently attest to the high quality of public education. Our school system attracts homebuyers, and that can mean thousands more dollars for you when you sell your home.

Taxes. Our school, city, and county taxes are among the lowest in the state.

Weather. Our city has a pleasant, year-round temperature range of 53° to 92°.

Scenery. From the town center, you're only minutes away from five state parks.

Access. Littleton offers the right mix of suburban convenience and city access.

Quality of Life. What the numbers add up to is a higher quality of life. A home in our town is a terrific value that offers outstanding educational and community opportunities.

My associates at James Real Estate and I invite you to visit Littleton and learn more about these amenities and the outstanding home values we offer. Please call our office and begin the search for your new home with a James associate.

We look forward to serving you and welcoming you to our community.

Sincerely,

Kevin James

MODEL LETTER 2.19

Why Pay Rent When You Can Own?

Given the resident turnover at many rental properties, this letter can be effective in periodic mailings to the same addresses.

Dear Friend in Apartment 114:

It's the first of the month, and there goes another rent check. You must have said this to yourself time and again. You probably have very valid reasons for postponing the purchase of a home, but let me explain some reasons to reconsider.

Equity. The equity you've been building is not your own. Home values are rising, and indications are this trend will continue. Instead of lining your landlord's pockets, consider making an investment that will let you keep more of what you own.

Affordability. Owning a home can be more economical than you may think. Depending on your personal finances and the type of mortgage you select, you may have more after-expenses money when you buy a home than when you rent.

Security. Insurance companies recognize it: apartment dwellers are more likely than homeowners to sustain property damage or other losses. Your auto and personal property rates may actually decrease when you move into a home.

Comfort. A house will give you room to breathe—a place for you, your growing family, a yard, and covered parking—at no extra charge.

Sound convincing? If you're interested in moving into homeownership, give me a call today. We'll determine your needs and price range and start looking for your new address.

Sincerely,

Bart Cole

Model Letter 2.20

Locked into a Bad Real Estate Deal?

Expressing your empathy with prospects' adverse circumstances shows you understand their problem and may offer a worthwhile solution.

Dear Property Owner:

Changing market conditions can change the way we look at a transaction. The home that seemed like a terrific value a few years ago today may have you locked into a mortgage with a balance that exceeds the value of your home.

RAH Real Estate Associates understands your dilemma, and we have partnered with Allied Finance to offer a way out. We have developed a comprehensive tradeout program that has already helped clients throughout the city. We would welcome the opportunity to evaluate your property and advise you on how the RAH/Allied program might benefit you.

Please call me to learn more details about your options. My associates and I look forward to serving you.

Sincerely,

R. A. Holmes

Using Technology to Extend Your Reach

Small innovations can make large differences in personal productivity. This section describes how two innovations—business card scanners and telephone databases—can enhance correspondence.

MODEL LETTER 2.21

Promoting a Time-Limited Offer
to Convention Contacts

A device that can scan your business card attaches to your personal computer and creates a database of addresses without tedious retyping.

Dear Cindy Reeves:

At Builders, Inc., we are excited about our new Swank plumbing accessories, and we're extending a special offer to you in appreciation for the interest you expressed in the line at the Home Accessory convention today.

Complete the enclosed credit application, and we'll discount all orders you place with us in the third quarter 20 percent. For the next three months—July 1 to September 30—you can save thousands of dollars on your construction projects just because you visited us today!

The construction market is booming throughout the Midwest, and this offer can help you prosper even more. And if you like this opportunity, visit us at the Home Etc. show next month in St. Louis and see what we have in store there.

Sincerely,

Terry Harper

MODEL LETTER 2.22

Providing Product Information to Convention Contacts

By sorting and then scanning a stack of business cards according to questions the contacts asked or material you promised to send, you can quickly prepare appropriate follow-up messages to a number of prospects.

Dear Ed Collins:

Thank you for completing the request for product information at Williamson Co.'s booth at the Hi-Tech convention today. I'm sending you an advance copy of our 19XX catalog. All products with code prefixes of ABC are shipping today. Those with DEF prefixes will be available June 1.

Our new line continues the high standards of quality and design excellence that have distinguished Williamson for more than three decades. Last year, Williamson won eight different awards from our industry, as the article on page 15 explains.

One reason we've been successful all these years is that we make a habit of listening to our customers. Whether you've been a customer for years or are just getting to know us, I invite you to call me at your leisure to express your reactions to our catalog and the extensive range of products we offer. I've sent a business card along with the catalog, and I'm hoping to hear from you soon.

Sincerely,

Pat Malone

MODEL LETTER 2.23

Follow-Up Convention Contact

This note looks personalized but is anything but. It can work equally well for 1,000 prospects or a half dozen.

Dear Linda Simms:

Thank you for stopping by Resonance Corp.'s booth at the SOS convention today. It's always great to hear what my colleagues in the industry are doing and what you think of our new line.

I have added your name and address to our database. Throughout the year, you will receive mailings to keep you apprised of our new offerings and promotions.

Again, I appreciate your taking time to consider Resonance's products, and if you're planning to be at the Next Time meeting in May, come see us there, too.

Sincerely,

Brandon Morgan

MODEL LETTER 2.24

Using Technology to Extend Your Reach

When you take on a new territory, phone book databases can be a valuable resource. These databases—with phone numbers from more than 10,000 U.S. phone books—are available on the Internet (for example, try www.Switch-board.com) and on CD ROMs. The CD version lets you search for companies by type of business, size of business, name, and other variables.

The mailing list for Letter 2.24 was drawn from a CD search for companies with the name Rainbow to market products with a rainbow design.

Dear Rainbow Inc. Manager:

Everyone loves a rainbow, and what a stroke of luck to have a business named Rainbow. Rainbows promise calm after a storm and maybe even a leprechaun's pot of gold.

Your customers can share the pleasure of your rainbow every time you use beautiful, laser-ready paper from Artcraft. Whether you're announcing a sale, answering an inquiry, or prospecting for new business, your message will have greater impact when you send it on our colorful rainbow paper. Use it consistently to set your correspondence apart from the crowd and build customer recognition. Who wouldn't rather open a warm, personal-looking letter than another plain vanilla bill or cheaply made flyer?

Artcraft provides fast, convenient service for all your desktop publishing supplies—labels, certificates, trifolds, and much more. We've been serving customers nationwide from Dallas since 19XX. We're so sure you'll be satisfied that we're offering special incentives when you begin using this beautiful rainbow paper before March 20, 20XX. The enclosed postcard lists volume discount prices available only through this offer.

There's no risk because we provide a money-back guarantee. We also carry an extensive line of pinfeed and laser products. Ordering is easy when you call or fax us at 567-555-7292 or visit us on the Internet at http://www.comuforms.com.

Sincerely,

Ron Campbell

PS. Hurry! Spring's the time for rainbows. Save when you order five or more packets of laser paper before March 20, 20XX!

(Courtesy of Ron Campbell, Dallas, Texas.)

Selling Outlook
Direct Mail: A Tool to Grow Your Business

Your company may already practice sophisticated direct-mail marketing techniques to support the sales division. Even so, an understanding of direct-mail principles and resources can benefit enterprising reps who want to experiment with new sources of prospects.

If you decide to try a mailing on your own, one of these direct-mail classics might be helpful:

- Burnett, Ed. *The Complete Direct Mail List Handbook: Everything You Need to Know About Lists and How to Use Them for Greater Profit* (Englewood Cliffs, N.J.: Prentice Hall 1988).
- Deloitte and Touche. "Managing Database Marketing Technology for Success: A Study of Leading Marketing of Experiences and 'Best Practices' in Leading Marketing Organizations," for the Direct Marketing Association, 1992.
- Nash, Edward L. *Direct Marketing Handbook,* 2d ed. (New York: McGraw-Hill 1991).

Two Internet sites can also help you locate list brokers and other resources:

- Direct Marketing Association—http://www.the-dma.org
- Direct Marketing Product & Services Directory—http://www.dmplaza. com/ps2.html

Letters That Get Appointments and Build Goodwill

So much of selling relies on really simple concepts—like please and thank you. *Please* take some time to find out about my company, my products, and me. *Thank you* for listening and including me in your crowded daily schedule.

A letter that says "please see me" is a courteous way to get started. It indicates your professionalism and organized style, which can help set you apart from your competition. Thanking someone is a powerful expression that reveals humility and the ability to focus on someone other than yourself. A sincere, timely thank you is always appropriate and can be the perfect way to demonstrate your ability to solve the customer's problems.

As the letters in this chapter illustrate, there's no reason you can't complete one phase of the selling process with a thank-you note that includes a "please" to move the sale along.

Requesting an Audience

Often, a well-targeted, compelling letter that says "please take a minute to find out about me and my products" can a get a prospect's attention and set the sales cycle in motion. You want to send the right message and package it in a way that motivates the prospect. In chapter 2, we looked at direct-mail letters that could be sent to huge lists of prospects. The letters in this section are intended for much narrower lists of potential customers and should bear the recipients' names. Like the direct-mail letters, however, these may carry a headline above the salutation that sums up the message and encourages the recipient to take action, which in this case means committing to a meeting.

Chapter 3. Contents

MODEL LETTER 3.1

Why You Should See Me

Lynn Morrison put this letter in a coffee mug and delivered it by either dropping it off at the front desk of prospects' companies or by mailing it to them.

"Finally! Something new and good for the HR department."
"This is going to save time, and it's so easy."
"Definitely an improvement over what's out there now."
"An HR person must have put this together."

My name is Lynn Morrison, and I'm with the human resources division of Staff Up, Inc. I know that you are busy, but share a cup of coffee with me so that I can demonstrate why I've been hearing the above comments. Then you can see for yourself.

- What SHRM is now using to answer questions coming into their information center.
- What the HR departments in over 1,500 companies have switched to, or invested in, in the last three months.
- How you can get the free service of a $100 Toshiba quad speed CD reader.

I promise that our meeting will be worth twenty minutes of your time—and I can almost guarantee that it will save you fifty times that each year.

I will call you on May 1.

Sincerely,

Lynn Morrison

(Courtesy of Lynn Morrison, Richardson, Texas.)

MODEL LETTER 3.2

A 60-Second Fable

This letter is another example of Lynn Morrison's creative packaging. The letter was printed on a scroll, rolled and tied with a ribbon, and mailed in a tube.

A 60-Second Fable

Once upon a time, the Swiss produced over 90 percent of the world's watches. So the inventor of the digital watch first went to them with his proposal. The Swiss didn't bother looking at it because they knew that such a different idea would never catch on. The Swiss lost over 50 percent market share and millions of dollars to the Japanese, who did take the time to look.

The top three reasons SUI users should take the time to look at the new HR Coach from Staff Up, Inc.:

1. RHM is currently using the HR Coach to answer incoming calls to their information center.
2. In the four months since this product has been released, over 1,000 HR departments have made the switch to HR Coach.
3. Finally, a suite of products written in business language for an HR manager, instead of legalese that's geared to a labor law attorney.

Please don't be like the Swiss. Take twenty minutes to see how Staff Up, Inc., has created a better research package for the human resources professional.

I'll be calling next week!

Sincerely,

Lynn Morrison

(Courtesy of Lynn Morrison, Richardson, Texas.)

MODEL LETTER 3.3

A Few Minutes with Us Can Mean Weeks to You

Offer prospects a benefit—such as extra time.

**Guest speakers, menus, block reservations. . . .
How are your corporate meeting plans coming?**

Dear Steve Bridges:

If you'd rather be thinking about keynote addresses, competitive
strategies, and performance incentives than a do-it-yourself company conference, spend a few minutes with Meeting Masters. Last
year, we conducted meetings in 120 cities and resorts throughout
the United States, Mexico, Canada, and the Caribbean, and 78 percent of that business was from repeat customers.

We handle every detail—from airline reservations to tee times—
expressly to your specifications. So give us your hassles, and we'll
give you back your time.

I will call you next Tuesday to discuss how Meeting Masters can
help you stage your most productive conference yet.

Sincerely,

C. B. Good

MODEL LETTER 3.4

You Owe It to Yourself

An appeal to a prospect's emotions. Fear, guilt, and hope can be the catalysts for a sale.

Dear Robin Black:

You've heard it before: "Pay yourself first." And you've promised yourself you'd get started—any day now.

I'm Don Nichols, a certified financial planner, and I can show you some fairly painless ways to start building a financial foundation that will give you the security and rewards you deserve. And if you've already started building your nest egg, I can suggest some creative ideas to make your money work even harder.

So spend an hour with me, and together we'll assess your financial status and develop a strategy to help you meet all your financial goals. I'll call you next week.

Sincerely,

Don Nichols

MODEL LETTER 3.5

Why You Should Stop at Our Trade Show Booth

This letter encourages readers to visit the firm's convention booth and see a first-hand demonstration of the products critiqued in the publicity. The letter could just as easily ask the recipient to visit a store, order from a catalog, or call a representative to request a demonstration.

Dear Greg Kaye:

We don't like to brag—so we'll let others do it for us. At Innovations, Inc., we're delighted about the industry's response to our new line of graphite power tools. Just look at what people are saying:

> "Sets new standards for precision . . ." *Industry Weekly*
> "More durable than you'd ever think possible." *Industry Now*
> "Simply the best." *Critics Corner*

Judge for yourself next month in Seattle. Innovations, Inc., will demonstrate our full line at the Mechanics Quarterly Conference. Stop in and see us there.

Sincerely,

Miles Gibson

MODEL LETTER 3.6

The Market's Buzzing

We all want to think we are up-to-date on what is happening in our industries. That is what makes new product information so compelling.

Dear Lisa Majors:

Software upgrades come and go, so why's everybody talking about WePublish? I'd like a few minutes of your time to tell you why we're outselling every comparable product on the market. I'll demonstrate the package's new spreadsheet and charting capabilities and explain our site-license pricing structure.

WePublish has captured more than 55 percent of the market in the past eighteen months, and we're still gaining momentum. When you take a look at this exciting new version of the product, I'll think you'll understand why.

I'll call you Friday to talk about when we might get together.

Sincerely,

Joe Singer

Confirming an Appointment

A confirmation letter reminds your prospect or client of your meeting and clarifies the details about it. Here's a checklist of information to include in the confirmation letter:

- Time
- Place
- What you will be bringing, if applicable
- Who else will be attending, if applicable
- When you will reconfirm
- How the customer can reach you
- What you intend to cover
- What the customer will get out of the meeting
- A list of information for the customer to bring
- A caution about anything extraordinary, such as confidentiality of information or a requirement to sign a nondisclosure or confidentiality agreement
- An expression of thanks for the opportunity to meet

Model Letter 3.7

A Confirmation That Invites Input

A good confirmation letter can be confirmation that you are organized, attentive to detail, and eager to satisfy the prospect.

Dear Ross Montgomery:

I look forward to meeting with you and your R&D team in the Fairfax conference center next Monday, January 7, 1:00 P.M. Your assistant, Mitch Miller, and I agreed that the purpose of the meeting would be to review the information system's twenty-four-month development plan and to schedule delivery dates for Innovation, Inc., products to coincide with the R&D team's development milestones. The meeting should give all of us a clearer idea of who needs to do what, and in what time frame.

This meeting is a top priority for me and my company, and I appreciate your giving Innovation the opportunity to participate in this promising project. Please let me know of any concerns or special needs you may encounter between now and January 7. I can be reached through my messaging center, 502-555-9900. I'll call Monday before I leave my office to see if there are any last-minute changes or additions.

Sincerely,

Leslie Wynne

Confirming the Date, Time, and Place of a Meeting

Well-written, error-free letters help build your credibility before you even meet a prospective client.

Dear Julie:

This letter is to confirm our meeting on Friday, December 23, in your office. I will bring the material we discussed on the phone—last year's end-of-year figures, projections for next year, and demographic summaries for target mail lists.

I expect the meeting to take no longer than one hour. Thank you for taking time to see me. I think a brief face-to-face meeting will help us establish what needs to happen over the next six months and what each of us stands to gain.

I'll call you Thursday to see if there are any last-minute changes. Please call me if you need anything before then. My number is 555-6677. I look forward to seeing you on the 23rd.

Sincerely,

Pat Meyers

Model Letter 3.9

Confirming the Meeting and What You Want from the Customer

Providing all meeting participants with the names of other participants is a helpful gesture.

Dear Max:

The purpose of this letter is to confirm our meeting on December 15, 3:00 P.M., at the Fairmont Hotel. As we discussed on the phone, I will be bringing my manager, Larry Schmitz, as well as my marketing director, Ken Redding.

During our meeting, we would like to review our marketing plan, especially as it relates to our product direction. We are very interested in hearing any reservations you may have, and we hope this discussion helps us better understand the user's perspective. We also want to answer any questions you may have about where we are headed with our current product line and how it fits into your strategy.

We expect the meeting to last from two to three hours. I will call you to reconfirm the meeting early in the week, but please let me know before then, should a conflict arise in your schedule. My voice mail number is 800-555-3000, ext. 247.

Max, thank you for arranging this meeting in your busy schedule. We look forward to seeing you on the 15th.

Sincerely,

Mary Hodges

MODEL LETTER 3.10

Confirming the Attendees and Agenda

Answer as many questions as possible in your correspondence before a meeting.

Dear William:

The purpose of this letter is to confirm the logistics and agenda of the meeting we've scheduled for January 11.

As we discussed on the phone, this meeting will be the first in a series of strategic alliance discussions. The senior managers and marketing staff from our organization will attend, and, as you indicated, their counterparts from your company will also be present.

As for the meeting content, we will share our future product line with your organization and will seek your opinions about the viability of our strategy. The content of this presentation will require participants' signatures on a nondisclosure agreement. (I've enclosed a copy for the review of your legal department.)

The tentative agenda is as follows:

  8:30 Introduction of participants
  9:00 Corporate overview
10:00 Futures presentation
12:00 Lunch catered in executive dining room
  1:00 Presentation by Dave Winters, chairman and CEO
  2:00 Questions, answers, and response time
  3:00 Adjourn

William, your participation in this alliance meeting is critical to the establishment of our future direction. We hope you will share with us your reactions to these products and the industry assumptions they are based on. In addition, a discussion of your company's market direction would enhance the exchange for all parties involved.

I will confirm the details and attendees in the week of January 7. Thank you for making the commitment to enter into this alliance with my company. On behalf of everyone at ABC, we appreciate your participation in this event and look forward to seeing you in January.

Sincerely,

Erin Riley

Supplying the Customer Information in Preparation for the Meeting

Product information given to customers before a meeting can be the key to an efficient, productive discussion.

Dear Joe:

In preparation for our meeting with your staff and you, I am sending you the technical description of our software. You or your engineers may want to read this material before we meet on June 2.

We're all busy, I know, but it may actually save time if you have this information now. This way, your people can prepare detailed questions in advance, and our discussion can be as technical as you'd like on the 2nd.

Please call if you have any questions or need any additional information. Otherwise, I'll see you next week. I look forward to working with you.

Sincerely,

Lou Richards

MODEL LETTER 3.12

Asking the Customer to Prepare for the Meeting

This request is actually quite huge, and it would be a real coup if the prospect actually supplied everything. Nevertheless, on the theory that if you don't ask, you'll never receive, you can at least get started by outlining what you want from the customer. If they supply one of the three requests, you are better off than you would be by postponing the request.

Dear Dick:

In preparation for our meeting next week, I've compiled a list of information that would help my firm refine our strategic marketing efforts on your behalf. It would be very helpful to have these items at the meeting:

1. Expected growth figures for next year
2. Current and next year's project and priority lists
3. List of requirements and objectives

Dick, thank you in advance for preparing this information. I know it will be time-consuming to gather this material, but I really think your work will pay off in a more focused meeting.

I will follow up on Monday of next week to discuss this request. Thank you for your time and effort.

Sincerely,

Michael Allen

MODEL LETTER 3.13

Canceling a Meeting

Most people will cancel a meeting by phone. But written confirmation of the cancellation is appropriate in more formal situations.

Dear Tom:

This letter confirms our phone conversation. I am canceling our November 12 meeting because our product announcement date has been delayed. I will reschedule the meeting as soon as we set a new announcement date. I apologize for any inconvenience this delay causes you or anyone else in your organization.

I look forward to talking with you soon.

Sincerely,

Erin Riley

MODEL LETTER 3.14

Suggesting Another Meeting When the Customer Cancels

Immediate follow-up can help you recover after a customer cancels a meeting.

Dear Raymond:

I was sorry to learn that you had to cancel our April 15 product presentation. I understand how busy you are and know that running your own business must be your first priority.

I'm still convinced that our product is the key to improving your manufacturing process. I encourage you to take a look at it. We can meet with you at any time, and I know we can suggest creative solutions to your productivity challenges.

I will call in the first week of next month. I hope we'll be able to reschedule the demonstration some time soon. Thank you for considering XYZ Company.

Sincerely,

Allen Richards

Following Up After the Meeting

After the appointment, it's important to confirm expectations. The remarkable thing about meetings is how widely everyone's perception of the same discussion can vary: what went on, who said what, and what exact conclusion was reached? The more people at the meeting, the more opinions as to what was said.

Smart salespeople protect themselves from misunderstandings by writing down their version of what happened and sending it to everyone who attended the meeting. This works! What gets written down and circulated becomes the established record of events. If someone disagrees with your interpretation, that person will usually let you know and you can address any corrections that may be necessary.

MODEL LETTER 3.15

What Each Party Agrees to Accomplish

Brief letters made up of concise numbered or bulleted lists provide an effective record of your meetings.

Dear Bill:

This letter is to summarize the commitments agreed to in our meeting yesterday.

1. ABC Company will provide on-site support throughout the testing phase of our new product.
2. ABC Company will allow XYZ Company to test the new product for two weeks.
3. XYZ Company will make available to ABC Company the results of the tests.

Please do not hesitate to let me know if I have left anything out, or if your understanding is any different from the above.

I look forward to implementing our new product in your environment and appreciate this opportunity for ABC Company.

Sincerely,

Lou Gaines

MODEL LETTER 3.16

Reviewing Activities to Be Accomplished by Each Party

Clear up any misunderstandings early by writing a follow-up letter immediately after the meeting.

Dear Jack:

Thank you for meeting with me yesterday. I thought it would be helpful to follow up with a summary of the action items and schedule agreed to during the meeting.

ABC Company:

1. Review quantity discounts and see about getting an additional price break at the 1,000 quantity.
2. Check into the delivery schedule for new product line.
3. Provide both answers by November 15.

XYZ Company:

1. Re-verify quantity requirement of 1,000 for the first quarter.
2. Check with manufacturing as to preference for current versus newer model.
3. Provide answers to above at next meeting, after November 15.

Jack, I look forward to working with XYZ Company to satisfy your requirement for units in the first quarter. Please let me know if I need to check into anything else before our next meeting.

Thank you for your giving ABC Company this opportunity.

Sincerely,

Mary Hendricks

MODEL LETTER 3.17

What Will It Take to Get the Business?
The Postmeeting Summary

When you're not meeting face to face with a customer, this type of letter serves as a reminder of the stipulations the customer set forth for you. The advantage of sending such a letter is to refresh the other party's memory about what he or she said, to demonstrate how seriously you take the customer's instructions, and to document the services you have performed.

As you progress through the selling cycle, you may discover that the customer meant something different from what was said. But how would you realize the miscommunication without your confirmation letter?

Dear Matt:

We covered a lot of ground in yesterday's meeting! I thought the meeting was very productive, but it might be wise to review the expectations we discussed to avoid any misunderstandings.

To secure future business from your company, my company needs to position itself to do the following:

- Meet your delivery requirements of a shipment every Monday by 12 noon.
- Plan to stock the items in our local warehouse.
- Have one week's inventory available locally, at all times.
- Have a service person on call 24 hours a day, 7 days a week.
- Be prepared to pay a penalty of 20 percent, if any of the above criteria are not met.

Matt, I recognize that each of these points is crucial to your ability to run your company and our ability to do business with you. Please let me know ASAP if I have summarized anything incorrectly.

I will call you Friday to see if my summary meets your approval. Next week, I expect to present you a proposal based on our discussion in yesterday's meeting.

Thank you for your consideration of ABC Company for your material requirements. I look forward to working with you.

Sincerely,

Linda Forbes

MODEL LETTER 3.18

Following Up by Sending a Property Value Estimate

Routine details can be handled graciously—as this letter illustrates.

Dear Mr. and Mrs. Townsend:

Thank you for coming to our office and permitting us to show the Riverhill area and some properties on the market. As you can imagine, there is always a turnover of properties that are available as properties are sold and other properties come on to the market. The property that was your favorite on Oakland Hills Lane is still available.

Vicki and I enjoyed seeing your attractive home and 55-acre ranch. It is our opinion that the current market value of your property is in the $280,000 to $320,000 range.

Please let us know when you are ready to list your property and continue looking for a new home.

Have an enjoyable trip to Europe. We look forward to your return to Kerrville. Please let me know if there is any information that will be helpful to you.

Very truly yours,

William C. Hubbard

(Courtesy of William C. Hubbard, Kerrville, Texas.)

Model Letter 3.19

Keeping a Dialogue Going When You've Decided Not to Pursue the Business

For whatever reason, the prospect or rep may be unable to commit to a particular deal. It is wise, though, to continue correspondence for future possibilities.

Dear Robert:

Thank you for our meeting. I know your time is limited, and I want you to know how valuable our meeting was to me. It gave me several insights about the marketing concepts and graphic look I am developing for my line.

You seem to have a good grasp of the importance of both marketing and presentation. I would like for us to stay in touch because I think we can help one another on future projects. I am committed to a project that will keep me busy until March. After that, I will be available on a per-project basis.

I will call you in March to discuss your needs. Good luck in your new business endeavor.

Sincerely,

Annie Adams

(Courtesy of Annie Adams, Dallas, Texas.)

Saying Thank You
in Almost Every Situation

"Thank you" is a powerful message by itself or in conjunction with other selling tasks. Sometimes a concise, heartfelt note of thanks is appropriate. On other occasions, the thank-you letter serves as a transition from one phase of the selling cycle to the next. Does the customer need product information? Can you offer a reference or testimonial to convince the other party that your company has successfully solved similar problems for others? Writing a thank-you note lets you suggest a way to continue the sale cycle. So, offer a next step, and let the customer know you're willing to help any way you can.

MODEL LETTER 3.20

Thank You for the Phone Discussion

Thank-you notes are a courteous expression of your appreciation, and they help put prospects at ease.

Dear Connie:

It was a pleasure talking with you this afternoon. Thank you for your interest in ABC's solid-state system. I'm sending you a copy of our latest product brochure and a copy of *Focus,* our corporate magazine. The magazine describes several installations that may interest you.

As I told you on the phone, I would be happy to meet with you, possibly together with a systems engineer, to discuss any performance problems you may be experiencing. Please call me any time I can be of assistance.

Best regards,

Ann Street

Model Letter 3.21

Thank You for Meeting with Me

No matter what title we go by at the office, we all like to receive personal mail. A personal note after an initial meeting is a must for successful selling. It is your chance to remind the prospect who you are. More important, it shows that you value the other person's time. You don't take this person for granted—and you appreciate the consideration he or she showed. A personal note helps build the goodwill that creates long-term business partnerships, and that's what gets you business long after the initial sale.

Dear Joe:

Thank you so much for meeting with me last week and letting me tell you a little about XYZ Company. The information that you shared with me will be invaluable as I develop proposals to solve your manufacturing challenges.

I hope our meeting will be the beginning of a long, productive business relationship. Thank you for your time and your consideration.

Sincerely,

Mark Raymond

MODEL LETTER 3.22

Let's Stay in Touch

Don't let your efforts go to waste. Letters are a great way to remind potential customers that you will be there when they are ready to make a move.

Dear Mr. Solomon:

Thank you for visiting with me about your development projects this afternoon. As we discussed, I specialize in the sale of undeveloped single-family land to homebuilders.

I would like to stay in touch with you regarding the possible sale of single-family land in Little Creek, Stoneridge, and Lakeview. My business card is enclosed.

Sincerely,

Blake M. Reed

(Courtesy of Blake M. Reed, Dallas, Texas.)

MODEL LETTER 3.23

Thank You for Meeting My Manager

This note accomplishes two goals: it shows that you respect the customer's time and reinforces the multilevel coverage you're providing the account.

Dear Marty:

Thank you for taking the time to meet with me and my manager, Joe Smith, yesterday. Joe was very pleased to talk with you and see your operation firsthand.

Although I have discussed your business with Joe in detail, the personal contact with you helped him better understand your requirements and be better prepared to give you the special account coverage we want to provide.

I know that your time is valuable. Thank you again for spending some of it with Joe and me.

Sincerely,

Beth Gordan

MODEL LETTER 3.24

Thank You for Attending
Our Product Demonstration

Establish your next move by telling the customer when you will call again.

Dear Sam:

Thank you for attending our product demonstration last week. It was great to meet with you again. I hope that seeing the product in action was helpful. As you progress in your product acquisition process, please do not hesitate to let me know if you or someone else in your organization needs additional demonstrations.

Sam, I know how busy you are, and I truly appreciate the time you took to view our products. I'll follow up with you next week.

Best regards,

Terry King

MODEL LETTER 3.25

Thank You for the Opportunity to Respond to Your RFQ; You Are a Valued Customer

This letter was used to follow up with a senior-level person, when the actual work done on the request for a quotation was at a lower level. Such a letter can help you achieve the necessary exposure to the higher levels of the organization, while not alienating the people who are your regular contacts.

Dear Bill Davies:

Thank you for giving ABC the opportunity to respond to your firm's request for a quotation for our solid-state disk subsystem. I have enjoyed working with Pat Jones in addressing your firm's data processing issues.

We value you as a customer and appreciate the opportunity to work with you as you progress from our B21 to B22 subsystem. Please call me if you have any questions concerning our response to the RFQ. I can be reached at 214-555-7799.

Thanks again for your consideration.

Sincerely,

Michelle Robinson

(Courtesy of Michelle Robinson, Mobile, Alabama.)

Thank You for Telling Me About an Opportunity

The next letter is one of two follow-up thank yous from an awkward situation. Ann ran into a friend who happened to be the president of a company. The friend told her about an opportunity at his company. She checked out the lead and learned that his employees had just decided to order from one of her company's competitors.

Ann felt that two follow-up letters were important. First, she thanked her friend for the lead and encouraged him to consider her firm in the future. Second, she wrote the primary account contact to ask for future consideration and prevent any misunderstandings about the president's message. Here's the letter to the president.

Dear Peter:

Thank you for letting me know about the opportunity at Home Security. I have had conversations with both Keith Rogers and Larry Timms. They explained that a decision had apparently already been reached by the time I called. I regret that we were not calling on you earlier, and hope that we will have the opportunity to participate in future transactions.

Peter, enclosed is a card for your files. Thank you again for the lead. I will continue to follow up with Keith and Larry. I hope we can match a Home Security requirement with an ABC solution sometime in the future.

Sincerely,

Ann McIntyre

MODEL LETTER 3.27

Thank You for Your Efforts on My Behalf

Both decision makers mentioned in Model Letter 3.26 received this letter.

Dear Larry:

Thank you for talking on the phone with me about Home Security's information management system and your recent transaction. I regret that my firm was not calling on you sooner, and I hope that you will let us stay in touch and compete next time.

I will call you in December. By then, maybe our schedules will have settled down and we can meet to discuss your challenges. I've enclosed my card for your files. Please do not hesitate to call me if I may be of service in any way.

Sincerely,

Ann McIntyre

MODEL LETTER 3.28

Thank You for Helping Me Pursue an Opportunity in Your Company

The success of your sales efforts often depends on individuals in a large firm who help you break the ice with decision makers. It is important to let these helpful contacts know they are valuable to you.

Dear Steve Peters:

Thank you for your interest in ABC's automation system. Enclosed please find the information I promised. I look forward to discussing this material with you, and I'd be happy to answer questions and research any issues you'd like to address.

I am most appreciative of your help in my pursuit of opportunities in your company. Thank you for your ideas and introductions.

Sincerely,

Chris Smith

MODEL LETTER 3.29

Thank You for Letting Us Study Your Needs

This situation—when your company is studying the needs of a prospective customer—gives you an opportunity to remind the prospect how valuable your company is to them. Establish that the results could include some surprises, and tell them when you expect to complete the project.

Dear Barbara Summers:

Thank you for letting XYZ Company study your capacity requirements. Expertise in capacity planning requirements is one of our company's specialties. Our experience tells us you might find the results of our study both thought-provoking and helpful. You can expect the study to confirm what you already know in some areas and surprise you a bit in others.

We will be working closely with the staff you have assigned to this project and appreciate that you have made these people available to us. Please call me any time you have any questions or concerns.

We expect to complete our work in the first week of October and will be prepared to present the results at that time. Again, thank you for this opportunity and for your consideration of XYZ Company.

Yours truly,

Mike Hansen

MODEL LETTER 3.30

Thank You for Providing a Reference

When someone serves as a reference for you, a thank-you note is essential. The other person's gesture suggests that your relationship goes beyond a customer-vendor transaction and into a partnership, and it's wise to reinforce that partnership with an expression of your appreciation.

Dear Bill:

Thank you for discussing XYZ's products and services with our potential client, ABC. Testimonials from satisfied customers are very powerful and informative—they can be more persuasive than anything representatives of the company say.

Your remarks made quite a favorable impression on ABC. They may ask to talk to you again or even suggest getting together. Without clients like you, XYZ would not be able to reach out to potential new users. Please know that your support is highly appreciated.

Sincerely,

Linda Holmes

MODEL LETTER 3.31

Thank You for the Business

Here's the classic that is all too easy to forget.

Dear Pat:

Thank you very much for your recent order for 1,200 units. That is a very significant order for me personally, as well as for my company.

I appreciate your confidence in my company's product, and for your ongoing business and support.

Very truly yours,

Lynn Hartley

MODEL LETTER 3.32

Thank You for Selecting Us

Long-term customer–vendor relationships develop one step at a time, and well-timed thank-you letters can be effective bridges from one phase of the sale to the next.

Dear Cynthia:

I want to thank you personally for selecting Team Health and to pledge our commitment to earn your business every day.

Since 1984, Team Health has grown and flourished because we have established and maintained the highest-quality standards for all our services. We've made client satisfaction and service excellence our top priorities, and then we've delivered on our promises. Our commitment has paid off as we see the continued loyalty of our clients.

We make the same pledge to you. We will work with you in partnership to be certain that we provide the best care for your employees. At the same time, we will work to help you reduce your costs and grow your business. With your Team Health benefit plan in place, you will be able to attract and retain the best people, and in today's business environment, that can give you a real competitive edge.

Our goal is to provide you with a wide range of services that meet your needs today—and in the years ahead. Of course, this means that we must be prepared to grow continually and to enhance our service offerings. Since its creation, Team Health has grown into the largest independent managed care organization in the state. With the addition of St. Mark Hospital as an equity investor, you can be certain that we have the financial stability to bring those new services to you.

Most important, throughout our relationship, I want to be certain that you are satisfied with every aspect of our service. Your feedback is vital to help me accomplish this goal. Please be sure to contact me directly with any questions, comments, or suggestions. My direct number is 331-555-0044, ext. 321.

Thank you for joining the Team Health family. We look forward to serving you for many years to come.

Sincerely,

Pat Romboletti

(Courtesy of Pat Romboletti, The Write Sales System™, Dallas, Texas.)

MODEL LETTER 3.33

Thank You for the Opportunity
(To a Customer Who Chose Someone Else)

Earn the opportunity to compete for future business by expressing appreciation that the prospect considered you for a contract you didn't win.

Dear Libby Mann:

Thank you for giving us the opportunity to submit a proposal for your health benefit plan. Although you have selected another plan, I want to assure you of our continued interest in serving you.

Team Health offers a comprehensive approach to health care. We focus on providing flexible plans, affordable rates, a wide range of options, and attentive service. In addition, we continually enhance and expand our benefit options to meet the changing needs of our customers. I hope we will have an opportunity to demonstrate that to you in the future.

Thank you for your consideration.

Sincerely,

Pat Romboletti

(Courtesy of Pat Romboletti, The Write Sales System™, Dallas, Texas.)

MODEL LETTER 3.34

Thank You for Taking the Time to Complete Our Customer Survey

Talk to your customers at every available opportunity—especially when they do you a favor.

Dear Lisa Lawrence:

We appreciate your taking time to complete our customer survey.

Your positive response is a testimony to the dedication and commitment of every member of On Time Service Team. As your business partner, we know that our success depends on your success. As your needs change, please be sure to let us know if there are any additional options we can provide that would assist you and your business.

I welcome your feedback, and I can assure you that everyone at On Time Service will continue to strive to provide the highest level of service possible.

Sincerely,

Pat Romboletti

(Courtesy of Pat Romboletti, The Write Sales System™, Dallas, Texas.)

MODEL LETTER 3.35

Thank You for Your Participation

Your enthusiasm tells customers you're on their team.

Dear Lynn:

I want to thank you, your company, and your client for participating in the 1996 Summer Olympics.

The overnights and the press say this was the most successful Summer Olympics ever. I know I watched more than usual!

I hope your client's advertising strategies and goals tally a perfect score. On behalf of the stations you chose to run your advertising, thank you for the business. We look forward to working with your agency and your client in the future.

Regards,

Sally Lombard

MODEL LETTER 3.36

"Thank You for Visiting Our Store"

Retailing with flawless customer service is the trademark of Lester Melnick, a women's apparel store based in Dallas, Texas. This letter and the three that follow it are samples of how the store's salespeople reinforce their efforts with personal notes to customers.

Dear Mrs. Wells:

I'm so glad you stopped into Lester Melnick yesterday and that we had a chance to meet. I will keep my eyes open for a luncheon suit that would be appropriate for your upcoming charity fund raiser and will call you when I have a few selections for you to try. I look forward to helping you on your next visit to LM.

Sincerely,

Lisa Guimbellot

(Courtesy of Lester Melnick, Inc., Dallas, Texas.)

MODEL LETTER 3.37

"Thanks for Stopping In"

Even if a customer didn't mention a special request, you can still say thanks for browsing, as this letter illustrates.

Dear Carolyn:

Thanks for stopping into Lester Melnick yesterday. I'm glad we got a chance to meet, and I hope we can visit again the next time you come by. It would be my pleasure to assist you with your wardrobe needs or gift selections anytime.

Sincerely,

Lisa Guimbellot

(Courtesy of Lester Melnick, Inc., Dallas, Texas.)

MODEL LETTER 3.38

"Welcome Back to Our Store"

This letter encourages an occasional customer to drop in more often.

Dear Judy:

It was a pleasure to see you again yesterday. I have missed visiting you. I am certain you will enjoy the ensemble we put together. Just this morning we received a handbag that would look perfect with it. I look forward to showing it to you the next time you are in.

Thanks for stopping by; I hope to see you again soon!

Sincerely,

Lisa Guimbellot

(Courtesy of Lester Melnick, Inc., Dallas, Texas.)

MODEL LETTER 3.39

A Thank You for a Special Purchase

Thank-you notes are a good place to express your personal interest in the customer's satisfaction with the purchase.

Dear Mrs. Meyers:

I'm so glad we were able to find the perfect dress for your daughter's wedding. After your life gets back to normal following the festivities, I hope you will bring in a few photographs—I'd especially like to see one of you in your dress. I hope all goes well with the wedding and reception, and I look forward to seeing you again soon.

Sincerely,

Lisa Guimbellot

(Courtesy of Lester Melnick, Inc., Dallas, Texas.)

MODEL LETTER 3.40

Thanks for the Referral

Referrals are both a compliment to you personally and a vital boost to your business. Let your friends know you appreciate their efforts.

Dear Steve:

Thanks for referring Fiona Westgate to me! I am very pleased to have Fiona as a client. One of these days, I hope to have all the members of your clan as clients (particularly their patriarch—you).

Please call when you have time. I would be very interested in catching up on your activities. Thanks again for referring Fiona to me.

Best regards,

Ed Keith

(Courtesy of Ed Keith, Houston, Texas.)

MODEL LETTER 3.41

Saying Thanks Although You Are Declining the Project

Occasions arise when, for technical or other reasons, you decline to bid on business. In this situation, explain your reasons and state the conditions under which you would bid. In some cases, prospects will consider a change to accommodate you.

Dear Joe:

Thank you for including ABC Company in your Request for Proposal process for new power generators.

The technical specifications of this project are well suited to an ABC Solution; however, ABC must decline to bid for two reasons. First, your request stipulates that all products proposed must have been in production for six months, and our current generator of the specified strength has only been in production for two months. Second, you require service not only in Oklahoma City but also in Bartlesville, which is outside our service range.

It is with great regret that we decline this opportunity. Although this letter is intended as ABC's official response, it is also our opportunity to say that if XYZ would consider variations to the RFP, we would be pleased to present alternatives. For example, a reference list, including beta customers, may convince you that the product is stable, despite its short life cycle. Regarding service, we do have a certified third-party vendor handling Bartlesville, and referenceable sites there.

We hope that these suggestions will lead to further discussion, and the opportunity to prepare a customized bid. If that is not an option, thank you for considering ABC Company, and please continue to keep us in mind for future requirements.

Sincerely yours,

Margot Taylor

MODEL LETTER 3.42

Keeping the Door Open When the Deal Is Off

Market conditions change quickly, and a deal that doesn't work this year can bear fruit sooner than you think. That is why it is important to establish a dialogue and keep it going.

Dear Mr. and Mrs. Williams:

Thank you for working with us on the potential development of your property in Lake Town. We have decided, however, not to pursue this opportunity. Pending developments in the surrounding area influenced our decision, as did specific development issues that are unique to your property.

Several properties in your neighborhood are under development now. They include the Michaels property (50 acres) and the Taylor property (114 acres). Together these projects will yield about 650 homes in the $90,000 to $115,000 price range. We are concerned that this development will define the north side of Hwy. 2 as a first-time homebuyer's market. This trend does not bode well for the sale of custom homes along the north side of the highway.

We also considered the development issues related to your property. As you know, our primary interest is in a low-density, custom home community. Unfortunately, the land cost and the desired lot size, coupled with the costs related to off-site sanitary sewers and perimeter roads, push the average lot price to a level that we consider too risky in light of neighboring developments.

These considerations do not preclude the sale of your property, however. I have some ideas in this regard that we might discuss at your convenience.

I thank you for your patience and the opportunity to work with you on this project.

Sincerely,

Blake M. Reed

(Courtesy of Blake M. Reed, Dallas, Texas.)

Selling Outlook
Handwritten or Typed Thank Yous?
A Guide to What Is Appropriate

We've come to expect that business correspondence will be typed or, more accurately for today's office, produced on a laser printer. We regard crisp, highly legible typed messages as professional, and we've made sizable investments in a company letterhead and logos. The only handwriting we expect to see is the author's signature at the end of the letter, or, if you know the recipient especially well, you may sign your first name only or initial the letter.

Some situations, however, call for a different approach. Especially in selling, you may find occasions to trade in the typewritten letter for warmer, more personal correspondence—the handwritten note. Handwritten thank yous and other personal notes are more common in certain selling situations, such as retail and real estate, but they can be effective in many other fields.

People react to mail that looks personal, as countless direct-mail tests have proved. Ann found this out when a note-sized envelope addressed by hand arrived in her morning mail. The note looked so inviting, she opened it first. It was from an acquaintance who'd bumped into Ann's husband and decided to follow up by sending a business card and handwritten note that announced her new status in real estate sales.

Why was Ann so eager to read the personal note? "My first reaction was that this must be someone who really knows us. How rare, something personal among the impersonal junk that arrives every day. I was delighted that this person took the time to contact personally. She showed a lot more effort than merely adding us to her mailing list. If I were in the market for real estate, I'm sure we would call her first," says Ann.

Ann's story is one example of how a handwritten note can give representatives a competitive edge. Here are some guidelines for using handwritten notes effectively.

Guideline 1: *Handwritten notes are especially appropriate in sales directly to an individual decision maker, rather than to a business.* A handwritten note emphasizes your personal interest in the customer and engenders confidence and trust in you. Sales involving residential real estate, cars, cosmetics, plus personal services such as financial planning, can all be enhanced by occasional personal correspondence.

Guideline 2: *Handwritten notes work well for salespeople from one-person or small businesses.* Personal notes can be persuasive reminders of the benefits of working with you—a sales representative who provides one-on-one attention and can respond promptly to the customer's needs. This approach can be effective whether customers come from other small companies or from larger corporations because notes from you show customers they are important to you. It underscores your competitive strengths: you are not so big; the customer will have great status in your organization.

Guideline 3: *Handwritten notes help you cross the barrier between professional activity and personal sentiments.* In long-term relationships between customers and sales representatives, occasions arise that call for heartfelt expressions of sympathy, congratulations, and gratitude. Customers may retire, get promoted, or have a death in the family. You may want to acknowledge the customer's birthday or say thank you for a lunch, dinner, golf game, or donation to charity. On occasions that go beyond specific business transactions, the personal touch of a handwriting message is especially appropriate.

One word of caution about holiday cards: send out season's greetings only if you can add a personal note to each card. Otherwise, the message to the customer may not be the one you intend to send.

CHAPTER 4

Cover Letters

Think of a cover letter as the warm smile and firm handshake you'd extend if you were greeting customers in person. The cover letter needs to be friendly, courteous, professional, but most of all—effective. You want to focus the recipients' attention and move the sale closer to closure. The model letters in this chapter illustrate this principle at work in various stages of the sale.

As a sales professional, you understand the importance of reading customers to uncover the objections, fears, and other obstacles to closing. The purpose of this chapter is to demonstrate how to put that information to work in cover letters that allay fears, overcome obstacles, and say just the right thing for the situation at hand.

Perhaps you're sending a prospect introductory information in brochures or testimonials. You'll want to create interest and encourage the prospect to take action—to call you, to answer your call on a specified date, to attend your company's open house or demonstration. Whatever the occasion, a clear, concise cover letter can compel your prospect to take another step toward closing the deal.

Cover letters that accompany proposals, contracts, or other documents specific to a customer provide an opportunity to reiterate important selling points and to persuade. Direct attention to the customer's areas of special interest, as in, "The volume discount numbers I promised are on page 3. I think you'll find them highly competitive."

Why assume that a brochure will convince the prospect that your offer is the best? Provide evidence in your cover letter. What makes your company a good bet? Cite recent comments from industry experts, financial analysts, or satisfied customers. Maybe they like your offer, but what makes you the person they should be dealing with? Use the cover letter to sell yourself.

An *effective* cover letter focuses attention where you want it. It's certainly possible to write one stock cover letter to use on any occasion, and there may be times when your favorite, tried-and-true letter is the fastest, most efficient way to give customers what they need when they expect it. You'll find plenty of candidates for best all-around cover letter in this chapter, but we also encourage you to adapt our examples to all sorts of situations.

Our model cover letters vary in length, but one-page letters should be the rule. Brevity is the key to driving home your message. Make exceptions only when you feel it's essential to recap a number of issues for the various recipients of your document. Even your longer letters can be concise if you use subheadings and bulleted lists to organize information and then follow the tips for self-editing discussed in "Words That Sell" at the end of this part.

CHAPTER 4. CONTENTS

Cover Letters for Proposals and Pricing

Cover Letters on a Revised Proposal

Cover Letters That Accompany a Contract

Cover Letters for Proposals and Pricing

Model Letter 4.1

Introducing a Major Proposal

When a proposal is massive, the cover letter that accompanies it may be large as well. The following example is fairly lengthy and covers a lot of ground. It explains why you are in the market, how the product evolved, how you see the customer using the product, and your assurance that your firm is positioned to handle the business.

This letter is technical in content, but the approach works equally well in other types of sales. Subheadings are used to help tell the story and to break up long blocks of copy.

Dear Mr. Jenkins:

Storage Technology Corp. is pleased to respond to your request for an enterprise-wide solution to managing data archiving across multiple computer platforms.

A Leader in Innovation

For twenty-three years, StorageTek has been a leading provider of high-performance information storage and retrieval solutions in the IBM marketplace. Our customers have been the beneficiaries of this expertise in installations of DASD, Tape, ACS, and Printers. During the past four years, our expertise has expanded as we perfected our ability to cross computer platforms.

StorageTek believes in an open systems solutions approach, and we have used this philosophy in solutions that define industry standards. First, we delivered Tapeline products, including both cartridge and reel tape drives. Next came Printline products, both band printers and high-speed laser printers. Then we introduced the Nearline products—the only fully automated production robotics library on the market with full multihost connectivity to provide complete automation of cartridge mount/dismount operations. Our peripherals now successfully interface with sixteen different operating environments via native and non-native attachment.

Our commitment to full solutions did not stop there. In 19XX, we entered into a new phase of open computing. Our customers had previously asked for and received the cartridge tape and library—those processors considered to be part of the "glass house" environment. Growth outside the glass house was explosive, yet the same management controls did not seem to exist among the network clients. Tape management and archival status were less secure than in the mainframe arena, yet were no less important. StorageTek seized this opportunity to fill a void with Nearline, our hardware/software-based client-server approach to managing your network. Our ultimate goal is to combine the native mainframe attaches with a symbiotic network and attach to centralize all automated mounts through your mainframe.

The Nearline Systems should be the repository of all corporate intellectual property. When you accomplish this goal, you will have achieved far more than a darkened data center for all platforms; your company will have furthered its goal of maintaining the highest return possible on its investment in peripherals.

About the StorageTek Proposal

The enclosed proposal encompasses tried-and-true technology across your entire enterprise. It also includes philosophies of control and management that go far beyond any other solution in the market today. Most important, it is a total solution, with one vendor, StorageTek, that will handle your current and future storage requirements.

We feel that a staged program of installations will benefit the different challenges your needs present. We are ready to implement a plan that would automate the backup of a vast majority of your platforms during the next twelve months. This proposal encompasses our thoughts and should be used as a guide for further discussions. We are hopeful that we can begin to implement this proposal this year. Our studies lead us to believe that the best way to proceed is to begin with implementation of MVS, followed by VMS, and then UTS.

We hope you accept our enterprise-wide solution on its merits. We believe that the detail that follows in our proposal will show you why you can trust StorageTek conclusions and move forward to implement them. We look forward to answering your questions and to continuing our long and mutually beneficial business relationship.

Thank you for the time you and your staff have given us on this very important challenge.

Sincerely,

Ralph Greenlee

(Courtesy of Ralph Greenlee, Storage Technology Corporation, Louisville, Colorado.)

MODEL LETTER 4.2

Reasons to Act Now

Proposal cover letters can do more than describe what you are sending; they can encourage the customers to act now.

Dear Lance:

Thank you for considering Pearson Software products and for this opportunity to present the enclosed proposal.

When you have reviewed our offer, I am confident you will see its merits and the attractive price that is available during these favorable market conditions. By acting now—before anticipated year-end markups—you will be giving your company considerable cost savings on its advanced technology investment.

As you and your staff evaluate our proposal, it will probably generate some technical questions. Our product support team is available to address any concerns your operations staff may express.

I look forward to your response. I am confident our products will significantly enhance your company's productivity at a very reasonable price.

Sincerely,

Robert Downs

MODEL LETTER 4.3

Explaining Several Categories of Pricing

Pricing can get complicated. Customers will appreciate the effort you put into explaining your pricing scheme. Also, your willingness to provide additional information will also be reassuring to them.

Dear Jeff:

Thank you for your interest in MegaDisk's automated archiving system and for your patience while I prepared this information for you.

I have classified the pricing information you requested into three categories:

- Pricing for used MegaDisk components and related software
- Pricing for new MegaDisk components and related software
- Pricing for alternate hardware and software from one of MegaDisk's partners

Jeff, I look forward to discussing this pricing schedule with you. I hope this information is adequate at this stage of the budget cycle. If you need anything else, just let me know.

Best regards,

Michelle Michaels

Explaining a Preliminary Pricing Scheme

Often customers request preliminary pricing information to help them plan their budgets. In such cases, sales reps need to forewarn customers that, as you continue to explore their needs, a price change is possible. The cover letter for this information also gives you the opportunity to remind customers that you hope to study their needs further before you submit a final price.

Dear Mr. Richards:

Thank you for your interest in MegaDisk's automated archiving system. I have enclosed the pricing information you requested for use in planning your 20XX budget.

This preliminary pricing information is subject to change, depending on the result of MegaDisk's automation study. Our systems engineer is preparing the study and plans to have it completed in two weeks.

I look forward to working with you as you proceed with archiving automation. I am always available to discuss this pricing information, the pending study, and any questions you may have. Please don't hesitate to call.

Sincerely,

Lyle Griffin

MODEL LETTER 4.5

"We Are Pleased to Submit Our Proposal. . . ."

The confidence you convey in your ability to meet the customer's needs is enticing.

Dear Dr. Mitchell:

We are pleased to submit our proposal for catering luncheons, dinners, and break refreshments for your quarterly conference. I know that you have many factors to consider before making a final decision. As you review our information, if you find that any part of the proposal needs further clarification, please let me know.

With CityGourmet, you can expect every detail to be carefully planned and handled to perfection. Your event will be complemented by the finest cuisine and served in a setting beyond your imagination. We can confidently promise you an occasion that will exceed your expectations.

Long-term relationships are the foundation if our business and our success. We would consider it a privilege to include you as one of our satisfied clients.

Sincerely,

Pat Romboletti

(Courtesy of Pat Romboletti, The Write Sales System™, Dallas, Texas.)

Model Letter 4.6

"We Will Work to Meet Your Needs"

Use the cover letter to convey that your offer is exactly what the customer needs—at the right price.

Dear Jerry:

My suggested advertising package is enclosed. As we discussed today in our phone conversation, WHO-TV basically covers the southernmost counties of the San Jose area. The enclosed trading area map details these boundaries: the areas of interest to you are in our immediate coverage area.

WHO-TV is "Your Hometown Movie Station" and will work with you to design sponsorships that meet your needs. The station is very well received and supported by local advertisers, who are familiar with their hometown station. Buying a schedule on this station will enable you to increase your reach, frequency, and efficiency in the market at a cost that is very reasonable in comparison to what affiliate stations in the area charge.

I will call you soon to discuss how you feel about our proposed schedule. Please make any suggestion you think would be beneficial to your client.

I look forward to working with you.

Sincerely,

Susan C. Wagner

(Courtesy of Susan C. Wagner, Dallas, Texas.)

MODEL LETTER 4.7

Explaining Important Details

One strategy to help reduce confusion is to state clearly what your proposal includes and what it does not include.

Dear Mr. Smith:

BNG Company is pleased to submit a proposal in response to Meyerson, Inc.'s, Request for a Proposal dated April 15, 20XX. As requested, the information is provided in triplicate and includes a CD-ROM with additional specification information. The proposal includes an executive summary, product descriptions, and pricing.

Not included is an implementation plan, which we would develop with your staff during the Systems Assurance process. We recommend a three-month cycle to complete the Systems Assurance and Installation phases.

On behalf of everyone at BNG, we look forward to our continued discussions, and to welcoming Meyerson as a BNG customer soon. Thank you.

Sincerely,

Laura Redding

MODEL LETTER 4.8

Reinforcing the Strengths of Your Proposal

Point the customer to the executive overview in a complicated proposal; that's where you explain your features and strengths.

Dear Michelle:

BNG Company is pleased to submit the enclosed proposal for the comprehensive Sales Automation Project we have been developing for Regency, Inc., over the past six months.

The development of this proposal has been a cooperative venture between BNG and Regency. BNG is most appreciative of the extensive time and resources you made available to complete this proposal. The teamwork we can achieve will be invaluable as we implement this project.

The executive overview summarizes the global benefits of the program and explains why the Sales Automation Project will increase the productivity of your field sales force by, conservatively, 50 percent. The overview outlines the added benefits to all aspects of the organization and positions this project as the first step in Total Workforce Automation.

Our project team looks forward to presenting this proposal to the executive committee. Thank you for your participation in the proposal and for this significant opportunity.

Sincerely,

Marcy Adams

Model Letter 4.9

Reinforcing the Customer's Confidence in Your Firm's Capabilities

Cover letters give you a chance to tell the customer about your strengths and experience as a supplier. Your confident attitude will be persuasive.

Dear Mr. Jack:

Brix Company is pleased to present the enclosed proposal for a power generator for your San Diego manufacturing facility.

Brix Company has been making generators since 19XX and has been the leading supplier of large-scale generators since 19XX. Last year, 60 percent of all generators shipped were Brix. Over 40 percent of all installed generators are Brix. That's market leadership!

Brix, a wholly owned subsidiary of WNT Corporation, generated over $570 million in revenue last year, 35 percent of WNT's total. We offer financial stability and strength—key features you desire in a supplier. Brix commits to over 12 percent of annual revenues to development, ensuring product improvements and futures.

We believe Brix has the market leadership, financial strength, and product prowess that you need. We appreciate this opportunity to present a solution in detail and we look forward to your favorable response.

Very truly yours,

Martin Kelley

Cover Letters on a Revised Proposal

MODEL LETTER 4.10

"Thank You for This Opportunity"

Use bullets to clarify what is enclosed, especially when the enclosures are extensive.

Dear John:

Thank you for this opportunity to propose a MegaDisk solution to your upcoming networking project. I am sending several types of literature:

- Pricing for an initial configuration of components that will provide the capacity you desire now with room for expansion
- Technical data about these components
- Pricing for MegaDisk's next-generation drives, which are in beta testing

John, I look forward to discussing this material with you and providing whatever additional information you may need. I appreciate your interest in MegaDisk and am confident we can provide a superior solution to suit your needs.

Sincerely,

Louis Friday

MODEL LETTER 4.11

Adding a Special One-Time Discount

One-time discounts can sweeten a transaction without compromising your margins. When you offer such a discount, explain it clearly in your cover letter. Your letter should convey the importance you place on the customer. The letter should also distinguish standard pricing from this special offer.

Dear Norm:

Thank you for this opportunity to propose MegaDisk's automated system to InsuranceCo, Inc.

The pricing for the total automation solution is enclosed, in summary as well as detail form. As you will see, MegaDisk is offering a special one-time discount for implementing this total complement of equipment, software, and services. We hope this offer makes the transaction cost justifiable for InsuranceCo. It is our way of showing you how much this business means to us as well.

Norm, it is always a pleasure to work with you and everyone at InsuranceCo. Please know that I look forward to doing everything necessary to implement our solution. I will be delighted to have InsuranceCo as our newest customer in the state.

Sincerely,

Randall Allen

Model Letter 4.12

Summarizing Your New Position
on Some Aspect of the Proposal

One-sentence paragraphs strengthen the presentation of each thought in this letter.

Dear Leigh:

Thank you for your continued interest in MegaDisk's storage subsystem.

Enclosed please find the incremental purchase pricing for acquiring the system in 100 gigabyte increments, which we discussed.

In addition, you will be pleased to note that the software charge has been eliminated from the proposal.

As we have discussed, MegaDisk continues to be willing to allow Insure US to evaluate our system, as we believe that is the most effective way to understand the true benefit of this product.

Leigh, I look forward to our ongoing discussions and to answering any additional questions.

Thank you for your consideration of MegaDisk.

Sincerely,

Randall Allen

MODEL LETTER 4.13

Summarizing Your Revisions and Explaining Thier Benefits

Customers appreciate clear descriptions of changes, and if the changes help the bottom line, be sure to say so!

Dear Bill:

I have enclosed a revised proposal for the upgrade transaction that we have been discussing.

In this version, the VTS devices are not included, as per our conversation. Additionally, MegaDisk is now absorbing the full early termination charge of your current equipment and has extended the maintenance warranty from three to twelve months. This now makes the proposal $1,477.77 per month less than your current charges.

Based on our conversation of last week, this equipment has been placed on order for Spectrum Bank, for delivery November 1, 19XX. As the equipment is in allocation, please keep in mind that our ability to deliver may be hindered by any changes to that schedule.

Bill, this is a significant opportunity both for MegaDisk and for me personally, and I look forward to providing whatever service or assistance may be necessary to facilitate the transaction this year.

Thank you for your ongoing support.

Sincerely,

Lisa Brun

MODEL LETTER 4.14

Communicating a Guarantee

When you make a significant change, tell the customer you are doing it to get the business.

Dear Bob:

Thank you for your continued interest in our carbon gizmo product set. To encourage you to place an order with us this quarter, we are now willing to offer a twenty-four-month, unconditional guarantee of the product. This guarantee will cover all parts and service associated with any of the gizmos under proposal to you at this time.

Bob, I hope that this will be the enticement you need to do business. I will follow up by the end of the week, and hope we can place your order at that time.

Thank you for your ongoing consideration.

Sincerely,

Beth Wilson

MODEL LETTER 4.15

Explaining Highlights of the New Proposal

Your cover letter should clearly state the revisions you are making to the proposal. You want prospects to know what you are doing to accommodate them.

Dear B. J. Smith:

Thank you for your time last Wednesday. I enjoyed meeting you and learning more about the growth and stability of Southern Cellular.

Enclosed is a new revised proposal for Southern Cellular that concerns the marquee for the convention center. The notable changes in the revised proposal include specific placement of Southern Cellular panels on marquee, advertising of Southern Cellular on the matrix of the marquee, and exposure for the Southern Cellular Business Center on the southern wall of the center. As you know, the convention center neighborhood will get a lot of traffic this year after the new park and theater open. From an advertising standpoint, the marquee is in an ideal location.

If you have any further questions, please call me at 713-555-5555. The convention center and Ads, Inc. value our relationship with Southern Cellular and look forward to ongoing success. Thank you for the opportunity to be of service to you.

Sincerely,

Michelle Robinson

(Courtesy of Michelle Robinson, Mobile, Alabama.)

Cover Letters That Accompany a Contract

All contracts need a cover letter, and the cover letter is your opportunity to convey how much you appreciate the business and to give the customer details about how the contract will be processed.

MODEL LETTER 4.16

A Cover Letter for a Contract

When various forms are enclosed, help the customer by explaining the steps to take.

Dear Ms. White:

Thank you for your time last Friday and for your continued interest in our products.

Enclosed are the license agreements covering your purchase of SCH:HotBackup. To initiate the purchase, you should sign the agreements, complete the worksheet and shipping forms, and return all copies with a signed purchase order to SCH Technologies. SCH will return a countersigned copy of the agreement to you.

I want to thank you again for taking the time to review our products, and I look forward to hearing your comments at our meeting May 15.

Regards,

Mary L. Piper

(Courtesy of Mary L. Piper, SCH Technologies, Inc., Cincinnati, Ohio.)

A Cover Letter for the License Agreement for a Trial Period

Evaluations are an excellent selling tool. Your clear descriptions of what to do with the paperwork starts the evaluation on the right track.

Dear Ms. White:

Thank you for your time on Monday and for your continued interest in our products.

Enclosed are the license agreements covering your trial period for SCH:HotBackup. To initiate the trial, you should sign the agreements, complete the shipping and configuration forms, and return all copies to SCH. SCH will send you a countersigned copy of the agreement.

I thank you again for taking time to evaluate our products, and I look forward to hearing your comments on SCH:HotBackup.

Cordially,

Mary L. Piper

(Courtesy of Mary L. Piper, SCH Technologies, Inc., Cincinnati, Ohio.)

MODEL LETTER 4.18

"I Am Delighted to Send You . . ."

Let the customer know when you want to pick up a contract in person.

Dear Ms. McKee:

I am delighted to send you the enclosed agreement for assignment of equipment from MegaDisk.

If you have any questions, contact me (214-555-0990) or Terry Bachman, financial services manager (214-555-0991). Also, if you will call me when you have signed the contract, I will pick it up. This will expedite the process considerably.

Thank you for choosing MegaDisk products.

Best regards,

John Clinton

MODEL LETTER 4.19

Enclosing Contracts and Confirming Details

Use the cover letter to reiterate important points, such as shipping and billing commitments you have agreed to.

Dear Bill:

Enclosed are the contracts for the purchase of 2,500 gizmos. Please sign these at your earliest convenience, and I will then process your order for immediate delivery.

Following are pertinent details of that order:

- Exactly one-half of the above order is for delivery to your South Dakota plant, and one half for delivery to the Ohio plant.
- Full delivery of the order is required by December 1.
- For fiscal accounting purposes, ABC Company commits to paying in full for the 2,500 gizmos by December 20.

Bill, thank you for this important order. I hope that you are satisfied with our product, and I look forward to being your gizmo supplier as your requirements continue to grow.

Sincerely,

Sue Michaels

MODEL LETTER 4.20

Enclosing Contracts and Thanking
the Customer for the Order

A thank you is always a welcome message. Your cover letter on a contract is an ideal place to say "thanks."

Dear John:

Enclosed are the contracts for lease and maintenance of the fifty laser printers for your distributed processing sites worldwide.

After the signature process is complete, please call me and I will pick up the contracts.

Thank you for your significant support of our printing product line and your confidence in us as a supplier. On behalf of everyone at Expert Printing, I am very pleased with obtaining the business and look forward to continuing to support your printing needs.

Sincerely,

June Harris

Cover Letters That Accompany Product Information and Company Literature

Model Letter 4.21

Cover Letter for Commercial Real Estate Listings

Tell the customer where you think the other bidders stand.

Re: Site Analysis, Big League Stadium

Dear Stephen:

I am sending you a summary of the properties surrounding Big League Stadium. I have also included a sales brochure on the properties owned by Appreciation, Inc.

Sterling Properties is a London-based real estate developer with U.S. holdings worth more than $700 million. The company has owned two Big League Plaza properties for several years and carries them on their books at a low basis (see maps 11 and 21). Although both properties are available for $7 per square foot, I do not regard Sterling as a highly motivated seller.

Please call me if you have any questions about this information. Thank you.

Sincerely,

Blake M. Reed

(Courtesy of Blake M. Reed, Dallas, Texas.)

MODEL LETTER 4.22

Networking Follow-Up

Suggesting a product demonstration can move the sale forward.

Dear Mr. Cain:

It was a pleasure to meet you at the Subcontractors Associated meeting last Tuesday. As we discussed, Information Management Systems & Services provides accounting and job-cost systems support services to companies such as Basic Drywall that do large commercial drywall projects. Your firm's list of recent projects is quite impressive, especially the work at Big League Stadium.

As promised, I have enclosed the *Sample Files and Reports* booklet. It shows the accounting information captured, as well as the reports the system generates. The booklet provides a good overview of the system's input and output features, but I would like to do a hands-on demonstration to show you how user-friendly the system is.

I will call to see if we can schedule such a demonstration, either on the demonstration system at my office or at one of our recent installations at a customer's office.

Thank you for your time. I look forward to working with you.

Sincerely,

Frank W. McIntyre

(Courtesy of Frank W. McIntyre, Dallas, Texas.)

MODEL LETTER 4.23

Replying to a Prospect's Request for Information

Let the customer know how extensive your service offering is.

Dear Mr. Chen:

Thank you for your time on Wednesday and for your continued interest in our products. SCH distributes more than 128 software packages from nearly forty-six developers worldwide. Our goal is to provide customers with the most advanced and highest quality systems support software at low cost and at low risk.

I have enclosed information regarding the automated tape robotics we discussed. If you have any questions after reviewing the brochures, feel free to contact me at 818-555-5555 or by e-mail at @not.really. You may also want to consider an evaluation of our software on your system. We offer a full complement of pre- and postsale professional support services.

I hope you find the enclosed information valuable, and I look forward to discussing robotic solutions in more detail with you.

Cordially,

Mary L. Piper

(Courtesy of Mary L. Piper, SCH Technologies, Inc., Cincinnati, Ohio.)

MODEL LETTER 4.24

A Cover Letter That Describes
the Strengths of Your Company

Your emphasis on customer service and support is the ingredient most customers seek.

Dear Ms. White:

Thank you for your call on Tuesday concerning your evaluation of SCH:HotBackup. I have enclosed the information you requested, along with some additional literature about other products. Please let me know how I can be of assistance.

Our involvement in the UNIX market dates back to the 1980s and is very important to us. We base our position in the market on not only having system software solutions available for UNIX, but also on our commitment to customer service and support. This relationship has been critical to our success over the years. SCH will continue to work with you and other UNIX users to provide solutions to your data processing needs.

If I can be of assistance in solving any current or future needs, please contact me at 818-555-5555 or by e-mail at @not.really.

Cordially,

Mary L. Piper

(Courtesy of Mary L. Piper, SCH Technologies, Inc., Cincinnati, Ohio.)

MODEL LETTER 4.25

Following Up with the Information
You Promised to Send

Follow up promptly. You will be laying the groundwork for a productive sales relationship.

Dear Mr. Holmes:

Thank you for taking the time today to talk to me. SCH Technologies has a variety of system support software products available for the UNIX operating system, and I am confident that SCH will be able to help you with solutions for your UNIX needs now and as needs arise in the future.

I am enclosing information regarding our system support product line for your review. If any of this proves of interest, or if you would simply like more detailed information, please feel free to call me at 818-555-5555 or by e-mail at @not.really.

Thank you again for your time and responsiveness. They were appreciated.

Cordially,

Mary L. Piper

(Courtesy of Mary L. Piper, SCH Technologies, Inc., Cincinnati, Ohio.)

Model Letter 4.26

Send Ads and Listings to a Phone Prospect

Here is a letter real estate agents can have ready for immediate follow-up to telephone conversations with prospects. As agents know, prompt response is essential after prospects reveal their preferences for price, location, and amenities.

Dear Judge and Mrs. Rector:

Thank you, Mrs. Rector, for calling our company and inquiring about property in the Riverhill area of Kerrville.

I am pleased to learn of your desire to live in Riverhill. As you know from your personal visits, among the many advantages to living in Riverhill are the people who reside here. They are very friendly and helpful and bring to our neighborhood experiences from living all around the world.

To help give you a feel for the type of housing available, I am enclosing a recent advertisement of our properties. Many of the properties do not meet your specifications but illustrate the wide variety and types of housing available.

Additionally, I am enclosing information sheets on properties that are on the golf course and meet most of your desires. These properties include both our company listings as well as the listing of other realtors.

Real Estate at Riverhill	**Other Real Estate Offices**
799 Oak Park	2200 Rocky Road
2308 Rocky Road	609 Rocky Road
509 Oak Park	404 High Plains Drive
519 Oak Park	

I look forward to your visit in early May. It would be helpful if you could give me one or two days' notice so I can give you the attention you need and deserve. Please let me know if I can help you with any questions.

Sincerely,

William C. Hubbard

(Courtesy of William C. Hubbard, Kerrville, Texas.)

MODEL LETTER 4.27

Following Up After a Phone Call

Turn the customer's phone call into an opportunity to send product information and to encourage the customer to ask you questions.

Dear Herb:

It was a pleasure talking to you yesterday. I have enclosed information on Model 500, which we discussed briefly. These brochures describe several product features. I will call you next week to elaborate on the benefits these features will bring to your organization.

Until then, please call me if you have any questions.

Sincerely,

Angela Green

MODEL LETTER 4.28

"Thank You for Your Interest"

Use your cover letter to draw the customer into the product literature you are sending. Also suggest where to look for additional information—such as a Web site.

Dear Fred:

Thank you for your interest in custom titanium golf clubs from Sports, Inc.

I have enclosed several issues of *Fore,* a magazine exclusively for Sports, Inc., customers, and our current product catalog. Page 56 of the catalog provides a detailed explanation of our manufacturing techniques, and the inside back cover illustrates how to measure the golfer for the perfect custom fit. You will also find us on the Web at www.notreally.com.

At Sports, Inc., we realized that the investment in our clubs is sizable, but you'll enjoy their superior performance with every shot. We encourage our customers to call our 800 number and discuss their concerns about custom titanium clubs with our experienced staff. What's more, if you are visiting the Los Angeles area, we will loan you a set for the day and let you experience the difference firsthand.

Of course, you won't really appreciate the difference of custommade clubs until you own a set of your own, so give us a call soon.

Sincerely,

Megan Moore

Model Letter 4.29

Why Your Enclosure
Should Interest the Customer

Using the opinion of an outside source is always an effective selling tool.

Dear Elaine:

The Charleston economy is booming! 20XX was a year of incredible economic growth for Charleston and the surrounding area. The latest issue of *Global Trade* ranked the city among the nation's hot spots for economic growth.

I am sending you an in-depth research piece that outlines areas of growth in the market. With all the new industrial growth, your television station is positioned to continue to meet your community's ever-changing needs.

Please call if you have any questions.

Sincerely,

Susan C. Wagner

(Courtesy of Susan C. Wagner, Dallas, Texas.)

Getting the Customer Interested in What You Are Sending

When market conditions are confusing, explanations are in order. Use an outside opinion to help explain the situation.

Dear Jim:

As you probably know, the Austin, Texas, market has presented a challenge to media buyers and planners over the past two years. The advertising community must deal with a market that, although ranked as the 64th largest DMA, has costs closer to those of a market in the low 40s. Additionally, last year brought a flurry of affiliation switches and the addition of two new stations to the market.

To give you more information about some of the dynamics particular to Austin, I have enclosed an excellent market overview that Lisa Brun, national sales manager of KOOX, developed. I am also sending you a preview of upcoming political activity and a partial list of Austin's newest retailers.

I hope this information helps in planning this dynamic market for next year. Please call if you have any questions.

Sincerely,

Susan C. Wagner

(Courtesy of Susan C. Wagner, Dallas, Texas.)

Model Letter 4.31

A Letter That Indicates Your Flexibility

You can pursue an aggressive sales goal but still leave room to compromise, as this letter illustrates.

Dear Ken:

The season has begun, and viewers are tuning in to KTV Channel 24 for exciting games!

I am enclosing sponsorship information for your review. The enclosure outlines a plan for your firm to sponsor the conference all the way through tournament games in March. The plan favors firms that utilize the entire package; however, we have inventory for every game and will be happy to work with you to meet your needs, as we have in the past.

I will call you soon to assess your interest and answer any questions you may have.

Sincerely,

Susan C. Wagner

(Courtesy of Susan C. Wagner, Dallas, Texas.)

MODEL LETTER 4.32

Explaining a Potential Problem
with the Enclosure

When you have an issue that needs to be worked out, tell the customer in the cover letter.

Dear Ken:

I've enclosed the sponsorship information, as requested, plus some other information that will help us plan the season.

I have also enclosed a list of general available spots and program schedules, just in case we can utilize some regular programming in some way to enhance sponsorship. Please note that basketball is the only sport we have running in the first and second quarters, and it does not fall within the dates you specified. I hope we can work around this factor.

Also, please find copies of correspondence regarding the basketball package. My agency is extremely hopeful that your firm can take advantage of this opportunity again this year.

I look forward to hearing from you.

Sincerely,

Susan C. Wagner

(Courtesy of Susan C. Wagner, Dallas, Texas.)

Model Letter 4.33

"As an Added Incentive"

Simple cover letters can be very effective—no matter what the price range may be.

> Dear Ken:
>
> Please consider the enclosed package proposal as part of your firm's holiday promotion.
>
> We can offer you frequency at a very efficient package cost. As an extra incentive, we will guarantee your post by running additional spots when available in acceptable programming at no cost.
>
> We appreciate your consideration and are eager for your firm to become a regular advertiser on WHO-TV.
>
> Sincerely,
>
> Susan C. Wagner

(Courtesy of Susan C. Wagner, Dallas, Texas.)

Cover Letters That Follow Up Phone Conversations and Meetings

MODEL LETTER 4.34

Enclosing Literature After a Phone Conversation

It's okay to be brief. Speed of follow-up is what's most important.

Dear Steve:

It was a pleasure talking with you yesterday.

I am sending you literature about our automated flight simulation module, which we briefly discussed. I hope that this information will be of interest to you.

Please call me if you have any questions.

Sincerely,

Pat Timms

MODEL LETTER 4.35

Enclosing Literature and Asking for a Meeting

Advise prospects of significant changes in your products and services.

Dear Don:

Thank you for your interest in MegaDisk's automated system. I have enclosed literature on our products. I hope that as you approach serious consideration of an automated solution you will allow us to review all our current products with you—our line has expanded considerably in the past eighteen months.

Also enclosed is a brochure about our User Group Conference, which this year will be held in Vail, Colorado, October 6–9. This is an excellent way to hear how current customers are using MD products and to learn where the product line is going in the future.

I look forward to meeting with you whenever it becomes appropriate. In the meantime, please call if I can be of service in any way.

Sincerely,

Sue Dreska

Model Letter 4.36

Enclosing Information the Customer Requested

Tell the customer exactly where the requested information is in the enclosures.

Dear Ms. Barnes:

In response to the action items assigned to me during our last meeting, I've included two pages of information on my firm's system. Page 2 details unique features of the K1 system. Page 3 details specifications of the 4.3 gigabyte drives that are internal in the K1 system.

Please call me with any additional questions, and thank you for your interest in MegaDisk products.

Sincerely,

Margaret Tag

MODEL LETTER 4.37

Introducing Several Items That Need Explanation

Add your personal touch to news articles and product literature by introducing them in a cover letter and asking for a "next step" to move the sale forward.

Dear Leigh:

Thank you for your ongoing interest in MegaDisk's disk array sub-system. As a follow-up to our meeting yesterday, I am sending you these items:

- An article that compares our products with those of our competitors
- An account story about a large utility company using our product
- A technology matrix comparing our products with those of our competitors
- A list of references
- A customer's response to the *Wall Street Journal* article

I look forward to discussing the enclosed with you. I hope your firm will pursue MegaDisk's offer of a product trial, as we believe personal experience is the best way to know what a device can do for the data you process.

Leigh, thank you for your attention and your consideration of MegaDisk.

Sincerely,

Ann Griffin

MODEL LETTER 4.38

Information in Response to
the Customer's Questions

This letter demonstrates the representative's personal attention to the prospect's questions.

Dear Ed:

Thank you for your interest in MegaDisk's system for remote vaulting.

I am sending you several types of information, based on questions you asked in our meeting yesterday. The material I have enclosed provides comprehensive product detail and information about MegaDisk's support, service, and training.

I look forward to discussing this proposal with you and your staff, and to implementing this solution at your firm.

Sincerely,

Ann Griffin

MODEL LETTER 4.39

A Cover Letter for Favorable Publicity

A good time to send customers copies of favorable publicity is immediately after the article is published. It is appropriate, however, to send out older articles that still provide current, accessible descriptions of your products. (Note: Ask the publisher of an article for permission to make and distribute copies of articles.)

Dear Norm:

Did you see the article about my company's latest product in yesterday's *Wall Street Journal?* I tried to call you yesterday but failed to reach you. The article featured comments from one of our XB3-model users since last May. As the article mentions, the user says our product led to a 25 percent productivity increase!

What would your business look like with such a productivity gain? Let's talk about it next week. I'll call you on Monday.

Sincerely,

Chris Smith

MODEL LETTER 4.40

Enclosing a New Brochure
About Product Enhancements

Your notes to customers are lasting reminders of your attention to their needs.

Dear Annette:

Thanks for calling to ask about our new fall cosmetics. Enclosed is our new brochure with the autumn color scheme you've been asking for. Also, we are now offering the green toner that helps mask out the red skin tones, which I know you have wanted for a long time.

I'm pleased that we have items you requested, and hope you like what you see in the brochure. Please call with any questions. I'll be in touch next week.

Looking forward to talking soon,

June Bennet

Selling Outlook
Why Cover Letters Are So Important

When you can't be present, your cover letter will be your ambassador. Use cover letters to sum up your finest assets and persuade recipients at critical decision points.

A well-written cover letter can serve several purposes:

Focus You've sent the customer certain material at a certain time for a reason; use the cover letter to focus the customer's attention on your goals. When thinking of a customer, salespeople tend to think about what it will take to close a transaction. Meanwhile, the customer is probably thinking of what the product can do for his or her business. By clearly introducing your topic in the cover letter, you direct the customer to the focus you choose.

Review your action and suggest the next step   Explain what you've done and what you think should happen next. This practice helps you establish that the ball is in the customer's court and lets the customer know what you'd like to have happen next. For example, you might take the opportunity to establish a time frame. Because you're doing this in writing, the message can strengthen any discussions you've had on the subject, and if there is any confusion later, you've provided a written point of reference.

Summarize your position   A summary gives the customer perspective on where the sale stands in regard to your company.

Express thanks and use a personal touch   People like to be called by name, and they like to be recognized for their effort. Both concepts can be powerful persuaders in a cover letter. We place a high value on something written expressly for us. That's why it's a good idea to use the recipient's name in the body of the letter, not just in the salutation. It shows you are talking directly and personally to this customer. And when you speak to the customer, something you might say is "thank you." This person is giving you an audience, is considering your proposal, and, if you make a sale, will become an essential partner in your success. There are lots of reasons to say thank you to customers. Here are some ideas:

- For considering your product
- For looking at your proposal
- For considering your offer
- For executing your contract

Reinforce important points   In a cover letter, you have an opportunity to reiterate an important point or say something new. Here are some messages you might want to include:

- The advantages you and your product offer
- Your guarantee
- Your next action based on the customer's intent
- How much you want the business
- Your willingness to accommodate a special request
- Reasons the customer should act now
- Benefits of your product
- Assurance that you are positioned to handle the business

- Assurance that you will do what is necessary to obtain the business
- A warning when something may change

Reinforce your professionalism The cover letter is an extension of your overall selling style. It's another opportunity for you to put your name in front of a customer. It won't replace the face-to-face meeting, but it's certainly more personal than a business card. Use the cover letter to remind the customer who you are and how well you can handle their needs. Use it as an ambassador.

Words That Sell
Ten Steps for Clearer, More Effective Writing

Communication is the measure of effective writing. Did the reader understand the author's message, or did the message confuse customers or staff at the home office?

By learning to write better, a professional salesperson can reduce opportunities for misunderstandings.

These ten tips will increase your chances of sending letters your clients will look forward to reading every time they see your corporate envelope in their inbaskets.

1. ***State your purpose clearly and creatively.*** Experiment with different ways to state your purpose in your opening remarks. You don't want every letter you send the same client to begin the same way or convey a sense of monotony.

2. ***Edit yourself.*** Have you repeated the same words or expressions too often? Repetition leads to monotony. Look at the big picture. Do your sentences flow in a logical progression of ideas? Something professional writers know that others often don't is that you should plan to rewrite. Hardly anyone produces a perfectly organized, compelling letter on the first draft.

3. ***Accuracy is utmost.*** Keep accurate files of name spellings, addresses, and every item you mention in a letter. Mistakes, no matter how they happen, stay in corporate files for years. One way to help yourself be more accurate is to make a computer file where you record information about your industry, your competitors, your clients. Refer to it for quick reference when mentioning specifics in your letters. Your customers will notice the attention to detail.

4. ***Help yourself get started.*** At some time everyone has to write a letter or report that is hard to get started. Write something—anything—that you know will be in the letter. The beginning, the end. Gradually break up the small pieces and write them down. Sooner than you realize, you'll have a complete project.

5. ***Double-check your work.*** Perhaps you are rewriting a letter you've sent fifty times to different prospects. Believe it or not, you are more apt to make a mistake in this situation. Mistakes happen when they are least expected, so double-check your work.

6. ***Test your results.*** Ask a colleague or family member to assess different examples of your work. What are they eager to read, and what do they read

to appease you? This approach can be especially helpful when you are working out problems or prospecting for new customers.

7. *Save your successes.* You will adapt letters in this book to suit your own style and situation. Save them, revise them, ask others what they think of them. You will be building a model letter library of your own.

8. *Know your strengths and weaknesses.* Are you a good speller? Do you write first drafts in the passive voice, then go back to make sentences more interesting? Do you need to reorganize paragraphs after writing a first draft? Study your own pattern and write a checklist for yourself for future reference.

9. *Study language.* Almost every writing guide advises writers to write in the active voice. But what does that mean? When you analyze what makes some writing better than other writing, you'll notice the difference between sentences built around strong, active verbs and those where all the action takes place somewhere else.

10. *Read other people's work.* Whether you like business books, fiction, or coworkers' sample letters for the same situations you face, you can learn from both good and bad examples.

Part 2

Letters for Overcoming Obstacles, Keeping the Sale Going, and Closing and Confirming the Sale

CHAPTER 5

Persuading the Customer to Move Forward

Persuasion is the art of convincing someone of something, and persuasion is the essence of sales. Successful selling requires finesse and savvy about what is appropriate during the prolonged period that is sometimes necessary to close a deal. How do you sustain the customer's interest despite an onslaught of competition from other vendors and a legion of other demands on the customer's time? How can you keep the cycle going and sustain a sale to closure?

Many types of selling become drawn-out processes. The challenge becomes keeping the cycle going. This involves keeping yourself psyched, keeping the prospect interested in you, your product, and the pursuit of a solution. Letters can help this part of the process. Letters are a tool for getting your name and your ideas in front of someone again. Letters are a way to present information in a format that the prospect can study, think about, and refer to. In letters, the salesperson has an opportunity to craft the message carefully. Letters also insulate the salesperson and the prospect from the emotional stress that is potentially and normally present in all face-to-face communication. Letters, therefore, allow both parties to contemplate their dealings within a relaxed, reflective, and comfortable context.

Use letters to summarize the benefits of your solution. Although you may feel a letter is redundant considering your many verbal presentations and discussions, remember that competitors have been in to visit the prospect since you last talked to him or her. A written reminder of your strengths causes the prospect to reflect on your company's solution.

In any complex decision, keeping the benefits of the various alternatives straight is challenging for even the most sophisticated decision maker. Help make it easier by formatting your message clearly in a letter. In complex sales situations, more than one decision maker is usually involved. Letters provide a way to be sure that each person receives the same message—the undistorted message you intended.

Everyone knows that writing a letter takes effort, and the effort you expend to communicate with your prospect is one more indication of your interest and your desire to find a suitable solution. Letters tell your prospect you are willing to work hard to win the business. That message is often more significant than the details of your product.

Use the letters in this chapter to help you rejuvenate a stalled-out effort, remove obstacles and concerns, and persuade customers to your solution. Remember, the question in the prospect's mind is always, Why should I buy from this person? Answer the question in a believable way, and you'll be pleased at the results.

CHAPTER 5. CONTENTS

Rejuvenating a Stalled-Out Effort

MODEL LETTER 5.1

"My Clients Rely on Me Because . . ."

This letter is a written reminder of why it makes sense to work with this rep. "Looking out for your best interest" is a positive approach.

Dear Mr. and Mrs. Lee:

My clients continue to rely on my knowledgeable advice to help them achieve their financial objectives. They know that I am carefully monitoring their plans and that I am always looking out for their best interests.

They like the personalized attention that I give them, and they appreciate the consistent approach that I take as I help them reach their goals. My broad knowledge of the financial marketplace has enabled me to build their portfolios from a wide range of investment products.

I hope to have an opportunity to provide the same level of service and expertise to you. Working together, we can create a secure financial future for you and your family.

Sincerely,

Pat Romboletti

(Courtesy of Pat Romboletti, The Write Sales System™, Dallas, Texas.)

MODEL LETTER 5.2

Giving Prospects Reasons to Talk to You Again

When your company makes improvements that make you a more viable supplier, sending the news in writing is a good way to regenerate interest.

Dear Joseph:

In response to the demands of customers such as you, ABC has developed two new capabilities. When we last talked, you needed a supplier who could produce a gizmo made of 150mm carbon. ABC was not then positioned to do so. Since that time, we retrofitted our factory to handle such requirements. We have been fulfilling 150mm orders for leading manufacturers since the first quarter of this year. We have state-of-the-art equipment and technology, and can now fulfill your 150mm carbon needs. Additionally, you required distribution capability for the continental United States. Recent additions to our distribution network now fulfill your requirement. Through Nationwide Industrial Distributors, we can deliver our product to you within forty-eight hours.

I will follow up with you by phone next week. I look forward to talking with you then, and hope we can be your 150mm carbon gizmo vendor. Thank you for giving ABC Company a second look.

Sincerely,

Tom Howard

MODEL LETTER 5.3

"Others Worry . . . My Clients Enjoy Peace of Mind"

Remind customers of what you do for them with a "keep-in-touch" letter.

Dear Mr. Temple:

While others worry about having enough money for their future, my clients enjoy the peace of mind of knowing that they have a plan in place that will give them the financial security they desire.

Each plan is different, depending on the age, family obligations, retirement goals, and risk tolerance of my clients. But one thing is the same—the personalized service that I give to every client. My clients count on me to manage every detail of their account today so that they are prepared for tomorrow.

I hope to have an opportunity to use my skills as a certified financial planner to guide you toward a secure future as well.

Sincerely,

Pat Romboletti

(Courtesy of Pat Romboletti, The Write Sales System™, Dallas, Texas.)

MODEL LETTER 5.4

"Some Time Has Passed Since We Visited"

When trying to rejuvenate a dialogue, it helps to remind prospects of the success of your solution.

Dear Jeff:

Although some time has passed since we visited with you about ABC's line of automation tools, we want to talk with you further if the timing is appropriate and if you are still interested in automating your company's warehousing process.

I have enclosed several brochures that may help trigger questions or additional discussion. Also enclosed is a brochure for ABC's user convention, which will be in San Francisco the first week of July. I highly recommend attending the convention if you are seriously considering our product line. The meeting will be well worth your time and will put you in contact with hundreds of companies that already have implemented our solutions.

I will call you during the week of May 20 to verify your receipt of this information and to see if you are interested in meeting again to discuss automation solutions.

Best regards,

R. A. Harris

MODEL LETTER 5.5

Reasons to Reconsider an Unfavorable Decision

As the newness begins to wear off your prospect's relationship with a competitor, a well-timed letter can put you back in the running.

Dear Maurice:

This letter is to follow up on your interest in ABC's advanced printing capabilities.

As you suggested, I contacted David Brown, but he indicated that he had already chosen a printer. Even so, I want you to be aware of our product offerings because I believe our investment in technology lets us provide superior quality at an attractive price. I have enclosed a catalog of our services, some recent samples, a dozen desk calendars for your staff, and a press release about the printing awards our work won for our customers last year.

I hope you will think of us the next time you need printing services. In the meantime, I would like to meet with you to discuss your publishing program and how we might fit into it. I will follow up with you again on Friday, August 23.

Thank you for your interest in ABC Printing.

Sincerely,

Art Reed

Model Letter 5.6

Giving a Prospect Reasons to Use Your Service

What's the prospect missing by *not* using your services? This letter spells it out in black and white.

Dear Sarah:

Finding sound investments that provide the best possible return without undue risk is not easy. It takes thorough research to identify the best products and careful monitoring to keep them on track. That's why my clients rely on my knowledge and expert guidance.

They know that I always watch out for their best interests, and I provide the personal attention and service that they expect. I have earned their trust and continued business by never losing sight of their objectives.

I hope to have an opportunity to earn your trust as well. I know that you will appreciate my commitment to developing a comprehensive financial plan to meet your specific needs.

Sincerely,

Pat Romboletti

(Courtesy of Pat Romboletti, The Write Sales System™, Dallas, Texas.)

MODEL LETTER 5.7

A Reminder of What You Will Do
for the Prospect

Your self-confidence is persuasive evidence that the prospect should consider your offer, as this letter illustrates.

Dear Beth Michaels:

Every day, I help my clients make the most of their money so that they can achieve their financial goals.

They count on me to keep a close eye on the short-term results so that they can reach their long-term objectives. Working with their financial team, I have helped them build a comprehensive plan that carefully balances the reward against their tolerance for risk.

I look forward to demonstrating how I can assist you as well. I am confident that my knowledge and commitment can help you achieve a secure financial future.

Sincerely,

Pat Romboletti

(Courtesy of Pat Romboletti, The Write Sales System™, Dallas, Texas.)

MODEL LETTER 5.8

Moving Forward with Information About Your Market

Interesting quotes and facts from third parties make persuasive openers for sales letters. This example uses a newspaper quotation to underscore the message of the letter.

> "We're looking at real strong economic growth in Austin with no real indication of a slowdown in the near future."
>
> —*Texas Perspectives,* economic newsletter

Dear Travis:

As you well know, today's healthy advertising climate is creating a particularly heavy demand in the Austin, Texas, market. In Austin, a strong local economy, combined with heavy political spending, has made inventory a scarce commodity over the past few months. And with major gubernatorial and senate races coming in November, this trend doesn't appear to be letting up any time soon.

If your planners, your supervisors, or you need more details about what is going on in Austin, please see the enclosed literature. I thought these brochures might be of interest because they explain why Austin is such a unique market and why our costs per point are generally more in line with much larger markets. Without a doubt, planners need to be aware that this market is in the middle of a strong growth spurt, and they must take this fact into account when putting together media plans that involve Austin.

Please call me if you have any questions or need any additional information.

Best regards,

Susan Wagner

(Courtesy of Susan Wagner, Dallas, Texas.)

Removing Obstacles to the Sale

MODEL LETTER 5.9

Responding to Customer Requirements

Some customer requests involve complex issues that take time to work through. Your letter to the customer shows that you are serious about finding a workable solution.

Dear John:

I am writing to follow up on your request for maintenance options in remote locations, primarily Seoul, South Korea; Tokyo, Japan; Kuala Lumpur; Malaysia; Sweden (north of the Arctic Circle); and Alaska.

We need to ask your organization several questions as we develop a response to your request:

1. Are the remote sites manned, and if so, how technical is the staff?
2. What are your uptime requirements?
3. Will your company be sending regular or emergency supply transports to these sites?

Depending on the answers to these questions, we may suggest that your organization enter into a self-maintenance plan, controlled out of Dallas, and that we provide education, diagnostics, and backup support. If you are planning on supporting your own equipment from Dallas, this solution may make the most sense.

Alternatively, we can enter into a multinational service agreement and rely on our company and our subsidiaries in Tokyo for Tokyo, Seoul, and Kuala Lumpur; Seattle, Washington, for Alaska; and Stockholm for the Arctic Circle location.

John, I look forward to discussing this further with you and will be happy to arrange an additional meeting, perhaps with our maintenance management, to discuss in greater detail your options for maintaining our equipment in these locations.

Sincerely,

Ann McIntyre

MODEL LETTER 5.10

Offering to Do a Cost-of-Ownership Analysis

Your ability to help the customer justify the cost of your product can jump-start a stalled sales effort.

Dear Ben:

Thank you for your ongoing interest in OurCo's products.

Several times you have expressed concern about how your financial staff will view your decision to buy our system. I can offer you a tool to help explain the cost benefits of our products.

We have developed a cost-of-ownership model that defines both the tangible and intangible benefits to be derived from our system. The model is simple to run but requires your manufacturing cost figures. I understand this information may be confidential, and to safeguard that confidentiality, we can tell you how to code those cost figures in the program so that only your staff has access to them. I believe this model is a reliable and credible tool that will give you the ammunition you need to win your financial people over to this solution.

Ben, we can run the cost-of-ownership model at any time. I suggest we proceed as soon as possible so that we have the information we need before the next budget cycle begins.

Thank you for your interest and your support. I look forward to working with you soon on this project.

Best regards,

Lynn Morris

Model Letter 5.11

Offering Trial Use of Your Product

When, despite your best efforts, you still haven't closed the deal with an important prospect whose needs match with your offering, get the product in this prospect's hands on a trial basis. This way, the prospect and you can work together to convince any doubters that your product best fits their needs.

Dear Ed:

The purpose of this letter is to make a formal offer to SBS to try ABC's newest device, the PQR, for sixty days. I believe an evaluation is the most effective way to understand the true benefits of this product in your environment.

I learned in my discussions with your operations manager that your company has an immediate need for PQR and wants to begin testing its features and performance as soon as possible. I welcome this opportunity and can deliver equipment by November 1.

PQR pricing is enclosed, and I can give you lease rates on request.

Ed, I am eager to discuss this proposal with you and your operations manager. I am confident that after testing our equipment, you will be convinced it is the perfect solution to your needs.

Sincerely,

Cindy Reed

Model Letter 5.12

Offering to Extend the Evaluation Period

Although you cannot extend trial periods forever, some situations call for flexibility.

Dear Brad:

I am writing to confirm the offer I made by telephone on Monday, June 24, 20XX, regarding XDX's evaluation of our SmartWorks product.

The SmartWorks evaluation period ended June 15, but XDX had not completed its business justification and needed additional time. My company offers to extend the evaluation forty-five more days, until July 31, 20XX. However, we ask XDX to pay maintenance on the installed unit beginning June 16, at the rate of $5,677.05 per month. When XDX either purchases or leases (on a long-term basis) this equipment, a ninety-day warranty will apply.

If you agree to these terms, we will forward the appropriate paperwork to Jo Williams. Thank you for your attention to this matter and for your interest in SmartWorks.

Sincerely,

Jane Bridges

MODEL LETTER 5.13

Moving Forward While Your Company Develops the Product

In some situations, clients key their business plans off developments your firm has promised. When clients need confirmation of a product's status, a letter is much more reassuring than a verbal update.

Dear Tim:

ABC is pleased to present Heartland Bank with a quote for the suite of Spider management software and services recently installed in your Sedona Data Center. The success of the pilot program was directly related to the commitment Heartland Bank made to this project and the planning that went into it.

ABC greatly appreciates the joint effort that went into the initial Sedona installation and is looking forward to working with your bank as you expand the Spider solution throughout the enterprise.

The prices are quoted as if the Sedona installation were a single entity. This transaction would be grandfathered into an enterprise license agreement to be finalized early next year. The enterprise license will offer Heartland Bank a partnership agreement with ABC and give Heartland Bank a purchasing structure based on the needs of the enterprise over the next three years.

ABC realizes that there are a number of issues that need to be resolved before Heartland Bank will be completely comfortable with the Spider as an enterprise solution. We are working on these issues and have presented our timetable for integrating them into the products or delivering the needed feature as a professional service offering.

ABC also realizes the magnitude of Heartland Bank's two gigabyte file size limitation and your need to see it resolved. We will present Heartland Bank with a formal commitment on this issue in December.

Presenting this quote will in no way slow down our efforts to complete the enterprise agreement. Likewise, Heartland Bank will suffer no adverse effects by purchasing software and paying for the services rendered in Sedona before the enterprise agreement is signed.

Please call me at 404-555-5555 with any questions or concerns you may have.

Sincerely,

Bob Campbell

(Courtesy of Bob Campbell, Dallas, Texas.)

MODEL LETTER 5.14

Providing an Inactive Customer with a Technology Compatibility Update

Frequent updates help sustain prospects' interest.

Dear Truman:

It has been several months since we last talked about the compatibility of Hi-Tech's products with products from other vendors. Many improvements have developed during this time.

I have enclosed a table that summarizes our product's compatibility across computing platforms, and I will keep you apprised of further improvements. Please keep me posted, too, as you pursue various alternatives, and do not hesitate to ask for additional information.

Sincerely,

Kim George

MODEL LETTER 5.15

Persuading the Customer to Reevaluate Price

A homeowner's asking price for a home, though critical to the sales effort, is a delicate and personal subject. This gently persuasive letter asks the owner to reevaluate.

Dear Mrs. Wiggins:

Thank you for visiting with me yesterday about your property at 358 Englewood Drive in the Riverhill area of Kerrville. As we discussed, another company listed this property at a price of $279,500. That listing agreement has expired, and you are interested in listing the property with another real estate firm.

Your property is unique and offers many attractive selling features:

Outstanding location—a spectacular view of the lake and golf course frontage on the 11th hole.
Exemplary maintenance—the house is in near-perfect condition, and professionals have performed most repairs and routine maintenance.
Open, spacious feeling—with cathedral ceilings and a see-through stone fireplace in the living room and dining room.
Enjoyable outdoor living—the first-floor patio and second-floor deck overlook the lake.
Large master suite—the first-floor bedroom has an oversized bathroom and walk-in closet.
Home office—with custom cabinetry to accommodate files and computer work space.

My major concern about marketing your property is the asking price. In my opinion, your asking price is substantially above the market price for similar properties.

Of course, the marketplace establishes the selling price. My goal is to provide you with information about sales of comparable properties, current real estate activity, and the area. You, as the owner, establish the asking price. At $279,500, your 2,300-square-foot home is priced at more than $87 per square foot. Sales of similar and comparable properties vary between $70 and $75 per square foot. A lower price on your property should help you attract more prospective buyers.

Please give this issue careful consideration and share your thoughts with me. I look forward to working with you and will call you on Tuesday after you return from Connecticut.

Very truly yours,

William C. Hubbard

(Courtesy of William C. Hubbard, Kerrville, Texas.)

MODEL LETTER 5.16

Overcoming the Price Obstacle:
"What Will Happen If You Don't Buy?"

Pointing out the risks of not moving ahead is one way of suggesting action.

Dear Mr. Kirk:

I think you will agree with me that a system that accurately and efficiently captures, processes, and reports accounting and job cost information will be very beneficial to Basic Drywall—and a great improvement over the current system. But about now you may be wondering, Will the system be worth $125,000?

One way to answer the question is to look at the alternatives. One alternative that, on the surface, appears less expensive is to continue using your current system. Of course, this choice means that you won't have information about your materials and labor costs. Your bottom line may look more profitable than it really is, or it may look like a given job is unprofitable when in fact it is making you money. Errors in either direction lead management to inappropriate responses to real problems. The consequences could be disrupted relationships with suppliers, customers, and employees, and unnecessary stress on you and other managers. The ultimate result of inadequate information about your company is suboptimal financial performance.

A second alternative is to hire additional personnel to compile materials and labor cost information manually. This choice will certainly increase your overhead payroll costs—eventually far more than $125,000. Manual information gathering produces information in a tedious, time-consuming way that discourages future requests for information. With the IMSS system, information is at your fingertips anytime you need it to make a decision, not days later when your window of opportunity may have closed.

As you increase the accuracy of cost estimates by using the IMSS system, you will realize other benefits as well. Given Basic

Drywall's current volume of business, a 2 percent increase in overall cost efficiency will pay for the IMSS system in just eighteen months. Experience shows that the system helps clients increase volume without a corresponding increase in cost overhead. I would be happy to give you the names of IMSS clients who can attest that the system more than pays for itself.

As you can see, an alternative way of looking at the cost question is to ask, What are the costs of working without the system? I am confident that no other vendor offers a comparable package of software and services for less money. I am equally confident that the proposed system—at the proposed price—will exceed your expectations.

I will call next Tuesday to see if you have any questions about the proposal and to provide names of clients who will tell you about their experience with it. I look forward to working with you.

Sincerely,

Frank McIntyre

(Courtesy of Frank McIntyre, Dallas, Texas.)

MODEL LETTER 5.17

A Letter to Allay the Customer's Apprehension

People are apprehensive about change. Address that apprehension boldly!

Dear Lee James:

Several months have passed since IMSS proposed a system configuration and price quote for your new accounting and job cost system. If you are like most business owners I have encountered, you are experiencing apprehension about the acquisition of a major capital item. My clients assure me, however, that their apprehension was worse than the pain.

Key issues in a new installation such as yours typically are the following:

1. Preparation of the files needed for the initial installation
2. How the system will affect employees' day-to-day routines
3. Whether the system will require the hiring of additional personnel
4. Initial cost

You may be apprehensive about other issues as well. Identifying and addressing concerns is one way IMSS customizes our system to each client's needs. As part of our installation process, we address concerns one by one until we arrive at the solution you desire. For example, we might suggest a lease or lease-purchase plan to resolve the issue of cost. We study each company's personnel needs and tailor a plan to meet the client's needs with existing and, as necessary, temporary specialists.

I think a face-to-face meeting would be very helpful to us at this point. We can identify how you will prepare for the installation, who will enter information into the system, and who will use the information from the system. By discussing these issues, we can move closer to the customized solution that will best suit your organization.

I will call you next week to see how your schedule looks.

Sincerely,

Frank McIntyre

(Courtesy of Frank McIntyre, Dallas, Texas.)

MODEL LETTER 5.18

Trying to Mend a Relationship

This letter points out that, despite recent problems, the client–vendor relationship was once exemplary and can be so again.

Dear Mr. Sawyer:

I understand that today's competitive environment makes it difficult for professionals like ourselves to meet as often as I would like. Therefore, please accept this short letter as a method of better communicating the long-term benefits of working with Digital by Design.

Digital by Design has a long history of working with Sawyer, Inc. As a matter of fact, our relationship goes all the way back to June 1986. We provided peripherals to Sawyer for integration into the phone switches that were being developed. At one point, Sawyer was on our top-ten account list.

Two years ago, we had an account manager assigned to you who was not up to our quality standards. That person is no longer with DBD, but I fear there may be some lingering effects from the experience. All I can do is give you my commitment as a thirteen-year DBD employee that I will do everything possible to earn your trust and respect.

My concern is not of a transactional nature but of a relationship nature. While I hope we can supply your requirements for a peripheral upgrade, I am more hopeful that I can work with Sawyer, Inc., on the data management needs of your entire computer network. I would like to schedule a meeting with you to learn if there are any obstacles that would preclude us from doing business together. The objectives of the meeting would be to discuss pricing, better understand your long-term data management plans, and begin the process of rebuilding the DBD/Sawyer relationship. I will call you on Tuesday at 9:00 A.M. to see if we can meet.

Please feel free to contact me or F. S. Westgate, your original DBD account manager, now vice president of sales, at 212-555-1616.

Sincerely,

Derrick Gamradt

(Courtesy of Derrick Gamradt, Plano, Texas.)

Persuading Prospects to Your Solution

MODEL LETTER 5.19

Four Reasons to Act Now

Depending on the circumstances, prospects may be ambivalent about buying or selling. Your well-reasoned letter states your case in a lasting, written format that the recipient can weigh carefully.

Dear Mr. Jones:

I am a commercial real estate broker who specializes in the sale of undeveloped single-family land and vacant developed lots to home-builders in southeast Benson County. My recent phone call to you was about your property in Pecan Grove, Louisiana.

I am writing to suggest that you consider selling the southern portion of your property for single-family use. This portion of your property is particularly well suited for low-density single-family development. Additionally, now is a good time to sell single-family land in Pecan Grove. My reasons are as follows:

- **Adjacent property use:** Your house to the north and the proposed elementary school to the south, together with existing residential developments on the east and west, make single-family use logical.
- **New infrastructure:** The improvements associated with the development of adjacent properties have brought roads, bridges, and utilities closer to your property. These improvements have enhanced the access to your property and reduced the potential off-site costs associated with its development.
- **Natural amenities:** The property's creeks and trees add value to low-density residential development.
- **Market considerations:** New home sales in Pecan Grove are at near-record levels. Many market analysts, myself included, believe that we are approaching the top of the residential market cycle.

For these reasons, I think that now is a good time to consider the sale of your property to a financially capable homebuilder who will develop a low-density residential neighborhood for moderate to high-priced homes ($200,000 to $350,000).

This letter is not a request to list your property for sale. Instead, it is an idea for your consideration. Please call me to discuss this idea in greater detail.

I've enclosed a summary of my recent activity and will gladly provide references on request. Thank you.

Sincerely,

Blake M. Reed

(Courtesy of Blake M. Reed, Dallas, Texas.)

MODEL LETTER 5.20

Reminding the Buyer of Reasons
to Accept Your Offer

Is the customer stalling? Maybe some reassurance from you will move the sale forward.

Dear Mike:

When you have reviewed the enclosed summary of single-family lot sales in Pleasantville, I am confident that you will find the HomeCo offer on Pleasantville West to be competitive. The strengths of the offer include the following:

- Aggressive takedown of lots for cash.
- Substantial earnest money of $100,000 plus accrued interest, which is not released until the final lot in Phase VIII is taken down.
- The least desirable sections of Pleasantville West, Phases VI A and B, are the first to be closed.
- Pleasant Oaks, where home sales are running ten per month, provides an excellent marketing window for the sale of homes in Pleasantville West, Phases VI A and B.
- Increased home sales in Pleasantville West, Phases VI A and B, enhance the value of Phases VII and VIII.
- HomeCo's reputation for quality and value will bring traffic to the subdivision, thereby enhancing the value of the remaining phases and the commercial reserves.

Taken together, these factors make the HomeCo offer very attractive.

I look forward to your response. Please call me if you have any questions.

Sincerely,

Blake M. Reed

(Courtesy of Blake M. Reed, Dallas, Texas.)

MODEL LETTER 5.21

Reminding Prospects of Your Strengths

Sometimes the vendor that wins the business is not the one with the superior product. Instead, it is the vendor that most frequently told the prospect that the vendor's product was superior. Use letters as one more reminder.

Dear Joe:

As you get closer to a decision on a vendor to supply your warehouses with packaging materials, I would like to take this opportunity to remind you of a few of the many reasons why I think KPG Packaging Systems should be your vendor of choice.

As we discussed in our meetings, KPG Packaging maintains a tradition of producing a quality product and has a futuristic approach to innovation and cost control. We are proud of our reputation for quality and service to our customers. To maintain our reputation, our product managers constantly look for new solutions to old problems. Our management's willingness to invest in the risk of a new product has paid off by providing us with a line of packaging products to meet needs our competition has not even thought of. At KPG, we utilize our past successes to invest in our future. New product development receives 10 percent of our annual revenues, which equates to continued new ideas that become cost-efficient new packaging systems for you.

You were one of our first users in the Los Angeles area, and we value our past business relationship. We strongly desire to continue to be your packaging vendor. We believe you should select the vendor best positioned to fulfill not only your needs today, but also the one who will continue to enhance your business options in the future. We believe KPG is the best vendor for you.

Thank you for your consideration of KPG Packaging Systems.

Sincerely,

Ann Marx

MODEL LETTER 5.22

Telling Prospects about Quality and Process Improvements

When you have made improvements to your production or distribution processes, tell your prospects about those improvements in writing. Process improvements affect your ability to get the business.

Dear Mr. Johnson:

In 19XX, ABC decided to seek the Emery Award for Excellence in Manufacturing. As I am sure you are aware, this award is both prestigious and difficult to attain. Seeking the award involved reeducating both management and factory personnel to a whole new way of looking at their work. We are proud to announce that ABC was selected a first-runner-up for the award. Our goal, of course, remains to win first place, but rarely do companies win on their first try. More important, we have made process improvements that ensure quality products for our customers. We are very excited to share this news with our current and prospective customers.

In addition, we now offer an expanded product line, better suited to meet the requirements of XYZ Company. Specifically, we can now accommodate your requirement for the 150mm carbon, which I know is key to your manufacturing process. Our factory was redesigned and retooled late last year to accommodate that line of business. We now have the most state-of-the-art 150mm carbon manufacturing facility west of the Mississippi.

I will follow up next week, and hope to meet with you in person to discuss further how the changes at ABC will benefit XYZ. Thank you for your interest and your consideration.

Sincerely,

Tom Howard

MODEL LETTER 5.23

Providing Names of Satisfied Users

Your professionalism will be evident in a letter that helps a prospect make contact with your reference.

Dear Spencer:

This letter is to follow up on our conversation last week when you indicated an interest in talking with users in your industry who have implemented our product.

I have arranged for you to talk with David Jones, executive vice president of the Jones Company. They were an early user of our product (implementing it three years ago), and, most important, are running the same applications you run. David can be reached at this address and phone number: David Jones, Executive Vice President, The Jones Company, 911 East X Street, New York, NY 10000; 202-555-2476.

I know that talking with David will give you the user perspective you are seeking. After you two get together, I would like to visit with you again to address any remaining issues.

Thank you for your interest and your attention.

Sincerely,

R. A. Harris

MODEL LETTER 5.24

Why Yours Is the Offer to Accept

Don't hesitate to clearly list reasons your solution is valid.

Dear Mrs. Pearson:

In view of the competing offers on the Pleasantville West Addition, Phases VII A and B, I am writing to encourage your consideration of the following facts regarding HomeCo's long-standing interest in the property:

- HomeCo's interest in the property predates the competition, as demonstrated by the Letters of Intent dated June 8, 20XX, and April 19, 20XX. Three of these offers were unsolicited.
- HomeCo has a competitive offer on the table to purchase all 125 lots in Phases VII A and B.
- Pleasant Oaks, HomeCo's subdivision at the northwest quadrant of Pecan Drive FM 182, is the most successful subdivision in Pleasantville and provides an excellent marketing window for Pleasantville West Addition. The competition does not have a market position in Pleasantville, much less a location such as Pleasant Oaks.
- There is no confusion within the ranks of HomeCo's management team. Liz Carter and Earl Means of the North County Division have been with the company for several years and are thoroughly familiar with the Pleasantville West Addition.

In fairness to HomeCo's long-standing interest in the property, and with the hope of reaching an agreement that can be satisfactory to everyone involved, I am requesting a meeting with you to discuss this matter in greater detail.

Please call me at your earliest convenience. Thank you.

Sincerely,

Blake M. Reed

(Courtesy of Blake M. Reed, Dallas, Texas.)

Reinforcing the Client's Interest in a Particular Location

In real estate, a letter reminding your client about the benefits of an area or specific houses of interest can keep the client excited and interested in what you have to offer.

Dear Bob:

Thank you for coming to our office and permitting me to show you the Riverhill neighborhood in Kerrville, the country club, and some of the properties new on the market. I enjoyed meeting and being with you very much.

Riverhill is a wonderful place to live, and I believe you would enjoy being here. The subdivision offers many advantages:

- Riverhill is in Kerrville, an incorporated city with city police and fire protection, city water, and city sewers (no septic tanks).
- Kerrville is the home of Schreiner College, a small, liberal arts school, and many summer youth camps.
- Good medical facilities are available, including a large community hospital, Veterans Administration, and a Texas state hospital.
- Kerrville offers proximity to San Antonio for advanced medical services, major shopping, and access to quality international air service but lacks the problems associated with living in a major city.
- The Riverhill Country Club is an equity club, owned by the members, who very actively support and use the club facilities. The club facilities are primarily for the members' use and enjoyment.
- Most important are the people who live here. They are very friendly and helpful and bring to our neighborhood experiences from living all around the globe.

Please let me know if there is any additional information that would hasten your return. I look forward to your next visit.

Very truly yours,

William C. Hubbard

(Courtesy of William C. Hubbard, Kerrville, Texas.)

MODEL LETTER 5.26

Reasons to Consider
What Your Company Is Developing

Sometimes your product features are key to closing the business now.

Dear Joe:

With so many carbon unit vendors in the market, selecting the right one for your needs can be difficult. Before you make your decision, though, you may be interested in knowing about a series of products my company is developing. We expect to market these products in six months, and they will be completely compatible with our current line.

As you know, ABC Company has 55 percent of the current carbon unit marketplace. Although this market share makes us the clear leader, we are taking steps to ensure that we dominate the marketplace even more completely with our next product family. We intend to leap over a whole generation of technology and bring you interactive units by the middle of next year.

As the only vendor taking this approach, we are confident it will solidify our market dominance.

The Hersey Company, an independent organization that reviews manufacturers in our industry, has reviewed our development direction and has given us a four-star rating on our product strategy and development plans. You can reach that company at 800-555-1000 for more information if you are interested.

I also invite you to participate in the nondisclosure presentation about these products we are planning for select customers. With a couple of weeks' notice, I can arrange a private presentation in your facilities.

I hope we can arrange the presentation as soon as possible. When you see what we are working on, I believe you will understand why ABC Company plans to be the undisputed world leader in carbon units and the appropriate vendor for your carbon unit needs.

I will call next week to discuss the presentation.

Sincerely,

B. J. Smith

Explaining Why Your Offering Is the Superior Choice

Lists of benefits help summarize and clarify your product strengths.

Dear Dan:

This letter is to recap the benefits of the solutions ABC has presented to XYZ. We believe our product offerings are second to none in the industry today. We also are confident that, after considering the alternatives, you will select XYZ—the industry leader—as your carbon unit vendor.

As we demonstrated in our last meeting, ABC products offer these benefits and more:

- Durability
- Serviceability
- Performance
- Investment protection through upgradability

We look forward to your favorable decision after your directors meet on May 8.

Sincerely,

Joel Allen

MODEL LETTER 5.28

A Reminder of the Benefits of Your Proposal

By putting written reminders of your benefits in front of prospects, you give them the luxury of thinking about your proposal at a time they find convenient.

Dear Mr. Kirk:

There never seems to be enough time in the day or an end to the worries about the bottom line.

I know that this is an extremely busy period for you and that you have not had time to meet with other key people in your company to seriously consider the IMSS proposal for your new accounting and job cost system.

Perhaps when you have a quiet moment, you can consider these benefits of the system and see how it can save you time and minimize your bottom-line worries. Here is an overview of the system benefits:

Reduces Duplication in Data-Entry Tasks

- *Saves time processing accounts payable and calculating job costs.* Each line-item entry on a purchase order flows through to update both the relevant accounts payable system files needed to pay your material vendors and the job cost files needed to report the actual material costs of the work in process.
- *Saves time processing payroll.* Each line item in the payroll time-card entry flows through to update both the relevant payroll system files needed to pay your employees and the job cost files needed to report the actual labor costs of the work in progress.

Reporting and Control

- *Alerts you to potential overcharges for material* with side-by-side comparisons of material suppliers' quoted or customary

prices and the prices charged in the invoice to your company.
- *Uncovers possible cost overruns* with side-by-side comparisons of material and labor estimates to actual costs, presented in terms of both unit quantity and unit cost.
- *Helps ensure profits on tight-margin jobs* by providing early warning of material overcharges or cost overruns.

Of course, these are just some of the benefits the system offers. The publication included with the IMSS proposal, *System Files and Reports,* describes additional attributes. Once the system is installed, I am confident you will have many more quiet moments to reflect on ways to use your financial information to make Basic Drywall a more profitable, smooth-running business.

I will call you in a week. Meanwhile, please call me if you have any questions about the system or the IMSS proposal.

Sincerely,

Frank McIntyre

(Courtesy of Frank McIntyre, Dallas, Texas.)

Staying in Touch
When Business Isn't Pending

MODEL LETTER 5.29

Professional Activities That Give You Visibility with Clients

Always thank prospects for taking their time to attend your function, even when the information benefits them.

Dear Janice:

I appreciated your attendance last week at my roundtable session entitled "Measures of Performance." I hope you found the session to be stimulating and informative. As promised, I am sending you an unedited version of the session notes.

Please do not hesitate to contact me if you have any questions about the notes or issues discussed in the session, or if you need consulting assistance related to reengineering facilities management.

Very truly yours,

Thomas H. Wenkstern

(Courtesy of Thomas H. Wenkstern, Plano, Texas.)

MODEL LETTER 5.30

"I Haven't Heard from You Lately— How's the Product Working?"

Sometimes just pausing to ask about the product you sold is a reassuring gesture that shows you appreciate the customer's business.

Dear Ms. Summers:

I haven't heard from you lately, and I wanted to make sure everything was working out well with your new copiers. Our customer satisfaction surveys have shown very positive feedback for the equipment you selected, so I expect you'll have years of trouble-free service.

As we discussed during my most recent sales call, we offer a complete line of facsimile machine/copier/computer printer combinations that would work well in your environment. I've enclosed a new catalog for your review.

Jana, it was a pleasure working with you these past few months. I hope we can do business again soon.

Sincerely,

Sue Myers

MODEL LETTER 5.31

Promoting an Advertising Opportunity

Dear Lisa:

WBOO has created a great promotional opportunity for Greek Fest Restaurants.

Did you know that a large percentage of news viewers watch news for the weather report? WBOO, in response to this finding, will soon provide the community with Weatherwatcher, a frequently updated report that will be available to callers twenty-four hours a day.

WBOO will promote Weatherwatcher at least twice a day (more frequently in the beginning). The promotional spot will say, "Weatherwatcher is brought to you by WBOO and Greek Fest Restaurants."

In addition to the on-air spot, the Weatherwatcher recorded message also will say, "Weatherwatcher is brought to you by WBOO and Greek Fest Restaurants." This amounts to 730+ mentions, not counting phone calls. The total investment per year is only $15,000, or $20.54 per TV mention.

WBOO is committed to this effort; therefore, you can be sure the Weatherwatcher spots will air in very desirable positions. And a look at the rating books will attest to the strength of WBOO in the Albuquerque market.

This opportunity is for a very consistent, inexpensive vehicle to keep Greek Fest Restaurants on consumers' minds.

I will contact you in a few days to see what steps need to be taken to secure Weatherwatcher for Greek Fest Restaurants.

Sincerely,

Sally Lombard

MODEL LETTER 5.32

Reminding the Client Why You're No. 1

People forget your strengths if you don't remind them.

Dear Cindy:

Why do viewers keep tuning in to KKXX-TV? One reason is that KKXX is the only station in the Portland market that has retained the same news anchors at 5:00 P.M. and 10:00 P.M. over the past thirteen years.

One KKXX competitor has announced anchor changes at 5:00 P.M., 6:30 P.M., and 10:00 P.M. Why? To try to capture some of the large KKXX audience share. But viewers know where to find their consistent, stable news source.

Dominance. Stability. Credibility. KKXX makes a difference.

Sincerely,

Sally Lombard

MODEL LETTER 5.33

A Note to Keep Clients Apprised of Your Improvements

Whatever your business, you can use news about your company to stay in touch with customers.

Dear Gloria:

As you know, since MegaMedia took over KKXX-TV, the improvements have been nonstop. Equipment upgrades for the news and sales staffs alone have cost more than $1 million!

KKXX is now proud to announce the newest addition to our news anchor team, Wayne Webb. Wayne brings eighteen years of television news experience. His extensive background in anchoring, reporting, and writing will help KKXX Channel 2 produce an even stronger newscast. Wayne is an award-winning veteran broadcaster who has worked in the Tulsa, Sacramento, and Buffalo markets.

Wayne will anchor weekday newscasts at 5:00 P.M., 6:00 P.M., and 10:00 P.M. He joins Anne Wilson, the popular and long-time KKXX anchor.

MegaMedia is committed to KKXX-TV, to our community, and to making KKXX the news to watch in the minds of viewers.

Regards,

Sally Lombard

Telling Clients About a Dramatic Improvement

Prospects are eager to learn of advances that can help them improve their profitability.

Dear Ted:

Watch for steady increases as more and more viewers turn to KMNM-TV!

On March 1, KMNM began airing from the station's new tower atop Lookout Mountain. Technical advances resulting from the change will dramatically improve the signal for Littleton viewers.

The enclosed articles will give you additional information about how these changes will affect the advertising market. I will follow up with a call next week to answer any questions you may have.

Regards,

Sally Lombard

MODEL LETTER 5.35

Reasons This Station Is the Strongest

Tell customers what makes your product strong. Your confidence will be persuasive and reassuring.

Dear Brenda:

Apart from their commitment to news and programming, KWWW remains a strong force in the Bakerstown market.

KWWW commissioned a report on cable penetration. Of the 109 cable systems serving 26 counties, KWWW is on all 109 systems— double the number of one competitor and 80 percent more than another rival station.

KWWW is the only VHF station, which is another reason it continues to dominate the competition. In the market's hilly terrain, UHF signals give a lot of viewers trouble.

The area's grocery stores tend to be outside the metropolitan area, which means they are outside the range of reliable UHF reception. In other words, they need KWWW's VHF signal to get their message to viewers.

Brenda, the station has the numbers, the programming, and a rate structure to allow you to easily place 85 percent to 100 percent of your television advertising dollars with KWWW.

Please let me know if you need any additional information on the market. I will be glad to help.

Regards,

Sally Lombard

Selling Outlook
FUD—Fear, Uncertainty, and Doubt.
Those Subtle Messages About Competitors

Chances are you are not the only salesperson pursuing a piece of business. Everything would be easier if you were the only contender, but our free-market, profit-oriented economy thrives on competition. Alternate vendors usually move quickly to replicate good products.

Your challenge is to distinguish yourself as the person customers prefer to work with. You have several tactics to accomplish this goal: distinguish your company as the leader, represent a superior service and support organization, exhibit personal professionalism that outshines other vendors' performance, or simply sell a superior product. Just remember: It's a war out there, and your competitors will be doing everything they can to shoot holes in your story.

How can you react gracefully and professionally, yet dodge their bullets? You learn to use FUD: fear, uncertainty, and doubt. FUD is information about your competition that you subtly and discreetly disseminate in a way that causes your prospects to be concerned, worried, even fearful about deciding in favor of your competition. FUD may come in the form of negative press. It may be in the form of a customer testimonial from an unhappy user who is willing to talk. It could even be a product comparison chart that clearly distinguishes your company's strength.

Selling takes strategy. Knowing the right approach in a given situation takes practice, skill, and finesse. At times, letters will be the best weapon in your arsenal to keep your name in front of customers, to keep them interested in you, and to combat the effects of the FUD that competitors are sending your way.

Letters to Help You Recover When Things Go Wrong

Most people who sell things for a living have thought from time to time that—had they known how many things could go wrong—they would have sought out a different career.

As the salesperson, you carry the bottom-line responsibility for product revenue, fulfillment, installation and training, the morale of your support team, product service, and ongoing customer satisfaction. If you sell a product that can have an impact on your customer's revenue, you live night and day with that responsibility.

Problems tend to be a large part of the job for many reps, especially if your product is complex and your sales cycle long and complicated. But even the simplest products get delayed, get bad publicity, and don't get delivered on time. The efficient management of challenging situations is a hallmark of a resilient, long-term rep.

But how do you keep the customer satisfied while working around the issue? Even if the problem is the customer's (as in a payment or credit issue), your goal is always to find a solution, keep order, and maintain positive communication.

The letters in this chapter can help you manage challenges. Customers will judge your ability to perform under pressure, and how you measure up can be more significant than your pricing or your product.

You will deal with many of the situations in this chapter in person, and your letters will serve as written confirmation of what you tell your customers. The importance of your letters is that they remain as the record of the incident and your attitude toward resolution. As with any situation involving error and human emotion, use extra care and sensitivity. These may be the most important letters of your career!

Chapter 6. Contents

Your Company Has Problems

MODEL LETTER 6.1

Explaining a Product Delay

When your company delays delivery of its product, come straight to the point in communicating the news. The customer will respect your honesty. Even if you lose the sale, you can save the relationship. In addition, try to find out the real reason for the delay and let the customer know whether it will be worthwhile to wait.

Dear Barney:

I am writing to let you know there will be a ninety-day delay in shipment of the new tape transports you ordered. Please accept my apologies. Our Quality Assurance Department discovered a design defect that, without correction, might have resulted in a failure of the transport. I know our delay is a disappointment; however, I believe it is preferable to having a component failure while you are relying on the transport for important data processing tasks.

Given this news, I will call to discuss alternatives. Please accept my apologies for the delay. Thank you for your understanding.

Sincerely,

Michael Harris

MODEL LETTER 6.2

Explaining a Shortage of Parts

By acknowledging the customer's problem, you demonstrate respect and concern.

Dear Juan:

The purpose of this letter is to follow up on your concerns regarding the lack of buffer units in the Los Angeles depot last weekend when you had a problem.

As we discussed by phone, Assemblers & Company has been challenged with getting an adequate supply of the buffers from our supplier. This product has been very well received, and we have had difficulty keeping up with the field demand for it. Nevertheless, the A&C purchasing manager assures that the critical phase has passed; we now have buffers in stock.

My apologies for the inconvenience this has caused. Please do not hesitate to call if you have additional questions or wish to discuss this issue any further. I appreciate your ongoing support and the confidence you have shown in A&C.

Sincerely,

Tina Lawrence

MODEL LETTER 6.3

Explaining a Modification to Your Plan

Your ability to foresee and communicate potential surprises can help keep customers satisfied.

Dear James:

Please accept this letter as a statement of variance to the Milestone project under way at ABC.

XYZ has learned from TGF that the support for Milestone will be available during the week of April 16 and only via the SCSI channel.

The impact to the server backup strategy at ABC is minimal. TGF backup tool will be able to manage all backup activities from a central node and will also be directing the automation from that node.

XYZ encourages ABC to continue working with TGF to help improve the availability of their support of XYZ Software, which is slated for late April, according to TGF. XYZ will provide necessary expertise to ABC to implement the feature when such support arrives. Kane Conrad, ABC, is in contact with David Foster, ABC project leader, to discuss the necessary changes to effect a smooth implementation of the modified approach. David has recommended the use of Platinum 5 as the TGF master node until the software support is available.

If you have any questions regarding this letter, please give me a call.

Sincerely,

Hanna Robinson

MODEL LETTER 6.4

Explaining a Change in What You Are Selling

Making a change in a deal after it has been agreed to is frequently awkward and can lead to fear, uncertainty, and doubt for the customer. Communication that is simple, direct, and timely can diffuse the hard feelings associated with a change in plan. Be sure customers are aware of your additional efforts on their behalf so that they do not feel that they are making all the compromises.

Dear Mr. Martin:

This letter summarizes yesterday's meeting regarding our plan to complete the DASD installation. As you know, our systems engineers have worked over the past couple of weeks, trying to determine exactly how much additional capacity you require. They have determined that your requirements can be met by providing an additional disk controller and cabinet.

We will still honor our original offer to provide additional usable capacity of 40GB for $2,086 per month for sixty months. We will fulfill that offer by providing the additional cabinet at no additional lease charge to you. There will, however, be an increase in the maintenance of $652 per month.

Thank you for your patience with us throughout this longer-than-expected installation process. We value your business very much and will continue to do everything we can to ensure a smooth transition to your new DASD.

Sincerely,

Emily Ciuba

MODEL LETTER 6.5

What to Say When Your Product Causes the Customer a Problem

When your product causes your customers a problem, real or perceived, you need to let them know immediately that their problems are your problems and that you are doing your best to solve them. An apology is always an appropriate first step. The next step is to offer to mitigate the damage and prevent a recurrence.

Dear Mr. Duffy:

I am writing to express how sorry I am that the failure of our equipment caused you to lose your largest customer. I am aware that the revenue impact to your organization is significant. While we do not have the ability to replace the revenue, we are working around the clock to identify and fix the problem with our equipment so that the problem never happens again.

Please accept my apology and my concern for what has happened. I will continue to monitor the problem and will be in regular communication with you as we sort through it. Do not hesitate to let me know if a response from a higher level of my company to a higher level of your company might be appropriate.

Thank you for your patience. I join you in hoping for a successful resolution of this problem soon.

Sincerely,

Richard Haygood

MODEL LETTER 6.6

Apologizing for Not Delivering as Promised

Dear Lynn Woods:

Please accept my apology for the problems that you had with your delivery. I know that if we fail to perform as expected, your business is affected.

When you selected Toute Suite Delivery Service, I considered myself and everyone in my company to be a part of your business, and therefore responsible for your success. That is why I take this lapse in service very personally.

After your call, I checked into the problem and learned that the delivery was dispatched on schedule, but the driver was delayed at the stop before yours; then no one was available at your office to accept the delivery.

I have taken specific steps to prevent the problem from recurring. Lynn, I want to stress my appreciation for your business and my commitment to provide excellent delivery service.

Sincerely,

Pat Romboletti

(Courtesy of Pat Romboletti, The Write Sales System™, Dallas, Texas.)

MODEL LETTER 6.7

What to Say When Your Service Organization Causes the Customer a Problem

When your service organization causes a problem, you need to acknowledge it, just as you would acknowledge a problem with a product. Your communication should facilitate a graceful reconciliation between your service organization and your customer's organization.

Dear Mr. Haas:

I understand that you have patiently endured several apparently incorrect diagnoses of software problems by our technical support staff. As a result, the time and money you have spent on the suggested solutions have been fruitless. I have reviewed the technical support notes and have brought the problem to the attention of regional management.

Please accept my deepest apologies for the inconvenience. I wish I could fix your problems by referring them to a higher level of technical support. Unfortunately, we already have our best people working diligently to solve what has proved to be a very unique set of circumstances. Please be patient with us a bit longer. Sometimes these things must be addressed by a process of elimination. In your case, there appears to be a rather complex combination of factors creating the problem. Be assured that we value your business and will do everything in our power to resolve your problem as quickly as possible.

Thank you again for your support.

Sincerely,

Bill Montgomery

Postponing a Training Session

Any time a schedule is involved, a written record is a must. It provides a reminder for everyone involved, and it documents your work on the account.

Dear Mr. Kirk:

A scheduling conflict has forced me to ask you to postpone the training session we scheduled for your new system next Saturday. I will not have a senior technician available to complete the session for at least two weeks.

I know this change will be a disappointment. Please let me know if I can do something in the meantime to minimize the inconvenience to you. I will call you before Thursday to reschedule.

Thank you for understanding.

Sincerely,

Frank McIntyre

(Courtesy of Frank McIntyre, Dallas, Texas.)

Explaining a Breakdown in
Your Company's Teamwork

Explaining a breakdown in teamwork requires sensitivity to the people issues on both sides.

Dear Mr. Pottenger:

Please accept my apologies for the recent breakdown in our internal communications regarding your upcoming system installation. We realize the importance of proper planning as a prerequisite to a smooth transition to a new system. We do not ignore important details.

As you know, we have been experiencing rapid growth during the past year, and we expect that growth to continue. Consequently, we have hired a number of new people who may not fully understand some of the steps we take during migration between systems. We both became painfully aware of a significant oversight by one of our newer staff members last week during our planning meeting with your systems administrator. That staff member will remain as part of the team, but we have added an additional senior technical support staff member to serve as a mentor to our newer member throughout the course of your system migration.

To ensure the success of these actions, I suggest we meet weekly to discuss support issues. Please recognize these meetings as an extension of our support for your business.

I will be at your office on Friday, so we can discuss this further. I look forward to hearing any additional ideas you may have to ensure the success of this installation.

Sincerely,

Trish Cane

MODEL LETTER 6.10

Explaining That Your Company
Is Filing Chapter 11

As with other challenges, Chapter 11 bankruptcy calls for honest, upfront communication to maintain customer confidence. Chapter 11 is a business reorganization carried out under court protection. It is a tool to restructure, rather than evade, business debts, which can make customers better off than they were before your firm filed for protection.

Dear Mr. Peterson:

This letter is to confirm the news you may have heard or seen in the paper. ABC filed Chapter 11 in the United States Bankruptcy Court on Friday. The news startled all of us who are employed by ABC, even though we have been aware of cash-flow problems that caused difficulties in filling orders over the past six months.

Management has assured us there will be no layoffs, orders will be shipped on time, and service contracts on installed products will be honored without interruption. ABC entered Chapter 11 to restructure some of its short-term debt into long-term debt. This move will improve ABC's cash flow and improve service to customers. At the same time, it will ensure that all of ABC's creditors are paid in full and improve the long-term financial viability of the company.

I promise to keep you informed of all developments. Thank you for your ongoing support while we reorganize. Please feel free to voice any questions or concerns.

Sincerely,

Elbert Hubbard

MODEL LETTER 6.11

Responding to Bad Publicity

When bad publicity hits, the credibility of your company is at stake. Part of the salesperson's job is to let the customer know what your company is doing to correct problems.

Dear Mr. Griffiths:

This letter is in response to a recent article in the *Wall Street Journal* regarding an unhappy customer we had in the Northeast. As you know, our newest product had early life-cycle troubles that caused problems for several of our customers. The particular customer described in the article seemed to have more trouble than most. Although it would have been better had the problems not occurred, we were eventually able to correct them. We also compensated the customer for his trouble. The most recent internal reports show the customer is completely satisfied with the solution and continues to order equipment from us.

I hope this summary satisfies your interest and concern about the *Journal* article. Please let me know if you want additional information, and thank you for your continued interest in our company.

Sincerely,

Trish Ferguson

MODEL LETTER 6.12

Maintaining the Business Relationship Despite a Dispute Between Your Customer and Your Company

It is possible that your company and your customer's company can be involved in a business dispute at one level and yet maintain an ongoing relationship at another level. Let your customer know that you and your company are willing and able to distinguish business issues. A dispute over one situation does not have to hinder other areas of the relationship.

Dear Mr. Edwards:

I am sure you are aware of the disagreement between ABC and XYZ over their respective obligations under the F-157 contract. I am confident that those disagreements will be resolved amicably through reasonable compromises on both sides.

In the meantime, I want to emphasize that our company considers that issue as completely separate from all others. I hope you and your company feel the same way.

Please consider my proposal on the F-160 purchase with the assurance that the existing disputes do nothing more than strengthen my resolve to work harder to avoid future disputes.

Sincerely,

Brian Downs

MODEL LETTER 6.13

Dealing with a Product-Availability Issue

When you cannot deliver everything customers ordered, the point to stress is what you can do for them. Show that you have thought about their requirements and intend to resolve the situation in a way that satisfies their needs, even if it is a compromise.

Dear Carryl:

Thank you for your recent order for an additional 9900 Robotics Unit and associated media.

We can ship the 9900 next week, and you can expect delivery by July 1. The media, however, are in allocation, and present a challenge. The media are manufactured for us by GBH Corporation and have been in allocation since the fourth quarter. We receive about 25 percent of what we need each week. The allocation situation is expected to continue through the rest of this year.

Due to the significant revenue tied to this order and your repeat business with us, we are able to supply you with a larger portion of media than other customers receive. Of the 2,000 boxes you ordered, 500 would arrive with your Robotics Unit. The remaining 1,500 will be shipped in increments of 500, over the next three months. Although I realize this is an inconvenience, by shipping your partial order, we can help you begin utilizing the unit immediately and begin your automation process.

Carryl, I hope this arrangement will satisfactorily meet your needs. Thank you for your patience and understanding during this phase. Please know that I am prepared to do anything I can to expedite the situation, it will be done.

Sincerely,

Carl Browning

MODEL LETTER 6.14

Dealing with Word-of-Mouth Bad News

Sometimes your competitors will say things about you that just aren't true. Set the story straight, honestly and directly. The customer will appreciate your professional attitude.

Dear Chuck:

One of the advantages of a competitive marketplace is the open flow of information about products, and much of it is brought to you by competing vendors. The benefit to you is access to a great deal of information; the drawback is sometimes questionable reliability.

I understand that one of the companies competing for your gizmo business may have indicated that my company has a supply problem, which would prevent us from fulfilling your order, should you decide to place it with us. I want you to know that our factory is running on a forty-five-day lead time, standard in our industry. In addition, if you needed a quicker delivery, we would probably be able to accommodate you. We are eager to prove our abilities as a vendor and satisfy your needs.

Chuck, your gizmo business is a significant opportunity for the ABC Company. We want you to have all the information about us that you need to make a sound business decision. I hope I will have additional opportunities to address any questions you have. Please do not hesitate to contact me.

Thank you for this opportunity, and for your consideration of the ABC Company.

Very truly yours,

Jack Fleck

MODEL LETTER 6.15

When You Ship the Wrong Product

Despite automation in warehouse procedures, sometimes the wrong product goes out the door. You can count on this happening in situations where timing is crucial and you cannot afford mistakes. Do what you can to remedy the problem, then explain it in writing. Seeing your written commitment helps alleviate pressure the customer may be experiencing.

Dear Bill:

As you are aware, you received an order from the ABC Company this week for 500 Type Z gizmos, when you had placed an order for 500 Type E Gizmos. My apology for the mistake, and for the impact the mistake may cause. Following is my plan to remedy the situation:

- By next Friday, September 15, you will receive 230 Type E gizmos. These will arrive by air freight, with ABC Company absorbing the cost of the extra shipping.
- The remaining 270 Type E gizmos will arrive by September 30, with expediting charges again covered by ABC.

Bill, if there is any way I can further expedite your replacement order, I will do it. Unfortunately, our factory is just ramping up again after our two-week August shutdown, and my options are limited.

Thank you for your support and your commitment to the ABC Company.

Sincerely,

Jeremy Gollop

MODEL LETTER 6.16

Beta Test Reveals Product Faults

Early life-cycle problems do occur, and it's best to be honest about them. Explain the plan for resolution, and you will keep the customer interested in you and the product.

Dear Margaret:

This letter is to inform you as a position order customer of some product problems that have recently arisen in the beta test phase of the new Ray equipment from ABC Company.

The beta test is designed to reveal product faults and is the final step prior to the general release of the product. The Super X 2000 is in beta test in three major hospitals across the United States, where the hospitals were asked to utilize the machine extensively. At two of the three sites, daily use of the equipment revealed a faulty inner lining, which will require a redesign of the lining.

Product engineering expects the redesign and final testing to take about three months. Although we regret the delay, we are pleased that the test process revealed the problem before general release.

I hope that this information will help your planning cycle. We are committed to making this a quality product and to satisfying your order. Please call with any questions or to discuss the situation in further detail.

Thank you for your patience and your support.

Sincerely yours,

Benjamin Kildare

Your Customer Has Problems

MODEL LETTER 6.17

When a Spending Freeze Delays the Sale

Reasons beyond your control can hold up a transaction. For instance, a spending freeze may surprise your contacts as much as you. The appropriate correspondence for this occasion is to reiterate your interest, mention what you have already done for the customer, and explain what you can do to hold on to your special offer.

Dear Bill:

Thank you for your notification about the capital freeze for the remainder of the third quarter. I am, of course, disappointed, after all the hard work that went into the proposal, from both your side and ours. I continue to believe in the benefits of the proposed solution and hope that you will have the chance to implement it when capital becomes available.

As you know, the pricing proposed expires at the end of the month. Our aggressive lease rates were tied to revenue recognizing a third-quarter transaction. Although I will commit to doing everything possible to again obtain attractive rates for you, I cannot guarantee where the market will be in one or two quarters.

On behalf of everyone at my company, I assure you that we appreciate the opportunity to propose our solution to you. We hope implementation becomes feasible again soon.

Sincerely,

George Buck

MODEL LETTER 6.18

They Ask for Special Concessions, Then Don't Buy

Sometimes after you go to the top of your company to get approval for a concession, the prospect decides not to buy. The situation is embarrassing to you, and you are furious with your prospect, but stay calm. Communicate your efforts to the prospect without showing your emotion. After all, if the prospect decides to revisit the decision, you will still be interested in the sale.

Dear Colin:

I know you are as disappointed as we were that your executive management decided to cancel the new building. Your team and ours spent considerable time and effort on the plans. I hope that as business gets better (it will!) they will proceed with the project, and we will participate again.

Unfortunately, I thought the project was "go." When I went up the ladder for the pricing concessions you asked for, I didn't realize this might happen. I am disappointed, but I understand your situation.

Best of luck to you during your downsizing and reorganization. I hope we will continue to work together on other projects, and thank you for considering us on this one.

Sincerely yours,

Dawn Andout

Model Letter 6.19

When the Client Causes Problems but Blames You

Who's really to blame? Unfortunately, this question sometimes needs to be answered. If it's your customer, state your position gently but clearly.

Dear Wendy:

I understand that the downtime you experienced on your system last weekend had a significant impact. In reviewing what happened, I discovered a couple of points I want to communicate.

Your system went down on Sunday. We received a call about the outage and responded on site within one hour. In reviewing the situation, we discovered that an operator had pulled the microcode out of the box, which caused the outage. Microcode intervention is strictly a service technician's responsibility, as you know. If an operator opens the box and begins adjustment, failure is likely to occur. Although we can't change what happened, we were disappointed to learn that the shift supervisor blamed us for the incident, claiming that the microcode was improperly installed and causing the operator to intervene.

Our teams have worked well in the past. I regret this miscommunication between your operators and our service personnel. I am also concerned about perceptions and roles during an outage and suggest a meeting to discuss what happened and how to handle these situations in the future. I hope you will join me in proactive discussion regarding this matter. I will call next Monday to arrange a time to meet.

Sincerely,

Noah Begoine

MODEL LETTER 6.20

The Customer Can't Afford to Buy and Asks for Your Help

If you offer a customer special terms, state how long the offer will be in effect—as in this example.

Dear Oscar:

This letter is a response to your concern abut your cash-flow constraints. At the moment, your firm's financial position is preventing your company from acquiring the materials you need to keep manufacturing at full production. As your long-term supplier of part 626, ABC Company is pursuing alternatives to enable you to continue acquiring materials from us.

ABC Company values the long-term supplier–customer relationship that we have shared with XYZ Corporation. Our profitability depends on customers like XYZ. We take your circumstances seriously and will review all available options to work through this challenge.

ABC Company, however, also has cash-flow challenges. Our first quarter was disappointing, and the continued resource outlay for our next generation of product constrains our options.

With that understanding, we propose that XYZ continue to take delivery of 10,000 parts per month, payable with ninety-day terms, instead of the usual thirty. This additional sixty days for payment should considerably ease your situation and continue to provide a consistent material supply. ABC can extend this offer through the remainder of this year.

Oscar, I hope this offer will be satisfactory to XYZ. My management and I are available to discuss this alternative, at your earliest convenience.

I look forward to our continued discussion and to solving your material issue soon.

Sincerely yours,

Cornelius Baggs

MODEL LETTER 6.21

Responding to a Breakdown
in the Customer's Network

Your company's ability to service your customer's needs effectively, efficiently, and profitably often depends on the customer's cooperation with your staff. Your letter should emphasize the customers' self-interest in cooperation.

Dear Ms. Thompson:

Now that we have signed the contracts to go forward with the MOUSE upgrade, we need to coordinate the efforts of our field engineering staff with your systems and operations staffs. Our field engineering manager has met with your systems and operations managers three times to obtain information that is essential to minimize the risk of an extended system shutdown during the upgrade process. In each case, written meeting agendas were distributed to the key players ahead of time. Unfortunately, at least one of your managers was unprepared in each meeting.

I am sure you realize the critical nature of this project. We want to be sure there is no unnecessary interruption in your service to your customers. A fourth meeting is scheduled between our staffs. Please help me ensure the smooth upgrade of your system by speaking with your personnel to ensure that everyone is prepared for the next meeting. I have enclosed a copy of the written meeting agenda to assist you. Thank you for your cooperation. Please call if you have any questions.

Sincerely,

Bobby Howard

MODEL LETTER 6.22

What to Say When
Your Customer Has a Credit Problem

Many companies with large and profitable accounts have reputations for paying debts slowly. When your customer has a credit problem, you need to protect your company from a potential bad debt yet preserve the opportunity for an immediate sale and future business. Telling the customers they have bad credit is insulting. A better approach is to simply state the payment arrangement your company requires for shipment and leave it at that.

Dear Mr. Moshier:

Thank you for your recent order. To process it for shipment, my company requires one-half of the purchase price with the order. The remaining half will be due on delivery.

Please call me if you have any questions. Thank you again for your order.

Sincerely,

Peggy Brandon

MODEL LETTER 6.23

Collecting Past-Due Accounts

Past-due accounts, like other types of credit problems, require you to protect your company's financial position and preserve the potentially profitable relationship with the customer. Your approach to collection will vary depending on the history of the individual customer. The following letter assumes the relationship is one worth salvaging.

Dear Mr. Wolf:

My company is trying to collect our invoice number 20348, which is four months past due. The invoice is for special services we provided when you moved into your new building. Although the charges had been approved in advance, these special situations apparently require another process in order to get paid.

I would appreciate it if you would make some calls within your organization to find out if there is some reason the invoice has not been paid. I will be happy to provide any additional documentation for the charges if there is any question about our services.

Thank you for your assistance.

Sincerely,

Sara Patterson

MODEL LETTER 6.24

Coping with Your Customer's Chapter 11 Bankruptcy

The same legal and business principles apply when your customer files Chapter 11 as when your company files Chapter 11. Obviously, you or your credit department must investigate the facts and circumstances to reevaluate the customer's credit-worthiness. Assuming your company decides to continue the relationship after such reevaluation, your letter must reflect your support of the customer's honest efforts to reorganize and, at the same time, set forth any new terms your company deems necessary to protect its interests.

Dear Mr. Wilson:

This letter is to inform you and everyone at XYZ Company that we are aware of your recent court filing for Chapter 11 bankruptcy protection. I regret that your firm has had to take this action. On behalf of everyone at ABC Company, I wish you success in your efforts to reorganize.

ABC Company is studying the possibility of continuing our vendor relationship with XYZ during this phase. Both our legal and financial staffs are preparing recommendations. Our roles have become more complicated because, as a vendor at the time of your filing, we are now a creditor in the bankruptcy.

As your sales representative, I am involved in ABC's internal discussions. We hope to decide on a course of action soon. I have greatly appreciated the business we have done in the past, and I hope to continue to serve you in the future. I will contact you as soon as I have further information to report.

Sincerely,

Ellen Ciuba

Model Letter 6.25

Offering Additional Training
for the Customer's Staff

Your ability to suggest potential solutions to problems is an essential selling skill.

Dear Mr. Kirk:

I know you are aware of the problems with the last three payroll cycles, and I know that your payroll clerk is unhappy with the way the system works.

However, my technical support staff has completed two error-free test cycles after the two most recent payroll periods. Their success leads me to conclude that the system works but that we may need to provide further training to address misunderstandings and questions about the system's payroll procedures.

Rather than plan an additional training session, I recommend scheduling a technician to be on site next Thursday at the beginning of the payroll entry. This way, we can walk your staff through the cycle, see any glitches they experience, and solve problems at the onset.

Thank you for your understanding. Please call if you have any questions.

Sincerely,

Frank McIntyre

(Courtesy of Frank McIntyre, Dallas, Texas.)

Selling Outlook
Maintaining Credibility Under Trying Circumstances

When the going gets tough, smart customers turn to sales reps who have proved themselves to be honest, dedicated, and innovative problem solvers. In business, setbacks are unavoidable, no matter how great the product or how dedicated the service team. It is the way the problems are resolved that determines their lasting impact on client–vendor relationships.

Over time, sales representatives either build credibility with customers or lose business to competitors, and to a large degree, it is the representatives themselves who determine which way a customer relationship goes. As a sales representative, you don't design the products you sell or run the shipping departments that fulfill your orders. You don't control corporate advertising or establish pricing policies. What you can control is your own selling style. Cultivate these traits, and you will do a lot to bolster your credibility with customers when the going gets tough:

- **Empathy**. Ask yourself what the customer expects to happen, and address issues from that perspective. If a shipment was promised on the 15th, even though your contract lets you deliver as late as the 25th, realize that the customer is disappointed.
- **Diligence**. It's difficult to help ward off problems if you don't ever check to see how your customers are faring with other parts of your company after the sale. Stay informed about your customers' experiences with your company and the progress of their orders.
- **Candor**. Even when the news is bad, it is crucial to be straightforward and forthcoming with information that directly affects the customer. Otherwise, you are teaching your customer not to rely on the updates you provide.
- **Creativity**. How well you navigate your way out of troubled waters can impress customers and encourage them to depend on you, even in trying situations.
- **Honesty**. Trust makes the difference between one-time sales and long-lasting associations. Trust takes a long time to develop and an incredibly brief time to destroy.

Letters to Help Disappointed Customers

Much of selling deals with managing disappointment and perception. Situations don't always work out as the customer or you would like. What separates the most successful representatives from the rest of the pack is how well you manage disappointment.

Successful representatives develop strategies for resolving problems before they derail a deal or cost a customer. Sales professionals work to polish the negotiation and conflict-resolution skills that preserve vital relationships. You recognize that every problem presents an opportunity to turn a situation around and possibly strengthen the bond with a valued customer.

As a successful representative, you know your future depends on keeping the customer interested in working with you. You have learned that most disappointed customers appreciate someone who will admit a mistake and take corrective action. A customer's respect for you may deepen when you've skillfully solved a problem.

Perhaps you are already adept at applying these skills in face-to-face meetings and on the phone with customers. This chapter gives you models of carefully crafted letters that can work to your advantage. Of course, whether you're communicating orally or in writing, your goal is to turn a disappointed customer into someone who is satisfied with your company and you, someone who wouldn't hesitate to place another order or renew a service contract. In other words, check your ego at the door, get past any thoughts about who is or isn't to blame, and look at what you can do to unravel the problem at hand without sacrificing your bottom line.

The letters in this chapter are drawn from many different industries to show a variety of pitfalls and ways to get past them. These examples have some common elements, however. They all express your high regard for the customer. They demonstrate your willingness to listen thoroughly and address the customer's complaint directly. They all suggest solutions to the problem and ways to continue the sales process. They demonstrate good-faith efforts that stop short of acceptance of liability. In short, they represent plausible solutions that take both parties' interests into account and help get the sales process back on track.

CHAPTER 7. CONTENTS

Resolving Payment Disputes over Claims That You Didn't Deliver

How to Respond to, "It's Not What We Ordered"

MODEL LETTER 7.1

R-E-S-P-E-C-T. Show a Little!

People react to problems with varying emotional intensity. For sales professionals, however, there is only one acceptable reaction, the one that comes with a cool head, courteous attitude, superior listening skills, dedication to solving the problem, and respect for the customer. In this model letter, the customer clearly expected something that was no longer available based on a misunderstanding of the vendor's promotion. The sales rep provides information to clarify the error and offers suggestions to satisfy the customer.

Dear David Brown:

This letter is a follow-up to our telephone conversation of October 21. As we discussed, there was miscommunication regarding your order of Real Fresh Dairy products. My understanding is that on October 20, you placed an order for December delivery based on the expectation that you would participate in Real Fresh's holiday promotional advertising. My sales associate explained that the co-op advertising was no longer available. I deeply regret this misunderstanding and hope you find my alternate suggestion equally attractive.

During my most recent sales call to Uptown Grocers' corporate headquarters (on September 15), I met with you and Kevin Hughes from your marketing department to discuss Real Fresh Dairy's upcoming promotional co-op for the holiday season. As I explained, the closing date for the co-op Christmas advertising was October 15.

The deadline is firm, largely because only a limited amount of advertising was included on the co-op plan, and that had been spoken for by the deadline. As a sales representative, I deeply regret not being able to accommodate a valued customer such as Uptown. As an alternative, you may be interested in Real Fresh's spring co-op program. I could offer the same terms we discussed for the holiday promotion at a 12 percent discount. I will call you later this week to talk about the possibilities.

Again, David, I am sorry about the misunderstanding, however it arose. You are an important customer to me and I want to make sure you are pleased with the products and services you receive from Real Fresh.

Best regards,

Liz Wilson

MODEL LETTER 7.2

"What Do You Think Is Fair?"

Getting the customer's view is a key step in satisfactory problem resolution.

Dear Carole:

As we discussed in our phone conversation Monday, your ad in Sunday's paper was a terrible disappointment. My agency prides itself on quality work, and I think that, after your years with us, you know that such problems are rare exceptions to a very reliable record.

As your account executive, I investigated your ad's progress through the production process. I learned from our art and copy staffs that proofs went through the routine checks at your office and mine. However, my agency accepted five copy changes by phone on Thursday, the day after the ad was to have closed. Because of the tight time frame, we agreed to bypass the normal proofing cycles. Instead, your assistant read and approved a facsimile of the ad you saw on Sunday. No one noticed the missing phone number.

As we agreed on Monday, the best long-term solution to prevent a recurrence is to forbid telephone alterations and to require higher-level approvals for any changes required after closing deadlines.

I am still thinking of several possibilities to make amends for Sunday's error. I must ask you, what do you think is fair? Agency staff clocked fifty-two hours developing the ad, then made the error trying to accommodate your need for last-minute changes.

Perhaps we can have lunch later this week and find a mutually acceptable solution. You know how much we value your business, and it's important to me that you have the highest levels of confidence in our ability and satisfaction with our service.

Best regards,

Bob Teague

MODEL LETTER 7.3

"I Said 24, not 100!"

Owning up to your company's mistakes keeps relationships on track.

Dear Sue:

I am sorry for the confusion that has arisen about your order for racks. You ordered four sets of cartridges, assuming the sets held six each, as they have in the past. We recently changed a "set" to be a pack of twenty-five. Unfortunately, our telephone representative failed to make this change clear to you.

I have brought this situation to the attention of the telephone sales manager. All telephone sales reps are being reminded of the need for clarity in their conversations with customers.

To rectify your problem, we will pick up the items delivered to you and reship the order, which we now understand to be a total of twenty-four units. As an expression of our regret for this misunderstanding, we will pay the freight for the mistaken shipment as well as on the reshipped order.

Sue, I hope this offer to pay all freight charges helps compensate you for the inconvenience the misunderstanding caused. Once again, my apologies, and thank you for your patience while we straighten out this problem.

Sincerely,

Frank Wynne

"Please Accept My Apology"

Sometimes the best solution is a straightforward apology.

Dear Ms. Mayhew:

Please accept my sincerest apology for the difficulties you experienced with our fulfillment department last week. I can assure you now that your order has been processed accurately and shipped by air freight at our expense. You should have it at your office Monday, March 10. I will call you Monday afternoon to confirm its arrival.

Frankly, I was surprised to learn that you had problems with your order. Our fulfillment group has an excellent record, and I am confident that you can expect flawless service from us in the future.

Please call if you need anything before I speak to you next week.

Best regards,

Lauren Bose

MODEL LETTER 7.5

Explaining How You Will Correct Your Company's Mistake

Step-by-step details about your plan to correct a problem can help smooth ruffled feathers.

Dear Ms. Clapton:

My technical associate, Tim Hodges, confirmed on his visit to your corporate headquarters that my firm had delivered several models of copiers that were not as specified in your order.

Your senior officer signed leases and service agreements for twenty copiers, ten collating units, and ten noncollating units. We delivered fifteen collating units and five noncollating units. On behalf of Copy Systems, I apologize for the mistake.

My installations manager and I suggest the following plan to correct the problem:

- The five noncollating units you need will be shipped from St. Louis on June 2.
- The week of May 26, I will call you to set up a time for Copy Systems to pick up the wrong copiers and deliver the right ones.
- Copy Systems will waive all delivery fees and lease payments through July on the five units that were not as specified.

I will verify with you that this is agreeable before I proceed.

Sincerely,

Kim Morris

MODEL LETTER 7.6

"It's Not What You Advertised"

If your product is oversold in advertising, your company and you must deal with the user's disappointment.

Dear Frank:

Thank you for your recent call to our customer service line. I regret that you are disappointed in your purchase of ABC software.

You commented that the software was much less feature-rich than our advertising brochures claimed it would be. I have forwarded your comments to our development and marketing departments.

ABC Company enjoys a strong reputation for customer satisfaction and, certainly, we do not want to jeopardize this status with over-stated or misleading advertising. As a token of our appreciation, I have enclosed a voucher worth $50 toward the purchase of any of our products.

Again, I thank you for the time you took to express your opinion, and I hope you will continue to give us feedback on ABC products and services. We value customer comments such as yours. They help us make the best products possible.

Sincerely,

Ray Robbins

When the Customer Is Unhappy with Your Firm's Performance

MODEL LETTER 7.7

Using a Performance Summary to Respond to Complaints

The letter demonstrates how to narrow points of controversy to one specific contract term, summarize performance in that area, and avoid blanket statements implying general dissatisfaction.

Dear Jerry Pearson:

This letter is in response to your stated concerns that my organization did not fulfill the integration services aspect of our contract for the installation of three Megadisk storage units.

First, I am very concerned that you have been disappointed in our service. We value the opportunity to do business with your company and believe we had structured this transaction to provide the support necessary for successful installation.

We expected to cover the proposed integration services in two ways:

1. Make available the assistance of my firm's installation staff
2. Provide a Megadisk Software consultant for one week to work through any and all issues associated with your Megadisk Software

In reviewing the installation process, we believe we fulfilled our obligations in the following ways:

1. Ron Ford, my firm's technical specialist assigned to your account, has provided ongoing support in person and on the telephone to David Lee and other members of your team.

2. Ron was on-site, as planned, whenever other Megadisk Software personnel were present to ensure that your firm received the necessary help from Megadisk.
3. Ron continues to have very regular contact with David Lee and other members of your staff. Ron's help, or the help of other specialists from my firm, will be part of our ongoing support of your account.
4. Linda Frederick, customer services engineer, has been on-site throughout this installation. In fact, she has logged 109.8 hours on your premises since this project began.
5. Donna Gold from Megadisk Software was on-site at your headquarters throughout the week of April 22. All indications are that it was a successful week.

I am aware that the timing of the Megadisk Software was not perfect. In checking that schedule, I recall your telling me that the week of the April 15 was too early and the week of April 29 would be too late. We knew that you wanted the units installed by April 15, but we did not understand that you wanted the software fully functional at that time.

I hope this summary helps you understand what my firm intended to provide your company and how we did it. My sincerest apologies for any miscommunication that may have occurred through my organization. We have enjoyed working with everyone in your organization and hope our partnership will continue to grow in the years ahead.

Sincerely,

Lynn Hubbard

MODEL LETTER 7.8

Going Forward with the Sale
After the Product Has Faltered

Every company has a product problem at some point. The key to keeping customers on board is to address their concerns immediately.

Dear Mr. White:

As manager of fleet sales at OK Cars, I want to assure you that the trucks you ordered will perform as promised. Like all our products, they have undergone excruciating performance tests and have lived up to the challenge. You can count on them for years of dependable use, and you can count on our service department for reliable maintenance.

Of course, I understand your concern about the recall and the publicity surrounding it. The recall will affect the models you are considering but shouldn't mean any delays in delivery of your complete order. I can assure you, though, we will make complete repairs related to the recall within three days, and all the trucks will be fully warranted.

It has been my pleasure to work with you as you completed the selection of trucks to replenish your company's fleet. I look forward to closing the transaction in the weeks ahead. I am confident you will be pleased with your selections. Meanwhile, I'm here to address any concern you may have about the recall or any other matter. Please phone me anytime.

Sincerely,

Bill Selph

Model Letter 7.9

The Customer Wants a Different Support Rep

It is possible to respond to complaints about an individual's performance without maligning that person or admitting fault—as this letter shows.

Dear Dick:

As of Friday, Terry Black, ABC's senior support representative, will be assigned to your account.

I was sorry to hear of the problems you experienced with your previous ABC account support representative. As you know, your previous rep has been with ABC for five years and has been assigned to your account for three. On several occasions during this period, you have expressed concern about the rep's performance. After your most recent complaint, we have decided to replace your previous rep with Terry, who has been with ABC for fifteen years. Your previous rep will no longer be in regular contact with your firm, although he will still be "on call" from time to time and could still conceivably handle one of your service calls, particularly a weekend call.

To ensure a high level of service, I have asked our service manager to be paged personally—on all three shifts—whenever someone from your company calls ABC to request account service. This is an added measure to give you extra accountability and coverage.

Dick, I hope this plan meets your expectations of us. My sincerest apologies for the inconsistent coverage you have received. I hope this new plan puts your disappointment in the past and increases your satisfaction with ABC.

I will stay in close contact during this transition period and will notify you immediately if any additional changes become necessary. Thank you for your support.

Sincerely,

Sue Rogers

MODEL LETTER 7.10

Explaining Why Your Firm Insists on Complete Payment

It's hard to imagine a business that operates so smoothly there is never a returned product or complaint about service. Still, there are times to make concessions to customers and times to stand your ground about refunds or price adjustments that seem unwarranted.

This letter illustrates a firm, diplomatic way to tell customers that you appreciate their business, you are sympathetic to their problem, but you think your company performed as promised.

Dear Mr. and Mrs. Watkins:

As your account representative at Hospitality, Inc., I was concerned to learn of your disappointment in our services.

The manager on duty during your corporate dinner last weekend told me you asked for an adjustment on your invoice. The message included these four complaints:

- A menu substitution was unacceptable to you.
- You thought portions would be larger.
- The party in the adjoining conference suite was noisy.
- You expected to have exclusive use of the lobby outside your conference room, but other parties were there as well.

I have reviewed your contract for the corporate dinner and am confident that Hospitality, Inc., fulfilled our obligations to you. The contract gives us some leeway to substitute food items that may be unavailable on the day of your event. In your case, salad, entree, and dessert items were as you specified. A substitution of appetizers was made because we did not receive the mussels you requested. We substituted a more expensive crabmeat selection.

The portions were the standard sizes you have had on previous visits. Also, I showed both of you the Preston Suite, which you agreed was the right size for the number of guests you anticipated.

As for noise, it appears that the biggest problem occurred in the hours after your dinner. The party next door to the Preston Suite was a dinner-dance scheduled to last until 1:00 A.M. Your event was scheduled to be over by 10:00 P.M., but apparently people stayed on for an hour or so.

Please know that Hospitality, Inc., values your business very much. We've come to rely on repeat customers such as you. Even so, we must insist on complete payment.

Please do not hesitate to call if you want to discuss this decision or other matters with me. I hope that, upon reflection, you will be pleased with our overall service and will keep us in mind when it's time for your next special event.

Best regards,

Lisa Manning

MODEL LETTER 7.11

Offering a Trade-Out Instead of a Full Refund

Creative problem-solving can promote future business rather than an immediate deduction from your bottom line.

Dear Mark Hansen:

As marketing manager for Better Printing, I want to apologize for the trouble we had in printing your brochure last week. You have been a valued customer of ours for many years, and I realize that my company delivered a project that was not up to our usual quality standard. As we discussed on the telephone, the registration was off on page 6 and the second color was darker than specified.

I am confident we will work out a mutually agreeable solution to the problem. Your tight deadline last week made a reprint out of the question. Still, I think Better Printing is justified in expecting full payment. What I suggest, however, is a printing trade-out of 30 percent. In other words, you pay us, and we'll take 30 percent off the invoice price of your next printing order. Does that sound fair?

I will contact you to discuss my suggestion and any other issue of interest.

Sincerely,

Jack Waters

MODEL LETTER 7.12

Making Concessions Without Caving In

Your firm may be at least partially at fault when a customer has problems. If so, your goal will be to appease the customer without accepting total liability.

Dear Mrs. Brown:

I read your letter of June 22 and was disappointed to learn of your problems on the Grand Cayman tour. You have been a valued customer of Fun in the Sun Travel for many years and have reported lots of enjoyable experiences on your travels with us. It is important that we resolve this issue to your satisfaction.

As I understand your complaint, you feel the hotel was not as advertised. Your room was smaller than you expected and had a double rather than king-sized bed. You also hold Fun in the Sun responsible for ground transportation that was not available as promised.

This is the first complaint we have received about the hotel. However, I discussed your comments with the hotel manager, who offered to credit your bank card $75.

As for the ground transportation, I am not sure how the confusion arose. Fun in the Sun paid for four limousines to transport your tour group to and from the airport on arrival and departure days. There apparently was miscommunication, and you were not aware of these arrangements. I deeply regret the inconvenience you experienced.

While Fun in the Sun cannot give you a complete refund, we can offer a 15 percent discount—up to $400 off—your next Fun in the Sun tour.

Thank you for your past support and your patience as we work together to resolve your complaint. We appreciate your business and hope to serve you again soon.

Sincerely,

Martin Reed

MODEL LETTER 7.13

Suggesting a Reduced Fee to Satisfy a Disappointed Customer

Sometimes the client and you simply see things differently. When that happens, an offer to compromise on fees may settle the issue. Be sure to quantify the value of your compromise with regard to your performance.

Dear Suzanne:

A number of months have passed since we last spoke and since RHMC delivered a draft report to you. We would like to issue a final report to you, and we will do so soon unless you have any further comments about the draft report we sent you October 1, 20XX.

I understand that you were not completely satisfied with our draft report. On October 30, 20XX, Tom Andrews and I gave R. J. Glass our responses to your criticisms. On balance, I believe that our draft report represented good work and that much of the criticism relates to the normal process when a draft report is reviewed by the client. I'm not sure that discussing the report in greater detail would really benefit either of us, but I am willing to do so if you desire.

The final matter to be settled on the engagement relates to the outstanding professional fees and expenses due to RHMC. Pursuant to our engagement letter dated January 31, 20XX, and subsequent amendment dated April 10, 20XX, our total fee estimate of the analysis of the Omaha and Memphis locations was $33,000 to $39,000, plus out-of-pocket expenses. Our actual fees at standard for the work are $35,590 plus $6,902 in reimbursable expenses. To date, your organization has paid $27,418, which after deduction of expenses results in an engagement realization of 59.31 percent of standard rates.

To address your comments on our work and to resolve the final billing of fees, I would be willing to discount our professional fees to 75 percent of standard, which would reduce the final amount you owe to $5,425.

I would appreciate your response to this proposal at your earliest convenience. My direct number is 202-555-2416.

Very truly yours,

Thomas H. Wenkstern

(Courtesy of Thomas H. Wenkstern, Plano, Texas.)

MODEL LETTER 7.14

Helping the Customer Understand a Benefit Tradeoff

This letter illustrates two helpful tactics. First, letter writers can borrow the technique of reflective listening to demonstrate their understanding of the customer's problem. That accomplishment alone can help you get past disappointment. Second, this letter is a reminder that technical information may be best communicated in writing. Written explanations or instructions can't be tuned out or interrupted. They can be shown to others and saved for reference, however.

Dear Mr. Cain:

I understand that you are very pleased with the information your new IMSS system is providing, although you have received complaints from your staff about a particular feature. Your accounts receivable workers are disappointed that they cannot look up previous invoices online. They considered this an important feature of the old system.

As we discussed, you prefer not to have us write a custom program to provide this feature with the new system. So I am writing to explain how the new system works and how your staff might use it to access information that will prove more helpful than old invoices.

- Sales history information is stored in a sequential file, which works fine for producing reports but is too slow to access for online hookup of transactions.
- The IMSS system does not store a complete image of each invoice after it is printed. The invoice is generated at print time from a transaction file.
- After invoices are printed, key information from the transaction file is posted to several files, including the sequential sales history file and direct-access open-invoice file. The transaction file is then erased to make ready for a new batch.
- When posting is complete, you can print an accounts receivable report from the open-invoice file.
- The sales history file lets you print several additional reports, including essential information from each invoice. This fea-

ture enables the user to produce sales history reports by various relevant categories. For example, you can call a report of all your sales activity between January 1 through December 31 sorted by customer—or even by job number.

Of course, I've given you a very brief overview of the information available from the sales history file. I think your staff and you will be amazed at the new system's power to refine your sales data into useful information.

If you agree, I would like to demonstrate these capabilities in a training session for your staff. I am confident that, given a little time and more information, your staff will be quite comfortable with the IMSS system.

Please call me to arrange a training session or if you have any additional questions.

Sincerely,

Frank McIntyre

(Courtesy of Frank McIntyre, Dallas, Texas.)

What to Say When Delayed Delivery Hurts the Customer

MODEL LETTER 7.15

"Thank You for Your Patience"

Information about what went wrong can help appease a long-time customer.

Dear Mr. North:

Thank you for your patience this week as we worked through the problems with your menswear order of January 10. I understand that the delayed delivery meant the merchandise you ordered was not available for your preseason promotion.

I have had an account services representative trace your order. She determined that half of your order was available at our warehouse on January 10 and was shipped to your Boise store January 17. Shipping records indicate that your warehouse received that part of the order February 1, a week before the promised delivery date.

The problems with the remaining half of your order began at the manufacturer's plant and continued en route to Boise. Our records reflect that a customer services representative called you on January 15 to confirm that Sports Line was sending a partial shipment. He also informed you that the remaining half was not in stock, but that Sports Line expected to ship it by the 20th. On the 18th, the customer service rep called to tell you the merchandise was still not available from the manufacturer, and that we would not be able to meet the February 8 delivery date. According to our records, you reconfirmed the order.

The manufacturer shipped the order directly to you on the 21st. However, inclement weather en route further delayed the shipment. It arrived at your warehouse on the 24th.

You have been a valued customer of Sports Line for many years, and I want to express my sincere regret for the problems you experienced. I think you will agree, however, that our track record has been good. I assure you, you can rely on us for on-time delivery in the future.

Sincerely,

Lance Goodman

MODEL LETTER 7.16

Your Company's Mistakes
Disappoint an Executive

Trust is the essence of a good customer–vendor relationship. When mistakes happen, trust is at stake. The following letter shows a clear understanding of the customer's position, a key first step in rebuilding confidence.

Dear Pat:

I am writing to let you know how sorry I am about the trouble and disappointment we caused when we had to postpone your upgrade at the last minute.

As you are aware, we had a breakdown in both communication and delivery with our factory. Unfortunately, we were unaware of these problems until the last minute, when we had to abort the upgrade. Although it is hard for me to change the way the factory works, I have made it clear to our managers that these problems have had a great impact on you and your organization. Additionally, we are assigning a new service manager to your account to improve communication with your organization.

Pat, I know that your organization looks to you for leadership, and that when a vendor lets you down, as we did last week, the loss of credibility is significant. Please know that our team understands our responsibility to you and will double our efforts to restore your confidence in us.

As we move forward from this incident, we will do everything possible to ensure that your trust in us is well placed. Thank you for your support through these difficult times and for the partnership we have built over the years.

Sincerely,

John Jones

MODEL LETTER 7.17

Warning the Customer of an Anticipated Delay

Sometimes preventive action helps salvage relationships. This letter warns of a "worst case" problem with enough lead time to help the customer mitigate damage.

Dear Mr. Smith:

I am writing to let you know that we have had a "stop in the line" at our manufacturing facility. This setback could mean a delay of up to three weeks in our getting the product to you.

Mr. Smith, I know delayed shipment of our products will limit your ability to meet your obligations to your customers. That is why I wanted to let you know about this potential problem as soon as I heard the word. Although I cannot change the situation, I do know that the stop line is evidence of our quality program's effectiveness in capturing manufacturing defects. Of course, all of us depend on this program for the zero-defects products you expect my company.

I will call you with an update when I receive more information. Please do not hesitate to call me in the meantime if you wish.

Sincerely,

Beth Wilson

MODEL LETTER 7.18

Explaining the Impact of a Strike

Events of third parties may cause problems at any point in the sales cycle. The representative's ability to provide information, alternatives, and solutions can help turn adversity into a stronger bond with the customer.

Dear Richard:

I'm writing to give you a heads-up about a potential problem with your order. We had agreed to ship your order on March 24 by ground freight. As you probably know, a truckers' strike is threatened for the 22nd. A strike could delay your shipment by two weeks or more, so I thought it would be wise to develop a contingency plan now.

We have several alternatives. First, we could agree to ship by truck at the earliest possible date, provided your need for the shipment isn't urgent. Second, we could substitute parts X2A for the Y3Zs you ordered and ship today. Third, you could keep the March 24 ship date and pay the extra costs of air freight.

Richard, we are flexible about alternatives for fulfilling your order. Please let me know what you think of these suggestions. You may want to consider additional options.

Call or e-mail me anytime.

Sincerely,

Don Perkins

MODEL LETTER 7.19

Advising the Customer of
a Delayed Insurance Payment

Written documentation of your company's reasons for postponing payment to a customer can help limit misunderstandings.

Dear Mr. Perkins:

After our discussion this morning, I confirmed the status of your firm's claim in the Montgomery accident.

Secure Insurance has placed a hold on your firm's claim pending the release of Montgomery County's investigation report. The county sheriff's office is looking into the cause of the accident that led to your loss. Our adjustors assure me the report is due next week and, assuming the investigators confirm the trucking company's liability, you could have a settlement by the end of the month.

Thank you for your patience, and thank you for allowing Secure Insurance to take care of all your corporate insurance needs.

Sincerely,

Lyle Robbins

MODEL LETTER 7.20

Why Beta Tests Delayed the Software Shipment

The term *vaporware* says it all: when products such as software are promised but not delivered, manufacturers lose credibility. Still, customers will appreciate the manufacturer's candor about delays that arise during product development.

Dear Nancy Biggs:

Systems Software's beta tests of YourBasic 7.0 have been very encouraging, and all of us here are tremendously enthused about the upgrade's enhanced page layout, chart design, and spreadsheet capabilities.

Our launch date has been moved back six weeks, however. This change came after beta tests uncovered a bug related to the year 2000 problem. The projected ship date on your order is now June 18.

Please know that Systems Software is dedicated to providing the highest-quality software solutions. We realize that this delay may inconvenience you, and we appreciate your patience as we perfect this major upgrade of YourBasic.

Sincerely,

Michael Taylor

Resolving Payment Disputes over Claims That You Didn't Deliver

MODEL LETTER 7.21

An Apology After Negative Feedback

Even when the news is bad, thanking customers for feedback is appropriate.

Dear Mrs. Patterson:

I appreciate your taking the time to complete our customer survey. Your feedback is vital in helping us honor our commitment to provide reliable, consistent delivery service.

Your comments make it clear that we failed to meet our usual high standards of performance. I will provide a full response within the next five business days.

Please accept my sincere apology. I assure you that I will work to resolve this problem.

Sincerely,

Pat Romboletti

(Courtesy of Pat Romboletti, The Write Sales System™ Dallas, Texas.)

MODEL LETTER 7.22

Acknowledging the Dispute and Informing the Customer When to Expect a Response

A letter breaks the silence after a customer lodges a complaint, and can limit damage—even when you admit no liability.

Dear Marsha Adams:

I received your letter of May 5, 20XX, which outlines the problems your firm is experiencing with the PC network Can Do Computers installed the week of March 12, 20XX.

According to your letter, your coworkers and you experience several system failures per day. You have requested an investigation by Can Do's support services to determine whether the network's resources are adequate for your needs. You have also asked that Can Do bear the expense of this investigation and the costs of system upgrades that may be deemed necessary.

Two members of Can Do's technical support team will investigate these problems next week, and I should be able to respond to your requests more completely by June 1.

Marsha, I want you know that Can Do appreciates the opportunity to serve your company and will work to ensure your satisfaction with our products and services.

Sincerely,

Jeanne Harris

MODEL LETTER 7.23

Advising the Customer of the Outcome of Your Company's Investigation

A letter that restates the outcome of your investigation brings closure to the episode and serves as a record of your efforts.

Dear Marsha Adams:

This letter is to confirm our telephone conversation of May 30. As we discussed, the problems your firm was experiencing with your PC network have not recurred since last week, when Can Do's technicians completed their investigation.

Our technicians determined that your network's resources are adequate for your needs and could support additional users without requiring system upgrades. A minor reconfiguration appears to have solved the problems you were experiencing.

There will be no charge to you for this investigation. The technicians' time is covered under your service agreement, and no system upgrades were necessary.

As always, it has been a pleasure to serve you.

Sincerely,

Jeanne Harris

MODEL LETTER 7.24

Explaining Why Your Firm Insists on Complete Payment

When you disagree with a customer, state your case succinctly and offer a "next step" to move the relationship past the conflict.

Dear Mr. Rogers:

As your account manager for Go Figure Accounting, I understand your request for a reduction in your tax preparation bill. You are being audited, and you feel Go Figure shares some responsibility for triggering the audit and should, therefore, reduce the charge of our services to you.

There has been no indication that the audit relates to any of the services Go Figure provided in preparing your federal income tax returns for the past five years. Therefore, we cannot adjust your bill. We will, however, offer whatever support we can as you prepare for the audit and during it, if you so desire.

Thank you for giving Go Figure the opportunity to serve you. We value your business and look forward to serving you in the future.

Sincerely,

Pat Miller

MODEL LETTER 7.25

Offering the Customer Future Discounts in Lieu of Partial Payment Now

Occasional problems that arise in long-standing selling relationships can be turned into opportunities. Had the author of this letter offered a cash refund, the client could have taken the money to a competitor. Instead, the account exec's suggestion of a generous credit toward future business gives the customer a strong motive for reestablishing a positive relationship with the vendor.

Dear Mrs. Watkins:

Photo Pros deeply regrets our mistake in processing your company's film last week. We realize that the error greatly inconvenienced you and that some photographs for your annual report must now be retaken.

As we discussed on the phone, Photo Pros agrees that your company is entitled to some form of adjustment on your invoice. We propose a $3,000 credit to be applied to future photographic processing (with no expiration date).

Our feeling is that, as a valued customer of long standing, you realize that last week's error was a rare exception to a record of excellent service. By extending your company a $3,000 credit, we will be compensating you for two photographer's sessions and the inconvenience this delay has caused.

I think it would be a good idea for us to talk later this week. Perhaps you are available for lunch on Thursday. Please check your calendar; I'll call you on Monday.

Sincerely,

Dilbert Good

MODEL LETTER 7.26

Responding to Your Customer's Offer for Partial Payment

Letters, friendly as they may be, provide documentation when selling situations get sticky. This letter illustrates a sale rep's effort to be sympathetic yet firm with a customer who hasn't paid up.

Dear Robert Franks:

Thank you for explaining the circumstances surrounding your firm's outstanding invoices. As we discussed on the phone this morning, your organization has suffered several setbacks in the past three months—first the earthquake and then the financial failure of your biggest customer.

I am confident that you and the company you have built will rebound soon. Still, I cannot change the terms of your sales contracts by accepting 60 cents on the dollar, as you requested. I must insist on payment in full. We will, however, accept partial payments as long as payments are made on an agreeable schedule, such as 50 percent this month, 25 percent next month, and the final 25 percent by May 15.

Robert Franks, Inc., has been an important customer both to me personally and to my organization for more than fifteen years. I appreciate your business and look forward to serving you in the years ahead.

Sincerely,

Bill King

MODEL LETTER 7.27

Why Your Firm Won't Ship More Orders Without Payment Now

A straightforward, succinct approach is the best way to deliver unpleasant news.

Dear Mr. Jackson:

Thank you for Hartley's order of twenty-four cases of Reliable supplies. We appreciate your business.

I need to advise you, however, of a Hartley finance policy. We cannot authorize shipment of orders to firms that have three unpaid invoices outstanding. According to our records, these invoices have not been paid:

Trace	Date	Amount
00921	01/05/98	$ 798.42
01024	03/10/98	$1,278.01
03032	04/20/98	$ 675.98

Please advise me if there is a discrepancy in our records.

When we receive payment, our fulfillment system will automatically authorize shipment of your order, and you can expect to receive the supplies you ordered within five working days.

Thank you for your support of Reliable products.

Sincerely,

Arthur Thomas
Account Executive

MODEL LETTER 7.28

Your Customer Withholds Payment and Claims You Did Not Deliver

When things go wrong, everyone sees the events and facts differently. It is important to put your version of what happened and the action you took to correct the situation into writing. Your written account lets the other party think about your point of view. It also documents your response in a record that others can read. Often, problems that arise during a sale are communications-based, and letters help clarify where communication broke down.

Dear John:

I was sorry to receive your recent communication indicating your disappointment in ABC Company. After all the years we have done business, it is both a shock and a disappointment to realize the extent to which we have let you down.

In the hope of rectifying this situation, I would like to offer the following:

1. XYZ expressed dissatisfaction with the performance of our product. Although the performance you are currently getting is less than what is specified in the product literature, our experts are continuing to research this problem, and the connections between your application and the characteristics of the device. We are pleased to note that the performance you receive, although less than expected, is still a twofold improvement over previous technology.

2. XYZ expressed dissatisfaction in the installation support from ABC. Unfortunately, most miscommunications contributed to the support difficulties. We at ABC think that we received different signals from various people in your organization about expectations. Because nothing was put into writing at the time, we unfortunately cannot accurately trace the miscommunication of expectations. We are sorry about what occurred but also want to note that as soon as we realized that we were not covering you, we sent people over immediately and stayed through the remainder of the installation. We have continued to follow up on the post-installation effort.

Norm, although I cannot change what has happened, I hope this letter at least explains some of this miscommunication from our perspective. My apologies again for what has happened. I hope we can discuss these issues in person, at your earliest convenience. Thank you for all the effort you have put into this project and for your business through the years.

Sincerely,

Liz Plant

MODEL LETTER 7.29

Your Customer Threatens Bad Publicity or Legal Action

If problems escalate, you must use your best professional judgment to determine when it is time to call for legal help.

Dear John:

This letter is to acknowledge receipt of your correspondence of July 5, 20XX, which outlines your disappointment in ABC's non-performance and your intended actions as a result.

John, after servicing your account for over five years, I was very sorry to receive your letter, and am responding in the hope that we can meet and come to a resolution.

Although I cannot change what you have gone through, I want you to know what a significant customer you are to ABC, and that we would like to do everything in our power to prevent the potential actions you indicated in your letter.

Due to the gravity of the situation, I propose a meeting that includes senior management as well as legal counsel from both our organizations, at the earliest possible date. As the exposure of your situation has been significant internally at our company, I am authorized to offer you a meeting at literally any time that your senior management can be available. Additionally, the meeting can be at your site, or we would be willing to send our corporate jet to pick up your management, if that would be of interest.

John, repairing this situation and our relationship is my foremost priority, so please do not hesitate to let me know what I can do to facilitate the earliest possible meeting.

Thank you for your attention and for your consideration of this proposed meeting.

Sincerely,

Michelle Plant

MODEL LETTER 7.30

When Someone Else Got There First

Sales of residential real estate involve some very personal decisions, and emotions can run high. When a couple offers to buy their dream home, rejection of that offer can cause profound disappointment: they won't be living in the house they wanted, or maybe the amount they had hoped to spend is not realistic. More disappointment comes when they realize that the energy they spent in the negotiating process is down the drain, too.

The salesperson's sensitivity at this stage is critical to continuing the sales process with these clients. By expressing understanding of their disappointment and by offering encouragement, you can keep them motivated to make another pass at another property and motivated to continue working with you.

Dear Patty:

I am writing to let you know that the property you were interested in was acquired by another firm in a cash offer that closed last week. I know that this will be both startling and disappointing news to you, and that the Riverwood property had virtually all the feature and location benefits that you seek for your new corporate office.

I will continue to look for properties for you and believe that this will only be a temporary setback. The time and effort you have put into determining your requirements will continue to benefit our search and should make it easier to arrive at some alternatives. Please call if you wish to discuss this; otherwise, I will be back in touch as soon as I have other prospective properties to view.

Thank you for your understanding and your patience.

Sincerely,

William C. Hubbard

(Courtesy of William C. Hubbard, Kerrville, Texas.)

When the Customer's Bid on a Property Is Rejected

This letter emphasizes the future—and what can be done to overcome a setback.

Dear Mr. Pringle:

The owners of the property at 101 Riverhill Boulevard have rejected your offer in your fax of April 22. They will not make a counteroffer.

I regret very much that your contract was not accepted and that you had trouble in trying to work out a deal to buy the Riverhill property.

Please know that Riverhill is still the place you need to be. We will keep working to find the right property at the right price and to make your move a pleasant experience.

Sincerely,

William C. Hubbard

(Courtesy of William C. Hubbard, Kerrville, Texas.)

MODEL LETTER 7.32

The Product Is No Longer Available

A letter that expresses your diligence in satisfying the customer can reassure someone who has received frustrating news.

Dear Dr. Turner:

The model you ordered has been discontinued. I know this will be
disappointing news, given the time you spent researching your decision. As a consolation, the manufacturer does offers three similar
models. I would like to discuss this with you at your convenience.

Although none of the three alternates has the exact combination of
features of the model you ordered, there are some attractive
choices that may more than compensate for the change.

Please know that I value your business very much and will work
hard to help you find a product that satisfies your requirements.
Thank you for your patience.

Sincerely,

Bruce Bonn

MODEL LETTER 7.33

"Here's How We Plan to Solve the Problem"

The more you tell customers about possible solutions, the easier it is to explain a problem.

Dear Mr. Leonard:

Thank you for your patience as we work out the problems with your November 15–19 conference here at Out West Resort. We are very excited that your sales staff will be meeting here, and I am confident you will be pleased with the alternate arrangements I suggest in this letter.

As we discovered last week, there was a mixup in your group's departure date. Your original request was for a November 18 departure, and our marketing staff booked the conference rooms you wanted on that day. Here is how we plan to solve the problem. Your meetings on November 15–17 are scheduled in Big Horn Lodge. As we discussed, the meeting rooms in the lodge will accommodate your audiovisual needs. The building is adjacent to our dining hall, so meals will be easy to handle.

My suggestion for the 18th is to move your group to a scenic, riverside tabernacle about a mile from the lodge. Our wagons would drive your crew to the tabernacle, and we would cater your continental breakfast, breaks, and lunch at no extra expense. I think this suggestion makes sense because your agenda on the 18th doesn't include breakout sessions. The tabernacle is on a beautiful site that would enhance the message of your motivational speaker. You'd be giving your reps a big sendoff.

If these arrangements are not acceptable, we have several alternatives. I'll call you on Tuesday, May 5, to see what you think.

Best regards,

Tom Rubens

MODEL LETTER 7.34

"Let Me Tell You About Upgrades"

Your enthusiasm can help a customer forget about a minor hassle and appreciate your efforts.

Dear Kenneth Mayes:

I received your order for 250 model 102A television sets. What a terrific incentive reward to give your top producers! The size of your order entitles you to a 15 percent discount off the invoice price.

I have some disappointing news, though. Model 102A is no longer available. The manufacturer upgraded that set by adding stereo sound—so can I interest you in model 201B? The before-discount price is $375 per unit, instead of $345 on the set you ordered. I think you would hardly notice the difference in appearance, but your reps would appreciate the great sound it offers.

Ken, it's always a pleasure to do business with you, and I appreciate the order. If for some reason the alternative I've suggested is not acceptable, I hope you'll let me tell you about other upgrades.

Sincerely,

Liz Hayes

MODEL LETTER 7.35

"Don't Let This Be the One That Got Away"

A customer who has been disappointed in the past may respond to a follow-up note about a new possibility.

Dear Mr. Rayfield:

I thought of you the moment that 44-foot cruiser left our showroom: he's missed another great one. I sold the yacht you and your wife looked at last weekend. I'm not a high-pressure sales type, but I know you'd be interested in a very similar boat I have coming in Saturday.

It's another 44-footer. It's been on Lake Michigan for five years and has not been used a great deal. It's absolutely beautiful, though, and it looks like a terrific value, too.

I encourage you to stop by our showroom again this Saturday. Don't let this be the one that got away!

Yours truly,

Pat Mars

Model Letter 7.36

Offering a Losing Bidder a Consolation Purchase

Stay-in-touch notes remind customers of your personal service.

Dear Mr. Jackson:

We opened bids this morning on the American Brilliant chandelier. Unfortunately, yours wasn't the winner. I know how disappointing it can be to miss out on a much-desired treasure. That is why I thought you might be interested in several similar pieces Antiques America has located.

I've taken the liberty of sending you pictures of three chandeliers. I've seen two of them, and, I promise, they are every bit as beautiful as the piece you bid on. If you're interested in one of them, please call me. If not, please plan to stop by our showroom on the 15th. We will have a new shipment of English pine.

Sincerely,

Beth Wilson

MODEL LETTER 7.37

Your Customer Thinks a Price Increase Is Not Justified

Although no one wants to see prices increase, you can ease such unfortunate news by appealing to the customer's business sense with plausible reasons for the increase.

Dear Dave:

I know you recognize the challenge all businesses face when it comes to providing quality service at a reasonable price. For us at XYZ Company, the decision to raise the prices we charge on maintenance contracts was a difficult response to changing business conditions. Of course, we knew that the changes might cause concerns such as those you expressed in your letter of September 19.

The price increase came largely as the result of two developments: our expanding range of products has required that we expand our staff, and the prices we pay for parts to maintain our equipment have risen dramatically in recent months. Once these factors made it clear that prices had to increase, our management's goal then became to keep the increase under 10 percent, which we managed to do. Although I know any increase has an impact, I am pleased that we could limit this one. I am also pleased to tell you that we have no plans for further increases. I know you are aware that our contract allows us to increase maintenance up to 15 percent annually, which we hope never has to happen.

Dave, I will be happy to discuss this with you further, at your earliest convenience or at our next regularly scheduled meeting, whichever is better for you.

Thank you for your understanding in this matter and for your continued business.

Yours truly,

Pat Meyers

Selling Outlook
Why "In Writing" Is So Important
When Customers Are Disappointed

Calling on the same companies year after year, sales representatives naturally develop cordial relationships with customers. After all, isn't that the point of face-to-face meetings? Yet the letters in this chapter are a testament to the range of problems that can crop up, even in long-standing client–rep partnerships. That is why, as your business law professor no doubt said, you need to "get it in writing."

Follow up sales calls, especially orders, with letters to the customer that specify every term you expect to fulfill and every qualification and requirement the customer has imposed. It takes discipline, but what a godsend such letters can be when disputes arise over what was promised, who made the promise, and who failed to deliver.

Months or years after an event, even in a stressful situation, written documentation adds to your professionalism by

- Clearly defining expectations
- Defusing the emotional aspect of the situation
- Removing body language, facial expression, tone of voice from the sales message
- Helping you trace events that vary according to everyone's selective memory
- Serving as a point of reference that you can read and reread long after the sales call

CHAPTER 8

Presenting Pricing

Letters that present pricing serve several important purposes. They clearly state the terms of the transaction—what goods or services will be exchanged for the stated price at the stated time. They demonstrate your knowledge of the customer's needs and explain your proposal to meet those needs, and they move the sale toward closure.

The models in this chapter illustrate two approaches to pricing letters. Some examples propose one pricing scheme with no alternatives, and other letters either present several options or explain that terms are flexible. The approach you choose will depend on the timing, competitive situation, and customer requirements in a given situation.

CHAPTER 8. CONTENTS

Letters for Decision Makers

MODEL LETTER 8.1

Using Your Pricing Cover Letter as a Selling Tool

Persuasive reps promote their sales message in every piece of correspondence, especially pricing cover letters.

Dear Mr. Burns:

The selection of a key supplier can be a worrisome decision in today's volatile market. That is why the Buchanan Corp. makes reliable customer service the cornerstone of our corporate values. From our front line to our boardroom, we measure success in terms of service to you. Our records for on-time delivery, product reliability, and customer satisfaction set the industry standard.

All of us on the Buchanan Corp. sales team hope you will become the newest satisfied customer. In the enclosed proposal, we address the specifications your company outlined in your request for a proposal of May 20, 19XX. As we explain in the executive summary, we think our proposal provides major improvements over your current arrangement at a considerable savings.

The Buchanan Corp. knows you have a choice in the market. That is why we work each day to earn customers' loyalty, trust, and business. We hope you will weigh our proposal and choose us as a key partner in your success.

Sincerely,

G. H. Jenkins

What to Say When You're Not the Lowest Bidder

You may sense that your proposal will not be the lowest bid the client will receive. That fact may work to your advantage if you remind the client why your proposal is worth the extra expense.

Dear Mr. Lewis:

Thank you for this opportunity to submit a proposal for the design and production of the Technology Company's 19XX new product brochure. I am confident that you will find the finished product even more appealing than the mockups you reviewed last week.

The enclosed proposal reflects the finished-goods costs for 20,000 copies of the 24-page, 6-color mockup you selected. For your information, I have also included estimates for reprints in 5,000- and 10,000-copy increments.

Mr. Lewis, I congratulate you on your selection: it will result in an elegant, effective piece. When you consider the importance of the communications that promote your new products to customers, I think you'll agree that our plan is the best option to convey the Technology Company image.

Taylor Design Corp. is an award-winning, full service advertising agency. Most of our business is from repeat customers, and we would welcome the opportunity to count you among our satisfied customers.

Sincerely,

Renée Taylor

MODEL LETTER 8.3

"Thank You for This Opportunity"

When you are especially motivated to get a particular piece of business, say so in your cover letter to the prospect.

Dear Mr. Lockheart:

Thank you for this opportunity to extend the enclosed bid on the Thompson Building air-conditioning renovation. We are particularly interested in this contract because of its timing and its location.

The renovation will be our top priority: we just completed several jobs and have crews available to begin immediately. Also, the Thompson Building is near one of our current projects and will be a very convenient worksite. Our proposal reflects this motivation.

The Thompson project presents several mechanical challenges:

- Western exposure
- Unsightly location of equipment
- Lack of space in the building

Bonaire Ducts has offered more than one option to address each of these challenges, as the proposal explains.

Mr. Lockheart, it has been my pleasure to work as a subcontract or with your firm on three past occasions. I am impressed with your growth these last few years and would consider it a privilege to work with you again.

Sincerely,

L. L. Taylor

MODEL LETTER 8.4

Conveying That You Are Flexible

When customers' situations make long-term commitments difficult, your flexibility can sustain their interest until their circumstances become more predictable.

Dear Mr. English:

From our conversations over the past few weeks, I gathered that your situation is somewhat difficult to predict right now and may remain so for at least the next quarter. I took this factor into consideration when I developed the enclosed proposal.

The proposal outlines contractual terms on a month-to-month basis and spells out the conditions for renewal and termination of the agreement. I think this arrangement might be the best approach from both our perspectives, at least until you resolve the issues related to your recent merger.

Mr. English, I am confident that this arrangement will be mutually beneficial, and I look forward to a long and rewarding business partnership.

Sincerely,

R. W. Hanes

MODEL LETTER 8.5

Exploring Several Categories of Pricing

Dear Howard:

This letter is in response to our discussions this morning regarding the TGP proposal. I requested the following items to help me complete your recommendation:

1. **Purchase/lease options**   The purchase price for the redundant Z unit is $46,240, compared with a monthly lease rate of $1,090. With either option, the monthly maintenance rate is $302.

2. **New product**   An attachment will be available for the proposed equipment in the third quarter of 19XX. The purchase price for the adapter is $14,950 per controller, or $209,300 for the proposed configuration. The 36-month lease rate is $425 per controller, or $5,950 for the proposed 14. The maintenance rate is $95/month/controller, or $1,327 for 14.

3. **Training**   ABC proposed training for four people, which may be utilized any time from when the contracts are executed up to twelve months after installation of the equipment.

4. **Maintenance charges**   I have been able to improve the hardware maintenance charges by 7 percent. The new hardware maintenance figure will be $21,683, beginning on the 13th month after installation (twelve-month warranty). In addition, ABC will commit to keeping that rate for the 36 months, provided that your organization commits to a 36-month maintenance term.

5. **Software**   The software maintenance charge will remain $1,075/month and will be applicable from the date of installation.

Enclosed please find the new detail sheets reflecting the lower maintenance charges.

Howard, I believe this offer resolves the open issues we discussed. Please do not hesitate to let me know if you or others in your organization need any additional information.

Sincerely,

B. J. Knoble

MODEL LETTER 8.6

Conveying Advantages of Your Product

Even when your message is for a technical audience, formatting can help clarify and emphasize important points. Letter 8.6, for instance, lists key concepts to get the reader's attention.

Dear Joe:

ABC Company would like to encourage XYZ Company to pursue automation by starting with the PQR platform and adding other platforms as they become available.

It is advantageous for XYZ to automate its operations using the 9300 for the following reasons:

- All mounts and dismounts would be automated at loader speed.
- All scratch volume handling would be automated.
- There is need for additional operations staff for tape handling.
- Consolidation of the number of transports is possible within a single frame.
- Two devices on separate PQR processors may access one device.
- Operations of all products can be centralized from the System Administration console.
- RRR Software provides automated tape management by maintaining scratch pool security for tape media; providing volume access control; providing quick, consistent, error-free handling of cartridges in either the backup or restoration process; providing mixed-media management.

By implementing automation early on, XYZ will take the initial step toward implementing a timely enterprise-wide solution. At any point, XYZ may choose to add the pieces needed to manage any of the following:

- Network via the RRR products
- Network via the ABC enterprise solution
- Direct connections to any of the eighteen different platforms

Automation is consistent with PQR and ABC's development and testing effort for the automated online backup of the PQR databases.

The following terms are suggested for the ABC equipment:

1. **Hardware:** one 9300, one 9311, one 4430, three 4700, one B workstation
2. **Software:** RR, RR Database, RR Exchange
3. **Length of evaluation period:** six months
4. **Charges:** equipment charge, $80,000; maintenance charges, $1,200; freight, $800; software charges, $24,000 (Total: $106,000)

By implementing automation at the onset, you ensure a smooth transition and implementation of other processors and software at XYZ. I look forward to discussing this proposal with you and to answering any additional questions that you may have.

Sincerely,

Roger Williams

MODEL LETTER 8.7

Explaining a Change

Brief business letters that get to the point immediately can have dramatic sales results.

Dear Don:

The purpose of this letter is to confirm to you the price of upgrading your subsystem, and to convey a change in a previous offer.

Assuming an April 1 lease-effective date, the additional capacity will be $700 per month for the remainder of the lease (54 months). The additional maintenance is $200 per month, as we agreed.

ABC is extending a new offer to you with regard to the 3333 equipment. Originally, we wanted to take that equipment back in trade when the upgrade is implemented. If you have use for this equipment and would like to keep it, however, we will execute a dollar buyout transaction, and you may keep the 3333s.

I am pleased that you are satisfied with ABC equipment and are planning this upgrade. Thank you for your ongoing support of the ABC Company.

Sincerely,

D. R. Jones

MODEL LETTER 8.8

Offering a Lease Buyout

Complex offers need not be difficult to understand.

Dear Kyle:

Thank you for this opportunity to provide a proposal for Apex X-ray equipment for your new medical offices. As you know Apex is the world leader in X-ray equipment. We shipped more than 85 percent of the total X-ray equipment in 1996. We welcome you to the Apex family and believe that you will be pleased with an Apex decision.

To facilitate your desired transition to the newest technology, Apex proposes the following:

- If you enter into a 36-, 48-, or 69-month lease with the proposed Apex equipment, Apex will pay your leasing company for the remainder of your current lease.
- The Apex charges are as follows: 36 months, $97,000; 48 months, $132,000; 60 months, $142,000.

The Apex Total Service maintenance charges will be $700 per month. The lease start date will be June 1, 20XX, or later. (Freight: FOB Orange, CA. Equipment proposed will be used equipment.)

Kyle, I believe this proposal satisfies your interest in going to laser technology and provides a means of releasing you from your current lease commitment. Please keep in mind that these proposed devices may be upgraded to work with any of our other family of products, should that become necessary.

Enclosed is a printout of the details of this configuration, as well as a summary of ways to cost-justify this move, which I hope you find helpful.

I look forward to discussing all of this with you. Thank you again for your interest in Apex, and this opportunity to present a solution to you.

Sincerely,

Bruce Hayes

MODEL LETTER 8.9

A Proposal to Extend a Service Agreement

Many technical aspects of Letter 8.9 have been simplified. What matters here is how complex information about schedules and fees is interwoven with the sales message.

Dear Mr. Vincent:

It was a pleasure to speak with you today about HM Consultants' ongoing site location study for the Miller cookie manufacturing plant. This letter will serve to amend our existing engagement letter with Miller dated December 26, 20XX, with respect to work steps, schedule, and professional fees.

In our telephone call and in your memorandum of January 10, 20XX, you conveyed two requests regarding additional work steps for completion by the end of this week. First, you want HMC to identify the three "best locations" for the plant based on labor costs, utility costs, taxes, and economic incentives, excluding transportation costs. HMC is to determine total annual labor costs for Miller based on a list of fifteen job titles that provide a benchmark for comparison in German labor costs.

HMC understands Miller's requests are to ensure that locations with an overall operational cost are not excluded through the study's initial screening process based on transportation costs. Given your desire for a quick response, however, we suggest a more cost-effective approach than providing the level of analysis that would conceivably rank all forty-eight contiguous U.S. states to identify the three best markets on an overall cost basis. Our revised approach is to determine the ten most cost-effective states for each criterion that can be compared with the markets/centroids identified by optimal transportation costs based on the top fifty markets for cookie consumption.

Outlined below are the work steps we will undertake:

1. **Labor**   HMC will investigate a variety of published data sources, including trade associations and online resources for national job-specific cost benchmarks to yield a comparison among

states. In the event the quality and quantity of data availability is not satisfactory, a follow-up step will be to contact and interview representatives of key selected cities (such as St. Louis, Kansas City, Omaha, and Oklahoma City) based on the transportation costs analysis.

2. **Utility costs**   HMC will identify five to ten states that offer the lowest average electric and natural gas rates in comparison with the national average rates.

3. **Taxes**   HMC will identify five to ten states that offer the lowest rates with respect to corporate tax, sales tax, unemployment tax, and inventory tax. Workers' compensation taxes will be benchmarked for a plant worker by purchasing "loss cost" data (or mandated rates, where loss cost is either not available or not applicable) from the National Council of Compensation Insurance. The purchase of this data will entail an out-of-pocket expenditure of approximately $140.

4. **Economic incentives**   HMC will summarize, in a manner similar to that in the interim presentation, the benefits offered by five to ten states with reputations for being the most flexible or generous, such as: Alabama, Kentucky, Mississippi, Nebraska, Ohio.

Schedule and Fees

HMC is prepared to commence work immediately and, assuming prompt sign-off on this agreement, will deliver the work products described above by January 21, 20XX. To the extent that parts of this work are completed before January 21, we will fax the results to you and Branden Miller in Germany.

We estimated our professional fees will be in the $5,000 to $10,000 range plus expenses. These tasks are viewed as advance work on Phase II, and these fees are in addition to the fees estimated for Phase II in our December 26, 20XX, engagement letter.

We look forward to continuing our working relationship. If you agree with everything in this proposal, please countersign below and send it to me. Please call if you have any questions (567-555-2000).

Very truly yours,

Tom Wenkstern

(Courtesy of Tom Wenkstern, Plano, Texas.)

MODEL LETTER 8.10

Explaining Your Mistake

As a sale moves toward closing, it is crucial to clear up any misunderstanding about the offer or product features.

Dear Michael:

Thank you for your continued interest in our Automated Backup Solution.

Please accept the enclosed revision of my initial pricing proposal, dated April 6, 20XX. Unfortunately, one key element, the UNT, was left out of the proposal. In this revision, the UNT is included, as well as two additional options for the control unit.

Also enclosed is pricing for the subunit we discussed at our April 1 meeting. We built the subunit with parts from our previous generation of equipment that have gone through an extensive refurbishment process. The parts are combined with new shells and electronics to provide a device that supplies all the features and functions of automation at a lower price level than a device with completely new components.

Michael, I look forward to our continued discussions, and to learning more about your operations and the role automation may play within your organization.

Sincerely,

Beth Andrews

When the Customer Requests
Several Price Scenarios

When you present several options in the same letter, format the letter to avoid confusing the customer. Labels on a tabular format in this letter make it easy for the reader to find various options and their associated prices.

Dear Mr. Smith:

MegaDisk is pleased to provide your company with MD0100 options for your data center in Midcity. As you requested, I am presenting pricing for several different scenarios.

	Equipment	3-Year Lease (per month)	4-Year Lease (per month)	Maintenance (per month)
Option A	56 basic + 2 upgrade units	$63,335	$56,369	$18,194
Option B	32 basic + 2 upgrade units	36,999	33,184	10,414
Option C	32 basic + 4 upgrade units	65,220	58,641	18,184
Option D	56 basic + 4 upgrade units	38,884	35,457	10,414

On behalf of MegaDisk, I thank you for your continued interest in our products. We want to earn your business as you upgrade your archiving technology. Our goal is be the provider of choice by offering products of exceptional quality surpassed only by our outstanding customer service.

Please call me or my associate, James Charles, if you have questions or need additional information. Either of us can be reached at 888-555-2342.

Cordially,

Patty Kelly

MODEL LETTER 8.12

"Other Plans Are Available"

The problem with presenting pricing is that it locks you into a narrow offer that the customer accepts or rejects. When you suspect that your offer may be too limiting, explain that other approaches are possible.

Dear Mr. Thomas:

I am pleased to present Myerson Inc.'s bid for Acme's 19XX fleet leasing contract.

The enclosed schedule spells out a precise number of compact, midsize, and luxury automobiles included in the fleet agreement. Also enumerated are the maintenance and end-of-lease terms.

Mr. Thomas, Myerson is offering Acme substantial incentives and has added two luxury vehicles to the fleet agreement free of charge. These gestures indicate our motivation to be Acme's leasing company of choice.

Myerson devoted considerable resources to developing the enclosed schedule, but I assure you that we offer a variety of leasing plans. If there are problems with any of the terms we suggest, I am committed to working out a satisfactory arrangement.

I look forward to discussing this proposal with you soon.

Sincerely,

Tom Patterson

MODEL LETTER 8.13

Announcing a Maintenance Price Increase

Make sure prices and terms are clear. Bulleted lists can help customers understand changes.

Dear Ms. Thomas:

Today ABC announced increases in monthly maintenance charges for ABC maintenance agreement service on selected products. The increase in monthly charges takes effect in July 20XX. Listed below is a summary of the products affected and the approximate change in rate:

- ABC products that will receive a 15 percent increase in monthly maintenance charges
- Increases apply to ABC Model Numbers: 1000-100, 1500-120, 1500-150, 3000-260, 3000-300, 4303-150, 5000-021
- New prices take effect July 1, 20XX. New monthly rates have been rounded to the nearest whole dollar after applying the percentage increase.
- This maintenance increase will be administered in accordance with your applicable ABC service agreement. If the new price differs from the terms and conditions of your contract, the conditions of your contract prevail.

If you have any questions, please contact ABC Company.

Sincerely,

Maurice Jenkins

MODEL LETTER 8.14

Announcing a Price Change to Customers

One benefit of long-term contracts is the predictable prices they make possible. Eventually, however, the price of almost everything rises. As contracts near expiration, sales reps may need to warn customers that a renewal will mean higher prices.

Dear Kelly:

It has been a privilege to serve as your account executive these past five years. Watching your firm develop has been especially gratifying to me.

As you may have realized, the term of our contract expires in four months. This is a good time to reevaluate the services we provide to you and to explore other ways my company might help you meet your goals.

I also need to discuss pricing under a new contract. My firm has raised prices several times during the term of your contract, as have our competitors. While it is likely that your service prices will increase, I have several ideas about how we might enhance your services to offset the effect of the higher prices.

I will call you next week to discuss your thoughts on a renewal.

Sincerely,

Robyn Davies

Model Letter 8.15

Explaining Price Differences

Prices can fluctuate at any time during the sales process, and sometimes customers will expect an explanation.

Dear Mr. Daniels:

As you may be aware, my company announced an across-the-board price increase last week. That increase applies to the sales terms we have been discussing, and I am writing to give you an update.

My most recent letter to you, dated April 11, 20XX, itemizes prices of the components you are considering purchasing. In the enclosures to this letter, you will find an updated schedule of prices for those same components and a copy of the press release my company issued last week.

The bottom-line effect is an increase of about 15 percent—still a very competitive price. As the press release explains, our price increase resulted from higher raw goods prices. Those prices have yet to level off, which makes another increase a real possibility. For that reason, I encourage you to consider ordering now.

I will call you on Friday to follow up.

Sincerely,

Brian Michaels

Explaining Special Offers

MODEL LETTER 8.16

"I Can Offer an End-of-the-Month Discount. . . ."

Customers will appreciate your candor when you explain that a price reduction is the result of a strategic business initiative, such as the desire to lower inventory of overstocked items and end-of-the-month models.

Dear Ms. Wilson,

I appreciate your support of KP's fall line of sportswear. Your reorders this season suggest that you would be interested in a sale my manager announced today.

Now through the end of the month, KP is extending discounts up to 50 percent off wholesale prices of many items. Some of the sport sets you ordered from us last fall are included in the offer. The catalog I have enclosed lists complete details. We are overstocked in many of these items, and we would rather pass value along to our customers than liquidate the merchandise, which detracts from the image of the line and undermines your sales.

I hope you will take advantage of this offer. Your success with our summer line is a good indication that your customers will be back to find end-of-season sales, and you can be ready for them by reordering before the end of the month.

Sincerely,

Lou Mitchell

MODEL LETTER 8.17

Offering Incentives for Volume Sales

The incentives and special promotions your company offers can be the basis of a sales letter to customers.

Dear Travel Agent:

In the Sky Airlines and Far Flung Travel are promoting Hawaiian packages from major markets with substantial cash discounts and unprecedented incentives for agents.

Throughout the shoulder season—from January 15 through April 15—we are dropping all wholesale prices $25 and doubling agents' incentives in bonus travel awards on all weekday flights from Chicago, Dallas, and Los Angeles to Hawaii. Our goal is to beat the majors in their own markets, and we are counting on all of you to help us.

Your potential bonus travel awards from this promotion could make a big difference on your bottom line—or they could mean an expense-paid trip for you and your family to Maui. However you use your bonus, it's never been easier to earn.

Sincerely,

Jay White

MODEL LETTER 8.18

Explaining a Closeout

When fast turnaround is important, fax special offers to customers.

Dear Joe:

Harper Electronics Distributors has acquired closeout models of several best-selling televisions and ministereos from nationally known manufacturers, and we are passing this opportunity along to our customers. I am confident that Charleston Bros. Appliances' turnover and margins make these prices especially attractive.

Harper's wholesale prices will be in effect for ninety days before we begin distribution of replacement models, giving you ample time to market the closeout items. Between June 1 and August 31, 20XX, Harper will discount the wholesale prices of the following television models by 15 percent, and our usual volume incentives apply:

Model	Unit Cost 1–20 Units	Unit Cost 21+ Units
X25	75	63
X34	150	135
NR52	450	405
WS22	900	810
GB21	1000	900

Also, between June 1 and August 31, 20XX, Harper is offering 12 percent discounts off the wholesale prices of these mini-stereo models, along with our usual volume incentives:

Model	Unit Cost 1–20 Units	Unit Cost 21+ Units
7825	50	45
3434	75	68
5652	88	80
1322	100	90

Joe, I know Charleston Bros. can move a lot of units at these prices. I will call you on Monday to discuss your order.

Best regards,

Susan Dreska

Selling Outlook
Complex but Clear: Two Strategies for Communicating Pricing

Pricing correspondence must tell customers everything they need to know without overwhelming them with detail. This task is becoming increasingly challenging. The complexity of products seems to increase with each new offering, and customers seek an expanding array of product features and financing options.

Consider two approaches to resolving this dilemma: first, format the pricing information in a way that helps the prospect sort through the various options without confusion, and second, present a narrow list of options you think will be of greatest interest to the prospect but explain that additional options are available.

Many of the sample letters in this chapter illustrate techniques for formatting letters in a way that enhances their clarity. Look, for example, for these features:

- Numbered and bulleted lists that highlight terms and options
- Subheadings that enhance the organization of large blocks of text
- Tables that show major options at a glance

Careful editing can also help simplify pricing information. For example, you might write out relevant pricing information in paragraph form only to discover in editing that the information would be much clearer in a table. Fortunately, when you have discovered what works best for your product line, you can devise your own best models and follow them again and again.

The time you invest in perfecting your pricing correspondence is time well spent. No one wins if a proposal is so clouded with detail that the prospective buyer cannot understand it, but clear, complete pricing correspondence increases your chances that the prospect will accept your bid.

Letters to Close the Sale and Confirm the Order

Closing a sale requires your concerted effort to overcome obstacles and resolve all the prospect's reasons for not buying now. A silent prospect isn't necessarily one without strong reservations about your product, your company—or maybe even you. To remove barriers to the sale, you must proactively seek out, listen to, and address prospects' reservations. Show prospects you are willing to do what is necessary to make them happy. Your concern for the other party's well-being can be the basis of a productive business relationship. After all, who would you rather do business with, a responsive, professional representative or someone who offers a solution before you ask a question? When you work on the prospect's behalf to find long-lasting solutions, you demonstrate sincerity, sensitivity, humility, and the desire to earn the business. Demonstrate your service-oriented approach to sales, and the closing won't end anything. It will begin a lasting partnership.

Most selling requires face-to-face closings. But letters can play several important roles. Written negotiating points, for example, can persuade clients who want to see things "in black and white." Letters can bridge the awkward silence that may set in after you've presented your proposal, and letters can confirm terms agreed to orally, and can thus prevent miscommunication.

CHAPTER 9. CONTENTS

Closing the Sale

A well-timed letter is frequently what it takes to convince a client to act. Your message may convey an appropriate sense of urgency, a limited opportunity, or the warm selling style that makes this prospect comfortable working with you.

Establishing a Time Limit on an Offer to Encourage a Decision

Time-limited offers provide several advantages: they encourage customers to try products; they can lead to future sales; and they create a sense of urgency.

Dear Ben:

I am pleased that you are once again considering ABC Company to be your office supply products vendor. I appreciate this opportunity to earn your business and hope that it will be a beneficial relationship for years to come.

I want to reiterate the time limit on the current proposal you are considering. The pricing is a special introductory offer that requires a firm order by June 1 for delivery no later than August 1. Ben, I know from our discussions that the additional discounts offered were a key reason you decided to do business with ABC. To ensure that you benefit from this offer, please place your order by the end of the month.

I will be happy to assist in whatever way possible in the placing and timing of this order, including picking it up in person instead of depending on the mail. Alternatively, we can accept a fax order, should timing get that close.

Ben, thanks for your vote of confidence in ABC Company! I look forward to working with you again.

Sincerely,

Justin Roberts

MODEL LETTER 9.2

Suggesting a Final Offer

Selling situations require your best judgment. Advice one prospect considers pushy could be the right message to help the next person avoid missing a terrific deal.

Dear Mr. Pratt:

This fax is to confirm our telephone conversation of this afternoon.

As you are aware, the contract for the purchase of the property has not been executed. The earnest money check for $1,000 is in my possession and the additional earnest money of $9,000 has not been paid.

The Schaffers have received another offer for their property. They believe it is appropriate that, since you have been trying to get everything worked out, you be given an opportunity to confirm in writing your last, best offer.

Your final offer is required by 5:00 P.M. CST, Tuesday, April 23, 19XX.

Sincerely,

Bill Hubbard

(Courtesy of William Hubbard, Kerrville, Texas.)

MODEL LETTER 9.3

Limited Availability Means
It's Time to Order Now

The combination of a letter and follow-up call is the right formula to move some customers to closing.

Dear Jack:

Thank you for your interest in ABC Company's sale of previously owned office furniture.

ABC office collections come on the market only after a business foreclosure. Thus, their availability is very limited. Other companies also have the opportunity to bid on the items you previewed; the company that benefits from this limited offer will be the one that places its bid first.

Jack, I encourage you to make a decision about the items of interest soon. What a disappointment it would be if the pieces you want were already sold!

Please let know now if you need any additional information. I will call you later this week to see if I can help in any way.

Sincerely,

Sidney Powell

MODEL LETTER 9.4

Encouraging the Customer
to Place a Position Order

Offering a way out, a way to reverse a decision, encourages some customers to more readily accept your new offering.

Dear Spencer:

Thank you for attending the product presentation of our new line of superprocessors. As we announced at the presentation, we plan to release the new line next spring.

We are now accepting position orders for the new processors. As you know from our previous product announcements, a position order is nonbinding and serves primarily to guarantee product availability. If there is any chance you will want to take delivery of this processor within the next calendar year, I strongly encourage you to place a position order now.

Thank you for your interest in the next generation of our products. I will follow up next week to discuss the processor and your decision about ordering now.

Warm regards,

Blair James

MODEL LETTER 9.5

Asking for the Order When the Customer's Evaluation Period Ends

Product trials can be the most powerful sales tool of all. The feasibility of offering such trials varies from product to product.

Dear Ken:

This letter is to notify your company that the software on evaluation will reach the end of the evaluation period at the end of this month.

In the regular status meetings that have been held throughout the evaluation I have gathered that the software appears to provide the features you are looking for. Therefore, I encourage you to get the full benefit of this product on an ongoing basis by executing a long-term contract and license agreement.

I will follow up by phone next week to see what I can do to firm up this evaluation for you. Thank you for your interest and for taking the time to evaluate our product.

Sincerely,

Marie Manning

MODEL LETTER 9.6

Completing an Evaluation Period with a Sale

The transition from an evaluation period to a closing can be very smooth, as letter 9.6 illustrates.

Dear Jeff:

Thank you for your continued interest in SCH and the products we offer. We appreciate the time you spent to evaluate our X20 system. Please complete and sign the statement below and fax back to my attention at 202-555-0000 so that I can send you an invoice and the permanent key.

_____ has evaluated _____ and would now like to purchase the product. Please send an invoice for $5,000 for the license fee, and $1,200 for maintenance, as per our signed contracts. It is our understanding that the permanent key will be issued once payment is received by SCH Technologies, Inc.

Mary Piper

Buyer's

_____ (signature) _____ (date)

(Courtesy of Mary L. Piper, SCH Technology, Inc., Cincinnati, Ohio.)

MODEL LETTER 9.7

Proposing a Contract Revision to Close the Sale

When it comes to negotiations, correspondence needs to be free of loaded words. For instance, letter 9.7 says "working out the wording of," rather than "compromising," because compromise can imply a tinge of disappointment for both sides.

Dear Thomas:

Although we did not agree to all terms in the Biggs Town joint promotion contract Monday, I am optimistic that we are close to working out the wording of the two clauses where we still disagree.

Soon after I left the meeting, I thought of two minor revisions that can get us past the questions of the percentage splits on distribution costs and the markup on movie tie-in promotional items. My suggestion is to stagger the terms so that Biggs Town Promoters receives the terms we requested for the first eighteen months, and thereafter, for the life of the contract, the percentage split and markup revert to the terms General Distributors requested.

My opinion is that we could make the transition of terms transparent to consumers, and each of our organizations would receive its preferred terms for part of the contract term. I think you will agree, Thomas, that these adjustments represent fairly minor changes to what should be a very lucrative partnership for both our companies.

If you like this idea, we can change the contract copies we used in the meeting on Monday and execute the contract by the end of the week. Please let me know your response as soon as possible. I know you are as eager as I am to bring this promising marketing idea to fruition.

Sincerely,

Mitchell Potter

MODEL LETTER 9.8

Reminding the Customer of Price Benefits to Encourage a Close

The silence that sometimes follows your offer of a contract can be unsettling. Such situations are the perfect occasion for letters that remind the prospect of the benefits of your offering.

Dear Reed:

As prices fluctuate over the next two years, my customers will have the advantage of locked-in prices for as many as 275 SKUs. The two-year contract General Distributors has extended to Principal Marketing offers benefits beyond the obvious price savings.

A contract with General Distributors represents our commitment to provide top quality products and exceptional service in a long-term partnership with your organization. A two-year agreement with us helps you plan costs and margins with greater certainty, a rare benefit in this market.

Reed, I encourage you to discuss the contract we have offered Principal Marketing with your marketing forecasters. I am confident they will agree that it represents an outstanding opportunity. General Distributors is aggressively seeking your business because we are convinced that the synergy a strategic partnership would produce would bolster the market stature of both our organizations.

Please keep me posted on the status of the contract.

Sincerely,

John Williams

Model Letter 9.9

Proposing an Agenda for a Closing Meeting

Selling situations reflect diverse corporate cultures. Some clients prefer to finalize details in a formal meeting that follows an agenda distributed a day or more before the meeting. Other clients work out details of the sale in long conversations over lunch or dinner.

Dear Mrs. McKee:

Medical Staffing, Inc., is pleased to address any concerns you and your staff may have regarding the contract MSI has offered General One, which was dated September 1, 19XX, and is valid for the next sixty days.

Perhaps the most expedient way to proceed is to arrange a meeting with you, your nursing supervisor, the director of nursing, and any other staff you choose to invite. I would bring my nursing division manager and technical support specialist. Please let me know your interest in such a meeting and tell me the best time to meet from your perspective.

I propose a discussion of the following agenda items, and I ask that you forward other issues you want to add:

Contract terms: Inclusions, Exclusions, Billing
Personnel: Specific resume files that make up the pool of nurses available to you
Compensation: Clarification of the levels of compensation in the available pool of nurses

Mrs. McKee, I look forward to executing the Medical Staffing–General One contract and to a long-lasting partnership between our organizations.

Sincerely,

Dianne Ashcroft

Confirming the Order

As you move toward a closing, it is wise to lay out the terms of sale carefully in a confirmation letter. Even when both parties have agreed about their price, warranty, delivery, maintenance, and all other relevant terms, a confirmation letter provides a document that can be invaluable if disputes arise later.

MODEL LETTER 9.10

Detailing the Implementation Process

Clearly explaining how you will proceed helps the customer plan. Any differences of opinion can be worked out before misunderstandings arise.

Dear Mr. Kane:

I am writing to let you know what to expect over the next few months as IMSS installs your new accounting and job cost system and trains your staff to take over its operation.

In our last meeting, we established that you are ready to go ahead with the purchase and installation of the system. Under the contract, IMSS agrees to install your new system with these two conditions:

1. To get the system fully installed and operational without disrupting your normal operations
2. To limit the amount of overtime required of your staff.

This letter elaborates on these two issues to help you plan for the transition and to avoid surprises during the implementation.

Getting the System Installed and Operational

IMSS has agreed to perform Item 1 for $125,000, but I need to be clear in explaining that this requirement depends on the diligence and cooperation of your staff and IMSS personnel in these specific areas:

1. **An understanding of accounting principles**   IMSS staff will
provide the necessary computer expertise, but to be successful your
staff needs a fundamental understanding of the accounting principles that underlie the new system. The professional backgrounds of
your current staff appear adequate for the job.

2. **The installation process**   Under our first-year System Support
Contract, IMSS personnel install system software in a directory
structure that is separate from your existing system. We conduct all
tests in a manner that is invisible to other users of the system. After
the software is initially loaded and tested to ensure that it communi-
cates properly with your network devices, IMSS provides approximately twenty hours of training to each person who uses the
system. At the same time, IMSS provides application installation
and training specialists who work side by side with your staff to implement each accounting subsystem.

3. **Twenty hours of training**   As part of the twenty hours of training, your system administrators and other users take a summary
course that provides an overview of the system in a single eight-
hour session. This class usually takes place on the first available
Saturday after IMSS field technicians complete software installation and testing. We use preinstalled sample data files for initial
training. Next, IMSS provides specialized courses for the individuals directly responsible for handling your payroll, job cost, purchase order/accounts payable, billing/accounts receivable, and
general ledger subsystems.

These courses last about three hours each and are offered when system users have completed the summary course. The courses can be
taught on weekends or after hours on weekdays. Typically, IMSS
schedules a class in conjunction with the loading of each
subsystem's master and transaction files.

The Need for Overtime

IMSS will provide two installer/trainers who will work full-time
with your personnel for ninety days. During this time, they will assist in loading your existing payroll, purchase order, accounts payable, accounts receivable, job cost, and general ledger information
into the system's master files. They will also enter transactions

such as time cards, purchase orders, and invoices, and they will perform additional tasks involved in taking the system through its various transaction cycles. During this process, the installer/trainers will teach your staff how to handle these transactions on their own.

If one of your employees quits, becomes ill, or is unavailable for work for some other reason, IMSS installer/trainers are available to fill in until the employee returns or a replacement is found. The IMSS rate for temporary assignment is $30 per hour.

IMSS cannot promise to eliminate overtime entirely. In our experience, however, the overtime of each person who is directly involved with the new system can be limited to about twenty hours, which includes evening and weekend training sessions.

I hope this letter addresses your concerns. I look forward to working with you.

Sincerely,

Frank McIntyre

(Courtesy of Frank McIntyre, Dallas, Texas.)

MODEL LETTER 9.11

Reviewing Product Alternatives and Getting Another Vendor Involved

When you need more information from a prospect, it is a good idea to put your request in writing. Your letter specifies the information you need and reminds the prospect of reasons to do business with you.

Dear Bob:

I am writing to follow up on your interest in a Fortress device and to ask you to consider several relevant points.

First, I need your responses to these questions before I place your order:

1. Would you like a two- or four-door model?
2. If you want a two-door model, do you want to add a loader feature as well?
3. How many interfaces do you need?
4. Is your archiving environment manual or automated?

Also, I need to advise you about these two issues:

1. **The media are in allocation**   At this time, the media are available only from ABC Company. I suggest you order the amount you need initially now. To place the order, please call our consumable department at 800-555-0000.
2. **Effective utilization of this product requires data-set stacking** You use Moward's product, which is not yet qualified for the Fortress device. I think the best way to proceed is for you to contact Moward and ask how soon they will have support. Since you are the customer and they want to keep you satisfied with their product, it is important that you, rather than ABC, contact the manufacturer.

Let's discuss these issues by phone or in person at your earliest convenience. Thank you for ordering this new product.

Sincerely,

Brenda Lewis

MODEL LETTER 9.12

"We Are Pleased You Accepted Our Bid"

The transition from prospect to customer is subtle but important. Until the order is signed, there may be tension on both sides about price, timing, and other issues unique to the sale. A warm letter confirming the sale can also help strengthen the customer–vendor bond.

Dear Mr. Charles:

We are pleased that Central Vending has accepted our bid for the sale of 250 cases of snack products per month over the next twenty-four months.

I have attached a detailed schedule of the products to be shipped, shipment dates, destinations of shipments, and freight terms. As we agreed, General Distributors can accommodate minor deviations from this schedule with written notice to your account executive at least two months before the scheduled delivery. We will also work with you to overcome any emergencies that arise.

We welcome you to the growing list of General Distributors customers. We owe our rapid growth throughout the Midwest and Central regions to repeat business from satisfied customers. Our signed contract is our commitment to provide you with quality products and exceptional service.

Sincerely,

Troy Bates

MODEL LETTER 9.13

Confirming a Verbal Offer

Letters that arrive before the final contract can help solidify the deal in the client's mind.

Dear Patti:

This letter is confirmation of the verbal offer I suggested on Friday regarding a one-year contract for advertising in *City Monthly*.

On Friday, I suggested that in exchange for your agreement to sign a one-year contract for advertising valued at $250,000, *City Monthly* would extend a 20 percent discount for the life of the contract, resulting in a savings to you of $50,000.

I have enclosed a copy of an electronic mail message from *City Monthly*'s executive vice president of sales and marketing authorizing this discount to AG Bankshares, provided a one-year contract is signed within the next thirty days.

Patti, I am confident we will work out the terms of this contract in a very few days, and that you will be very satisfied with the pull of advertising in *City Monthly*. The magazine's demographics are a perfect match with the group AG is targeting in your home refinancing promotion.

I am ready to send the contracts as soon as you give me the word. I look forward to hearing from you soon.

Sincerely,

Carol Lucas

MODEL LETTER 9.14

Confirming Contract Revisions

During a busy workday, it can be difficult to find a few minutes to write one more letter to a client. When you consider the payoff from a successful close, however, the investment of a little extra time seems like a very small price to pay.

Dear Patti:

Thank you for responding so quickly to my offer of a 20 percent discount off all *City Monthly* advertising for the next year. This letter is to confirm the changes we discussed this morning. We can modify the contracts dated May 22, 20XX, to reflect these changes.

Please write in these three changes on both copies of the contract, sign and date the contract, have your vice president of operations sign and date the contract, and return it to me. *City Monthly* will return one countersigned copy to AG Bankshares.

The changes are follows:

- January plan (page 3, fifth paragraph): change full page to inside back cover
- February plan (page 4, first paragraph): change full color to six color
- October plan (page 7, tenth paragraph): insert the phrase, "in the Christmas preview section."

Congratulations on the terrific promotional plan you have put together. I am honored that *City Monthly* will be part of it. We have a great lineup of editorial promotions and features planned for the year. I know you will be happy with the results of AG Bankshares' advertising plan in the magazine. I look forward to seeing mockups for the first two ads next month.

Sincerely,

Carol Lucas

MODEL LETTER 9.15

Confirming Terms of
a Consignment Arrangement

Consignment arrangements can be beneficial to all parties to a sale. In some cases, a straightforward agreement that itemizes consigned property and states terms of the consignment is all that is necessary to formalize an agreement.

Dear Matt:

Thank you for accepting HiCo's surplus office furniture on consignment. After our move to new quarters, there was really no place to put all the extra shelves, desks, and tables we had accumulated.

I have attached to this letter an itemized list with the approximate values we discussed. I can summarize our agreement as follows:

Consignment Values agrees to offer surplus office furniture belonging to HiCo Inc. for a period of six months at a 60/40 payment ratio (CV/HiCo). Prices are negotiable but should not drop below 70 percent of the value stated on the attached sheet. At the end of this term, HiCo is responsible for removing unsold furniture from CV premises within fifteen days, or ownership reverts to CV.

Matt, good luck with this arrangement. I hope it will pay off for both of us.

Best regards,

Terry Richards

MODEL LETTER 9.16

Confirming a Contract Addendum

Contract terms can be modified when all parties agree to the proposed changes. One expedient way to accomplish the change is to have all parties sign an addendum to the original contract. It is a good idea, however, to check with an attorney about when an addendum will suffice and when the situation calls for a new contract.

Dear Leah:

As we discussed, Annex, Inc., has agreed to change delivery terms during the second half of your contract term with the GTX Company. I have prepared an addendum to our contract that specifies the new delivery terms, including cost, freight arrangements, and a schedule of destinations.

To be on the safe side, I checked with our legal staff, and they assured me this document is as binding as the original contract. So, we are all protected by it. To complete the arrangement, you need to sign both copies of the addendum, return both to me, and I will forward a countersigned copy to you.

Leah, it is always a pleasure to do business with you, and I am happy to accommodate you with this modification to our original agreement. Please call me if you have any additional concerns.

Sincerely,

R. J. Brown

MODEL LETTER 9.17

Using a Letter Agreement to Confirm Terms

In some situations, letter agreements can have the effect of contracts—when, for instance, a technical writer agrees to perform a specific service at a stated price. It is best to consult an attorney when in doubt about whether to use a contract or a letter agreement in a particular situation.

Dear Mrs. O'Neil:

Your signature on this letter agreement signifies your agreement to terms stated below. We thank your for your dedicated efforts over the past year and look forward to working with you again.

Sincerely,

R. K. Harris

I, C. J. O'Neil, agree to perform technical writing services in support of the Midtown Electronics Group, from January 1, 20XX, through December 31, 20XX. I further agree to perform these services on Midtown premises during normal working hours. I understand that these services are to be performed on an as-needed basis, on a schedule agreeable to the technical writing supervisor.

Midtown will pay for these technical writing services at a rate of $55 per hour. For hours worked in excess of 40 per week, Midtown agrees to pay a rate 1.5 times this amount.

———————————— (name) ——— (date)

MODEL LETTER 9.18

Confirming the Sale of Depreciated Equipment

Some situations call for simple, straightforward letters.

Dear Mr. Barnes:

This letter confirms the J. C. Roger Company's purchase of the following equipment from JGD, Inc., at the prices indicated below:

Equipment Description	Year Put Into Service	Selling Price
Model XKY3 Bottler	1976	$11,000
Model 1237 Lathe	1985	2,500
Model 2879 Press	1975	15,000
		$28,500

Terms of delivery: J. C. Roger Company agrees to these items from JGD, Inc., premises by appointment between March 1 and 5, 19XX, during normal working hours, 8:00 A.M. to 5:00 P.M. Monday–Friday.

Terms of payment: Payment is due upon receipt of invoice from JGD, Inc.

Mr. Barnes, please call me if you have any questions and to tell me when you are ready to arrange a specific time to take delivery. JGD appreciates your patronage and will notify you when similar opportunities arise in the future.

Sincerely,

Myra Robbins

Selling Outlook
Orchestrating a Successful Closing

Success depends on making the right offer to the right prospect at the right time.

Having progressed through the prospecting and negotiation phases together, the prospect and you have developed an understanding of one another's needs and offerings. If a prospect resists committing to the sale and you don't know why, explore for hidden obstacles—resistance to price, pressure from a competitor, doubts about your product's reliability. Whatever the reservation, if you don't investigate, you won't be able to move on to close the sale. Use the obstacle as an opportunity to reiterate the value of your product, the reliability of your service organization, and your commitment as a representative to keep the customer satisfied.

When you sense that you have addressed the prospect's concerns, go ahead and ask for the business. You may discover another objection, or you may be delighted with an affirmative answer. What's certain is that you won't get a yes if you don't ask for it.

Words That Sell
A Quick Reference to Troublesome Word Pairs

In sales, just getting a client to the point of exchanging letters with you is a big accomplishment. By the time you bring the sale to closing, you and others in your organization have put in hours of work that is not remotely related to writing letters or grammatical nuances. When you do need to correspond with a client, though, you want your message to enhance, not detract, from the customer's impression of you. Attention to detail is essential, which is why the following list explains sometimes subtle distinctions between common words.

Some of these words made the list because their spellings are easy to mix up when you're rushing to meet deadlines and take care of business. Other entries are related to grammatical issues that experts continue to debate.

advice, advise   The similar spellings and meanings make it easy to overlook errors when the two are mistaken for one another: advice, a noun; advise, a verb.

altar, alter   altar, used in religious ceremonies; alter, to change.

among, between   "Among" applies to three or more things; use "between" to refer to two things (as in "honor among thieves"; "between you and me").

brake, break   brake, a stopping mechanism; break, to damage. The difference in meaning is clear, but people sometimes write the wrong word and then fail to catch the mistake.

can, may   Can means physically able; may entails permission. Unabridged dictionaries clarify many situations when the distinction can be confusing.

chord, cord   chord, musical notes; cord, a piece of rope.

complement, compliment   complement, to complete; compliment, to praise.

comprise, constitute   The whole comprises the parts; the parts constitute the whole.

connote, denote   connote, suggests; denote, means.

criteria, criterion   criteria, plural of criterion, for use with a plural verb; criterion, singular, for use with a singular verb.

desert, dessert   desert, extremely dry region; dessert, after-dinner sweet.

discrete, discreet   discrete, distinct; discreet, discriminating.

elusive, illusive   elusive, hard to catch; illusive, deceptive.

eminent, imminent   eminent, highly respected; imminent, about to happen.

enormity, enormousness   Enormity is often used incorrectly in reference to size: enormity, outrageousness; enormousness, great size.

ensure, insure   ensure, to make certain; insure, applies to insurance only.

farther, further   farther, refers to distance that is measurable; further means additional. A mile farther; a further point.

fewer, less   fewer, use with something that can be measured in specific units; less, use when something cannot be measured in specific quantities. "We have 5 percent fewer returns than a year ago"; "service is less of a problem this year than last year".

forego, forgo   forego, to go before; forgo, to give up.

its, it's   its, the third-person singular possessive pronoun; it's, the contraction for "it is".

lay, lie   lay, use for objects; lie, use for yourself and people. Lay down the cable to complete the installation; lie down and rest after a challenging tennis match.

lead, led   two tenses of the same verb that get confused with a metal. "We have led the market for the past six years"; "he danced with feet of lead".

liable, libel   liable, culpable, likely; libel, injurious written material.

principal, principle   principal, a sum of money, primary, the head administrator of a school; principle, a guiding concept.

proved, proven   proved, generally accepted as the correct verb form of to prove, as in "a test that proved the product's reliability"; proven, generally accepted as an adjective, as in "a proven sales strategy".

remunerate, renumerate   remunerate, to pay; renumerate, to recount.

that, which   Language experts do not agree on a standard. Use that in restrictive phrases—that is, when you are talking about a specific person, place, or thing. For example: "This was the demonstration that clinched the deal". Use which in phrases that describe but do not restrict the person, place, or thing, as in: "The presentation, which the customers loved, helped clinch the deal".

their, there   their, third person plural possessive pronoun, as in "their product"; there, an adverb, as in "over there" (can also be confused with they're—the contraction of they are).

who, whom   Use who for someone doing the action and whom when something is done to someone. "Who is coming to the sales presentation?" "To whom did you address the memo?"

your, you're   your, second person pronoun, as in "your bonus"; you're, the contraction of you are.

PART 3

Letters That Sustain Lifetime Relationships with Customers

Keeping the Customer Informed About Your Company

Keeping customers informed about your company is an important step in retaining the business you worked so hard to win. Remember fear, uncertainty, and doubt (FUD) from chapter 5? FUD creates emotional reasons that prevent a decision. When you use FUD, it is to keep clients from deciding on behalf of your competitors. When your competitors use FUD, it creates feelings of uncertainty and doubt toward your solution. Therefore, any hint of product-release delays, management turnover, layoffs, or service problems could unleash an onslaught of competitors' FUD. Open and frequent communication between your customers and you can help ward off the effects of FUD and sustain valuable relationships.

Depending on the size of your company, you may be able to draw on a public relations staff to support your efforts by preparing press releases, annual reports, and marketing brochures. But no amount of help from a PR staff can replace the goodwill that will develop when you take the time to write your customers to keep them apprised of events in your organization. After all, news about your company—good or bad—is better coming from you than from a competitor.

CHAPTER 10. CONTENTS

Letting Customers Know about Corporate Changes

Delivering News About Market Developments

Letting Customers Know about Corporate Changes

MODEL LETTER 10.1

Describing Changes in Your Management

Whenever possible, explain the positive reasons for changes in your company. This letter explains that management changes resulted from the company's growth. Without the explanation, the customer may wrongly assume your firm has a high turnover.

Dear Ted:

My firm's growth over the past eighteen months has led to several management changes.

Susan Jones has been promoted to manager of telemarketing, and David Jenkins has taken over Susan's previous position as manager of customer service.

Tony Piper, the New York area manager and the person to whom I have been reporting, has resigned from ABC Corp. Taking his place is Val Bazito, who has been managing the New Jersey area.

Ted, I think these management changes will bring fresh ideas and leadership to our organization, which means you can expect even better customer service and more product enhancements in the future.

Both David and Val are eager to meet you. I think separate meetings would be appropriate. I will call you on Friday to see how your schedule looks.

Thank you for your ongoing support.

Sincerely,

Trisha Morris

Model Letter 10.2

"Please Pass This Information Along. . . ."

When your company gains industry recognition, let your customers know about it.

Dear Jennifer:

Warning: Don't hold on to this letter too long because it is *hot*.

Media Winners of California, the group that administers the annual Hot Mike Awards, says that no single television station has so dominated the awards in the past twenty years. KOOO-TV has scored a near sweep, winning sixteen of twenty-nine Hot Mike Awards! (See details in the enclosed newspaper articles.)

Here is a recap of KOOO-TV's awards"

1. News broadcast, 60 minutes
2. News broadcast, 30 minutes or less
3. Sports segment
4. Newscast writing
5. Individual writing
6. Sports writing feature
7. Live news coverage
8. Documentary
9. News feature, series
10. News feature, individual
11. Economic reporting
12. News special
13. News videography of a hard news series or special
14. News videography of a single story
15. Videotape editing of a hard news series or special
16. Ongoing coverage of a hard news story

Jennifer, this is truly an honor for KOOO and further evidence of the quality of the station's nightly news programs that air from 8:00 P.M. to 11:00 P.M. The specials the news director has planned this season are sure to bring home more awards next year, too.

Please keep this information for your files, but pass along copies to media planners looking for smart advertising buys.

Stay tuned for more!

Regards,

Sally Lombard

MODEL LETTER 10.3

Changing Your Organizational Structure

Keep customers informed about changes in your organization. It is a great way to stay in touch and build the customer's knowledge of your company.

Dear Henry:

Some organizational changes in my company become official May 1, and I want you to be aware of them.

We are consolidating our marketing and service organizations under a central management that will report to our vice president of operations. We believe this change will improve communication throughout the corporation and lead to better customer service. Initially, you will probably notice little change. Over the long term, however, I am confident you will receive more focused and responsive support from us.

Thank you for your loyalty through the years and for your interest in our organization.

Sincerely,

Joe Long

MODEL LETTER 10.4

Changing Ownership

People appreciate the respect you show by notifying them in writing when major changes occur.

Dear Marge:

Effective July 1, ABC Company will become a wholly owned subsidiary of XYZ Company. XYZ markets and services wholesale textiles in the western United States. ABC's market is primarily in the Northeast. With this acquisition, XYZ is poised to become the U.S. market leader.

There are no plans at this time to change our sales team or our operating guidelines. If changes do result from the acquisition, I will keep you informed about them.

Sincerely,

T. B. Brown

MODEL LETTER 10.5

Changing the Customer's Account Team

A gracious letter helps smooth the transition when your changes affect customers.

Dear Ed:

Fountain Head Company has reorganized our internal support organization with the goal of achieving more rapid response at less cost to customers.

The reorganization will mean some changes on your account team. Joe Smith will assume responsibility for your technical support. (You may remember Joe from your upgrade project last year.) Conor Hubbard will handle all internal orders and the paperwork and billing associated with them.

Joe and Conor offer thirty combined years of industry experience and nine years with Fountain Head. They are conscientious, professional, and dedicated people, and I am confident you will be impressed with their abilities to serve you.

Thank you for your patience during this transition. All of us at Fountain Head look forward to the opportunity to serve you in the months ahead.

Sincerely,

Ron Jackson

MODEL LETTER 10.6

Explaining a Layoff

To make this message as timely as possible, consider sending it by fax or publishing it on the Internet.

Dear Bob:

ABC Company is notifying customers of the 500-person layoff we announced to employees this morning. The layoffs will occur between now and December 31 and will affect about 2 percent of our workforce. We arrived at this difficult decision after two quarters of disappointing profits. Bringing expenses in line with revenues now is the most responsible way to address the downturn in profitability, both for our customers and our employees.

You should notice little impact as a result of the layoff. Nevertheless, I urge you to call me if you have any questions or concerns.

Sincerely,

Beth Rogers

MODEL LETTER 10.7

Changing the Billing Process

Explain the benefits of the change you are announcing.

Dear Mac:

ABC Company is making several administrative changes that may affect you slightly. We are consolidating our billing function from numerous local offices to our corporate headquarters.

This change coincides with the implementation of a completely new, enterprise-wide accounting system. When fully operational, our accounting system will be smoother, more efficient, and more reliable than in the past. We also expect to see some benefits for our customers because of the system's flexible invoicing options.

By July 1, all billing will be handled from the corporate office. The first change you notice will be the appearance of your statement. Your billing representative will also change. Your new account representative is Angel Martinez, and her phone number is 800-555-1300.

I will be happy to discuss this change with you and to answer any questions that may arise. Please call me if I can be of service in any way.

Sincerely,

Emily Ciuba

MODEL LETTER 10.8

Changing a Service Process

A major service process change calls for a face-to-face meeting, but there are also several reasons to send a written message. Your customer may be curious about your changes before you visit in person. Your customer may want to show your explanation to colleagues, and you may use the letter to suggest a meeting.

Dear Jan:

I am writing to tell you about ABC's exciting new service process that will greatly enhance the service we provide our customers by cutting our response time to system failures by as much as 60 percent.

The process is a remote diagnostic system that enables engineers in Denver to examine your equipment in Los Angeles—or anywhere else. While the system helps solve problems quickly, it works equally well at preventing breakdowns by anticipating part failures.

Our implementation date for the new process is August 1. I am sure you and your staff will have many questions about this change, and I would like to arrange a meeting by July 15 to address the change and what it means to your company.

I will contact you in late June to arrange the meeting. In meantime, I have more detailed reports about the new process that I would be happy to send. Please call me at 800-555-6767 if you want them. Once you have seen what this new process can accomplish, I know you will be as excited as we are at ABC.

Sincerely,

Margaret Toy

MODEL LETTER 10.9

Letting Them Know You are Taking a Sabbatical

Dear Jusy:

After a personally difficult 1997, XXX Funds' management has graciously allowed me to take a sabbatical for a few months. It is with mixed emotions that I leave the work and people I love, including you as my client. I thank you from the bottom of my heart for the support you have given the XXX Funds and me over the past four years.

Although I may return to wholesale at XXX Funds, you can anticipate seeing a new XXX Funds wholesaler very soon. As has always been the policy with XXX, you can expect superior service and quality of funds. If you have any questions or need anything, please call Dealer Marketing Services at 800-000-0000. Our specialists will take care of you there.

Thank you again for the wonderful friendship and support you have given me. I hope your year is filled with success, joy, and love and that 1998 is your best year ever. And remember, keep selling those XXX Funds.

Sincerely,

Stephanie J. Chisholm

(Courtesy of Stephanie J. Chisholm, Dallas, Texas.)

MODEL LETTER 10.10

Announcing a Resignation

This letter is appropriate to send to anyone Libby worked with—clients, vendors, coworkers.

Dear Marshall:

After more than fourteen years of outstanding sales accomplishments, Libby McKnight has resigned from Associated Products effective May 15.

Libby has done it all. She began as a trainee and worked her way up the ranks to her present position as senior representative and my right hand.

I have been fortunate to have such an associate by my side all these years. I know you join me in wishing Libby the best in her new career in the homebuilding industry with her husband.

Sincerely,

Jack Jones

Announcing the End of a Partnership

Some news is almost certain to disappoint or inconvenience customers. Sales representatives can mitigate the negative effects of bad news, however, by offering solutions and reassurance.

Dear Don:

After May 1, 20XX, XYZ Company will no longer service or provide parts for ABC Company products.

Our partnership agreement with XYZ Company benefited both parties, as well as our clients, for more than three years. XYZ has announced its intention to enter the market as our competitor, however, and so the partnership must be dissolved.

All of us at ABC are working to ensure this change does not inconvenience our customers. We have secured XYZ's agreement to honor all service contracts written by ABC. We are also eager to address any other concerns you may have regarding this change.

Please call me to discuss any questions you may have.

Sincerely,

Lisa Moore

MODEL LETTER 10.12

Announcing a New Partnership Agreement

Tell customers how great your new partnership will be.

Dear Ellen:

ABC Corp. and XYZ Corp. today announced a partnership agreement to develop jointly a new generation of lighting and security products. The partners expect to establish a product development cycle shorter than twenty-four months.

This exciting partnership combines the talents and technologies of the two market leaders in their respective fields. The result should be unparalleled product choices for you, the user. As you know, partnering is the natural solution to the market's demand for continuous innovation in the shortest time possible.

I am delighted about the potential of this new ABC–XYZ alliance. I will continue to keep you informed about this relationship and the anticipated product offerings as I learn about them. Thank you for your interest and your ongoing support of ABC.

Sincerely,

Ann Ryan

MODEL LETTER 10.13

Announcing an Acquisition of Another Company

Emphasize the good news: an acquisition makes your firm larger and stronger.

Dear Bart:

Simms Recruiters has acquired Jones Technical Resources. This acquisition makes SR the largest technical recruiter in the Minneapolis area and enables us to provide our clients with expertise in all areas of technical and engineering placement.

At SR, our primary concern is to offer customers outstanding candidates who possess the skills customers need. With the acquisition of Jones, we add support and skills in all areas of computer programming. In addition, our new size and strength will enable us to attract the best talent and enhance our ability to satisfy your needs quickly.

We expect to complete the consolidation of Simms and Jones offices and phone lines by June 1. Until then, please continue to call either company, as you have in the past. We will notify you of our new contact numbers and addresses in the next few weeks.

We look forward to continuing to serve your technical staffing needs.

Sincerely,

Ellen Ciuba

MODEL LETTER 10.14

Announcing the Sale of
a Division of Your Company

Explain the improved product lines your company expects, and customers may welcome the news of a sale.

Dear Olivia:

Beluga, Inc., today announced the sale of our North Sea division to Glacier Company. The acquisition expands the selection of products Glacier can offer in the European market, and it enables Beluga to focus on specialized niche markets in the United States.

This sale concludes Beluga's six-month search for a buyer for our European division. The sale of the North Sea division frees us financially and enables us to reorganize and focus on our primary product lines. With the lower debt and operating expenses, we also have improved our ability to develop new product lines that complement our core competencies.

Glacier is a distributor of food products throughout Europe. The acquisition of Beluga's North Sea division enables Glacier to expand its offering of high-end specialty products. We expect to complete the transfer of operations by September 15.

Please let me know if you have any additional questions about the sale, or if I can help you in any way.

Sincerely,

Brad Miller

MODEL LETTER 10.15

Announcing the Sale of Your Lease Base to a Leasing Company

Users will consider a lease-base sale to be significant, and you should explain the action in writing.

Dear Gary:

SYC Corp. today announced the sale of our leasing division to Rogers Leasing.

The sale will benefit SYC Corp. in numerous ways. We receive $5 million for the asset base and will continue to extend leasing options to our customers through Rogers. The net impact of the sale should be transparent to you.

Rogers Leasing maintains a lease asset base of more than $100 million. The company's size gives it economies of scale that lower costs throughout the transaction cycle. SYC expects to pass these benefits on to customers by offering very competitive leasing arrangements.

Please forward this notice to anyone else in your organization who would find it of interest. I would be happy to answer any questions or related concerns you or your colleagues may have.

Very truly yours,

Conor Hubbard

MODEL LETTER 10.16

Announcing a New Branch Office

An invitation is always welcome.

Dear Cindy:

Please visit HiCo in our newest office at 1514 White Street, opening May 1 with a reception from 1:00 P.M. to 5:00 P.M.

Your continued support has helped make HiCo's latest expansion possible. HiCo continues to enjoy rapid gains in profitability. Throughout this growth period, however, we have strived to retain our focus on our core business and the customers who have been partners in our success each step of the way.

We appreciate your business and hope to have an opportunity to serve you soon.

Sincerely,

Renée Sanders

MODEL LETTER 10.17

Following Up After a Relocation Announcement

When your company announces a relocation publicly, it is best to follow up personally to open communication with clients. They naturally will have many questions at such a time.

Dear Ben:

By now you have probably seen news reports about MegaDisk's relocation announcement. I am writing to encourage you to discuss any concerns you may have.

I know the move creates some uncertainty. We have become accustomed to being neighbors in Jackson. I work with customers throughout the country every day, however, and our relocation to the West Coast will do nothing to change the high level of service and technical support you have come to expect from us.

Ben, it has been a privilege to service you these past five years in Jackson, and I look forward to many more years of a productive partnership. Please keep in touch. I will keep you posted as our move date approaches.

Sincerely,

Colin Hubbard

MODEL LETTER 10.18

Announcing an Office Consolidation

Dear Alise:

Changing demographics in Midcity have led Sales, Inc., to a difficult decision. After thirty-five successful years, we have decided to close our northside office and consolidate our business in East Midcity.

I apologize for any inconvenience this consolidation may cause you. Although I anticipate few difficulties as a result of the change, I encourage you to call us to work out any problems you may have.

Alise, we appreciate your continued support and look forward to seeing you in our East Midcity office.

Sincerely,

Barry Johns

MODEL LETTER 10.19

Announcing a New Subsidiary

Dear Thomas:

The success of United Distributors' direct-mail catalog divisions has led to the creation of a new UD subsidiary. Please look for a Distributors by Mail catalog in a mailbox near you soon!

Distributors by Mail will focus on the busy 30- to 45-year-old urban female who buys clothing and household goods for her entire family. This strategy has led to the subdivision's average annual growth of 15 percent for more than three years, and we have great expectations now that the subdivision has become a subsidiary.

Sarah Mitchell will head the new business. We have set ambitious targets for her, and she and her staff are working aggressively to achieve them. I will keep you posted on her accomplishments.

Sincerely,

Hal Thompson

Delivering News About Market Developments

MODEL LETTER 10.20

Announcing Good Financial News

Enthusiasm is contagious—share your excitement about good news.

Dear Jess:

Knowing that you are a keen follower of ABC Company's financial status, I wanted to tell you that we just announced our third-quarter earnings—a record $500 million!

As the press release explains, we had strong sales in all product lines. Our sales stood at only $415 million in the third quarter last year and at $450 million in the second quarter of this year. Along with gross revenue, profits were also up, compared with a loss last year in the third quarter.

After years of trying to break into the telecommunications market, we were delighted to receive a $25 million order from one of the major phone companies. We hope this is just the start of great things to come.

As you can imagine, the news made us ecstatic. Your continued loyalty and support helped make it possible. I very much appreciate the confidence you have shown in ABC and the business you have given us.

Very truly yours,

Beth Rogers

MODEL LETTER 10.21

Changing Marketing Direction

Write letters from the perspective of how the information benefits the customer.

Dear Jim:

Hi-Tech, Inc., has recently undergone an extensive business review with the help of an outside consulting firm. The result will be a change in market direction that will enhance our offering of products and services in the marketplace.

Traditionally, Hi-Tech has been strictly a manufacturer. Now we will provide integration services that enable us to offer turnkey solutions for our customers. This change of direction will benefit you as a user by providing "one-stop shopping" for all your automation needs. We expect this expansion of services and direction to enhance our competitive position, thus increasing our profitability. We hope you share our optimism and enthusiasm for this strategic shift in direction. I will continue to inform you of changes as they unfold. Thank you for your interest in Hi-Tech and for your continued support.

Sincerely,

B. J. Wilson

MODEL LETTER 10.22

Changing the Way We Market to You

Changes may be nerve-racking for you, but remember to contain your stress and emphasize the positive.

Dear Joe:

ABC Company has made an exciting change in the way we do business. Until now, we have been the exclusive distributor of our own products, and we have provided customers support through corporate account teams. Effective June 2, we opened a new channel of distribution by making our products available through local value-added distributors.

This change applies to all our consumable products and our products for the lower-end market. As a high-volume customer with outlets in all fifty states, you will most likely notice the difference in remote locations and subsidiaries. Local distributors will now handle this part of the business.

ABC is committed to this change because we are convinced it will strengthen our competitive advantage and add value for customers. Local distributors offer marketing expertise in geographically disperse markets, and by delegating this part of our business, our account teams have more time to focus on servicing high-end customers such as you.

Please call me if you have any questions. I am eager to hear your opinion about the change.

Thank you for supporting ABC. We appreciate your business and look forward to serving you again soon.

Sincerely,

Bill Gibbons

MODEL LETTER 10.23

Announcing Disappointing Financial News

Your confident attitude will mitigate the damage of disappointing news.

Dear Betty:

You may have seen the wire reports about ABC Company's disappointing second-quarter financial reports. The $2 million loss stems from the delayed release of our latest new product. Its development has taken more time and resources to bring to market than we anticipated.

Although a loss is never easy to absorb, ABC's cash position is still strong, and we expect to weather this period with no major restructuring. When we do release the next generation of our office products, our financial strength should be much more impressive. In fact, we are confident we can leap-frog our competitors and gain significant market share.

Betty, I would be happy to discuss ABC's financial status, our development projects, or any other issue with you. I will call you next week to follow up.

Sincerely,

Debbie Martin

MODEL LETTER 10.24

Announcing a New Service at BGH Financial Consulting

Clients should welcome news of expanded services.

Dear Brian:

For years, our customers have relied on BGH for help with tax preparation, estate planning, and risk management. We are now pleased to announce the addition of personal financial consulting to our range of services.

Personal financial consulting encompasses investment advice, goal setting, and strategic planning for your personal financial development. We can help you design a strategy to ensure success in meeting your financial goals, and that strategy begins with your decision to plan your financial future.

You may want money to send children to college, buy a vacation home, or retire early. BGH professionals will help you each step of the way. Two of BGH's most experienced CPAs, Jim Johnson and Teresa Brown, are certified financial planners as well. They will work with you to consider your objectives, age, tolerance for risk, and insurance needs, and then help you set saving targets, evaluate your present financial status, and build a plan.

Financial security begins with a financial plan. Call us now to arrange an appointment with Jim or Teresa.

Sincerely,

B. W. Timms

MODEL LETTER 10.25

Announcing the Discontinuation of a Product

Product lines don't last forever. Help customers adjust to changes by addressing their needs proactively and minimizing disruptions.

Dear Lynne:

In January, Tsunoda Electronics will discontinue manufacturing the line of electronic security devices that your construction company has used for the past five years. At this time, we have no plans for follow-up security products. Our management continues to review several options, however, and is aware of the demand for high-quality security devices.

For the next thirty-six months, we will continue to service the devices you have already purchased and installed. Parts will be available in our warehouses throughout the United States. Call 800-555-0000 for details about parts and service.

On behalf of everyone at Tsunoda, I apologize for any inconvenience this move causes you. Please understand that the competitive marketplace leaves us no alternative. I will continue to keep you apprised of our product offerings as information becomes available.

Thank you for your continued support of Tsunoda Electronics.

Best regards,

Paul Houston

MODEL LETTER 10.26

Announcing a New Corporate Alliance

This letter discusses a corporate change in terms of what it does for customers.

Dear Spencer:

I would like to take this opportunity to announce a bold and exciting alliance between StorageTek and Polar.

On July 1, 20XX, —— will become the primary worldwide channel of distribution of the Iceberg, Kodiak, and Arctic Fox disk array subsystems. They will also be the primary distributor of the IXFP, IXOF, and SnapShot products. We at StorageTek are very excited about this alliance for a myriad of reasons but in particular for the advantages it brings to you:

1. This is a joint development contract as well as a distribution contract. Therefore, it signals a tremendous future for the technology of Iceberg, Kodiak, and Arctic Fox, now backed by the resources of two of the leading high-technology companies in this industry.
2. It substantially expands the geographic service and support coverage for these products.
3. Application software developers in the —— environment working for you, TGF, or as separate companies will focus on the unique qualities of these products to create the most efficient solutions possible.
4. Iceberg, Kodiak, and Arctic Fox have an even greater potential of duplicating the long product cycles you currently enjoy with StorageTek libraries. And, as such, the potential return on your investment is significantly better.
5. These subsystems will incorporate ——'s "best of breed" disk drives, therefore improving capacity and performance.

This agreement with —— is an important step in the implementation of a strategic restructuring that we began at StorageTek in the fourth quarter of 20XX. The ultimate goal of this process is to provide your business with the highest level of competitive advantage possible with superior information storage and management technology whether our technology is delivered to you from StorageTek or indirectly through partners like TGF.

For StorageTek, this is clearly a testament to the power, performance, and reliability of StorageTek's Iceberg, Kodiak, and Arctic Fox technologies. It will significantly strengthen StorageTek's currently substantial financial resources. That, in turn, will support our aggressive research and development into future DASD technologies, as well as allow us to dedicate more resources to the development of new solutions for open-system, online, Nearline, and network-attached storage.

You will hear more of the new application programs we have been developing for various industry segments as they are announced in the very near future. Please note that this alliance covers only Iceberg, Kodiak, and Arctic Fox products. StorageTek will continue to provide complete direct sales, service, and support for our line of premier Nearline storage, network, and open-system DASD solutions. We will also continue to provide service and support for StorageTek Iceberg, Kodiak, and Arctic Fox products you currently have installed. We believe your decision to acquire Iceberg will bring even more benefits to your company because this alliance will allow us to introduce additional capabilities on Iceberg more quickly.

Finally, thank you for the confidence you have expressed in StorageTek through the years, as evidenced by your orders. We are a stronger, more robust company than ever before because of that support. This alliance allows us to expand our relationship with you in many ways. We are excited about the opportunity to grow our company, provide you with world-class products and services, and maintain a strong partnership with you for many more years!

If you have any questions, please do not hesitate to call me at 312-555-0000.

Sincerely,

John Williams

(Courtesy of John Williams, Executive Vice President, Storage Technology Corporation, Louisville, Colorado.)

MODEL LETTER 10.27

Asking for Participation in Your Advisory Board

Customer panels and focus groups are excellent ways to involve your customers in product plans. Customers provide insight into what will and will not be a viable product, and asking them to be part of the development process is a way of complimenting them.

Dear Travis:

You are cordially invited to attend StorageTek's 20XX Open Systems/Midrange Customer Advisory Board (CAB). As a valued member of our CAB, your participation is extremely important to us. The purpose of the meeting is to collect future strategic customer requirements and exchange information regarding future applications and market trends. In addition, we will share information on our product directions and strategies. Your input can have a direct effect on our future plans.

Enclosed is a proposed meeting agenda. If there are specific topics you would like to see covered as well as particular formats (such as breakout sessions, roundtable discussion, and so forth), please let me know.

The results of this meeting will help direct StorageTek's development and delivery of future storage solutions for your enterprise. The exchange of information should also help you in planning your future needs.

Thank you for supporting StorageTek. I look forward to your participation in this meeting. Your input is always helpful and appreciated.

Sincerely,

Margee Sullivan

(Courtesy of Margee Sullivan, Storage Technology Corporation, Louisville, Colorado.)

MODEL LETTER 10.28

Introducing New Services

Keep reminding prospects of the advantages of working with you.

Dear Mr. Kane:

Information Management Systems and Services is pleased to announce that we now support and service the two leading software suites. We have also developed templates for either suite that automatically interface with your existing customer, vendor, and employee master files. The interfaces allow you to send letters, announcements, and other correspondence more quickly and conveniently.

We invite you to a demonstration of these interfaces on Wednesday, May 7, at 10:00 A.M. in our offices.

We hope to see you there. Please call if you have any questions.

Sincerely,

Frank McIntyre

(Courtesy of Frank McIntyre, Dallas, Texas.)

MODEL LETTER 10.29

Announcing Your Representation of a New Client

A letter is a good first step to announce a new client. Follow-up phone calls would be a logical second step.

Dear Mike:

Lucia National is proud to announce representation of KVIV-TV in Jackson effective January 2.

KVIV's dominance as the news leader in Jackson enhances all aspects of the station's programming, giving us top numbers in early morning, day, access, prime, and late fringe.

I will contact you soon to discuss upcoming opportunities for you and your clients. KVIV-TV and Lucia look forward to doing business with you.

Best regards,

Susan Wagner

(Courtesy of Susan Wagner, Dallas, Texas.)

MODEL LETTER 10.30

Announcing a Client's New Affiliation

Customer demand for your product can begin the minute your prospect reads an energetic, informative letter about what you are offering.

Dear Julie:

We are pleased to announce that, effective July 1, KVIV has joined Central News Network as an affiliate. This move marks KVIV's return to the network after a five-year absence.

KVIV station director Pat Michaels explained the change: "Network affiliation increases our already strong commitment to news. It improves our ability to provide coverage of breaking news no matter where it happens." The network has been in operation for twelve years and includes twenty-five affiliates in the central states.

KVIV is the premiere news organization in Jackson and will be an important addition to the network. We invite you to enhance your Jackson schedules by including KVIV!

Sincerely,

Susan Wagner

(Courtesy of Susan Wagner, Dallas, Texas.)

Selling Outlook
Why You Don't Want Your Customers Surprised

Surprises—and the emotions that go with them—are best avoided in sales. Fortunately, sales representatives' clear and regular communication with customers helps mitigate the damage of disappointments that arise during the sales process.

One of Ann's worst experiences in sales came after she'd promised all was on-track for a product installation, only to learn at the last minute that essential parts were missing. She recalls: "The news that we had a problem—after I had told the top executive we were 'ready to go'—was not well received. My credibility and the credibility of our organization were compromised. Had I realized our situation and delivered the news to the customer, the experience would have been much more positive."

Customers depend on what sales representatives tell them. When the information you give a customer over time is consistently honest and reliable, the customer comes to regard you as honest and reliable. You have established credibility.

Surprises undermine that credibility. Surprises unnerve decision makers, divert attention from the selling process, and sabotage customers' confidence in you, your product, and their buying decision. As a sales representative, you can't eliminate every setback, but you can diffuse them by speaking openly and often with your customers. Successful long-term business relationships come from trust, and sales representatives who stay alert for potential problems and keep their customers informed along the way are laying the foundation of trust.

CHAPTER 11

Showing Continued
Interest in
the Customer

Some representatives' clients seem to follow them no matter what—through one product change after another, from one firm to the next. It's easy to envy such loyalty, but it is a lot more productive to emulate the habits that inspire it.

One strategy for sustaining business relationships is to stay aware of what is happening in your customers' organizations and to express your interest in timely correspondence. Customers appreciate the interest you show in their businesses. Your concern is an important element in your selling style; it establishes your relationship as one that transcends day-to-day sales orders and deliveries and demonstrates your desire to build a mutually beneficial partnership.

The letters in this chapter are evidence of such concern. Situations may call for congratulations, sympathy, or a simple acknowledgment. Whatever the circumstances, a letter from you can strengthen the client–vendor bond that is so crucial in sales.

CHAPTER 11. CONTENTS

Acknowledging Changes in the Customer's World

MODEL LETTER 11.1

Acknowledging an Organizational Change

You may want to keep a dialog going with someone who is no longer your primary contact. When you develop rapport with someone, you can look to that person for ongoing advice about your marketing efforts.

Dear Jack:

I learned about the organizational changes at your company, and I understand that you will no longer be my primary contact. My company now needs to focus its marketing efforts on your Chicago office.

Jack, I will miss having regular contact with you, but I understand the dynamics of such a change and the benefits that will result from your firm's consolidated purchasing arrangement.

I want to keep in touch with you and keep you apprised of our activities within your company. Your helpful, professional business style has contributed greatly to my company's successful relationship with your organization. Thank you for your support.

As my firm assembles the marketing team that will call on your Chicago office, I would like your recommendations on how best to approach a proposal to that group. I appreciate any advice you can offer. I will call you after my initial meeting with your Chicago staff, which is scheduled for the 14th. I look forward to speaking to you soon.

Very truly yours,

Bill Michaels

MODEL LETTER 11.2

Acknowledging a Change in Market Emphasis

Customers are looking to partner with vendors that can adapt to their changes. Show enthusiasm for change. It is an opportunity to serve the customer and solidify your relationship.

Dear Sherry:

Recently I learned that you are redirecting your business toward the European market. What an exciting, challenging shift! I understand that the Europeans are just beginning to express interest in the type of digital imaging services you provide—you will be in the right place, at the right time, with the right product.

Such a significant change will mean changes in what you require from my company. I want to address these needs proactively. We sell and service digital imaging systems throughout most of Europe and can provide you with considerable expertise about that marketplace. I suggest that we get together as soon as possible to discuss strategies and options.

Good luck in this new arena! After witnessing your incredible success in the United States, I'm sure you'll conquer Europe in no time!

Sincerely,

Janice White

MODEL LETTER 11.3

Acknowledging the Client's Acquisition of Another Company

By understanding the client's strategic focus, you demonstrate that your interest goes beyond your own bottom line.

Dear Mark:

Congratulations on your acquisition of ABC Company. I wanted to write you to express my support as soon as I heard the news. ABC's product line will enhance yours and establish you as the market leader. I am delighted for you and wish you the best of luck in the months ahead.

As you assess your business strategy and changing requirements that result from the acquisition, please keep in mind our interest in serving your business needs in whatever way possible.

Good luck to you in this new endeavor, and please let me know how I can assist.

Sincerely,

Ben Howell

MODEL LETTER 11.4

Encouraging a Customer About
a New Product Announcement

Letters reinforce the bond that distinguishes loyal clients from one-time customers.

Dear Eileen:

I was delighted to read the recent announcement about your expanded product lines. These new offerings should significantly enhance your profitability and market presence.

It has been rewarding to see your business grow over the years. You have made excellent strategic decisions that have turned your company into a market leader. Your most recent announcement is proof that more achievements will follow.

I congratulate you and wish you continued success.

Warm regards,

Ed Cooke

MODEL LETTER 11.5

Supporting the Customer Through a Period of Uncertainty

Over time, the contacts you establish in one firm may move on to other companies. In fact, your best customers may be the ones who continue to rely on your services no matter where they move in an industry. That is why you should always express your concern for customers' well-being and offer your support when appropriate.

Dear Martha:

Yesterday in a discussion with Mark I learned that your firm is considering eliminating the New York office and the functions performed there. What a difficult possibility to have to live with, and what a tough time this must be for you.

Please know that I sympathize with you and would be happy to help in any way I can. You have been supportive of me in many situations, and I would be delighted to reciprocate. With your energy and enthusiasm, you are bound to land on your feet no matter what happens.

Good luck in weathering the storm. I will call soon to touch base.

All the best,

Tim Johns

Model Letter 11.6

Acknowledging Milestones in the Client's Growth

Personal notes of congratulations remind customers you are part of their team.

Dear Judy:

Congratulations! I just read that your third-quarter sales topped $1 billion. Too bad I didn't buy your company's stock last year. Your growth has been dazzling, and I know ABC owes much of its success to you and your colleagues. Your vision and sound judgment have positioned ABC for even greater growth in the U.S. and Asian markets. Again, congratulations on this excellent achievement.

Sincerely,

Rex Henry

MODEL LETTER 11.7

Saying Good-Bye and Making Referrals When the Customer Is Relocating

It really is a small world, and it is amazing how acquaintances can re-enter our professional circles years or decades after we lose touch with them. Sooner or later, the help you offer a client who is relocating can yield dividends for you or others in your firm.

Dear Ben:

It seems that everyone has mixed emotions about Basic Products' move to St. Louis. I hate to see you go, but I know this is a good move for the company and for you personally.

I am passing your name along to Mike Rogers in our St. Louis division and will send him copies of your account file. Mike has been a sales all-star for several years. He will take good care of you.

Ben, I have enjoyed serving as your account executive this past year. You are a terrific asset to Basic—always cheerful, professional, and reliable. I wish you continued success in St. Louis, and please call on me if you need anything in Denver or if I can help in some way.

Sincerely,

Sharon Hodge

MODEL LETTER 11.8

Saying Good-Bye to a Client Who's Been Transferred

Dear Louise:

Congratulations on your promotion to branch manager of IncCo's new office. My only regret is that you must move to Tulsa to accept the position. I will miss calling on you—Tulsa is in our Midwest sales region. I have sent your phone number and account information to our Tulsa regional manager, Sally Briggs. I know she will want to meet you herself and introduce your Tulsa account representative.

It has been my pleasure to serve as your account representative since 19XX. As sorry as I am to see you leave, I am delighted to see your hard work pay off in a promotion. You will be a terrific branch manager!

Sincerely,

Joan Blanche

Congratulating Customers

MODEL LETTER 11.9

Acknowledging Good Financial News

Everyone likes to be rewarded for hard work, and your praise will add to the client's enjoyment of success.

Dear Bill:

Congratulations on your best year ever! I read the press release out on the Net yesterday and was delighted to learn the good news. Last year's cost-cutting and hard work paid off handsomely. I hope you and everyone in your organization are relishing your success!

I know your next challenge will be repeating last year's performance. Let me know how my firm can help you achieve your goals. We want to be your partner in whatever way possible.

Please pass on my congratulations to all your staff and take time to enjoy your achievement!

Sincerely,

Kimberly Myers

MODEL LETTER 11.10

Congratulating the Client for an IPO

It never hurts to remind clients that successful vendor relationships like yours contribute to their success.

Dear Jerry:

You must be terribly excited about your initial public offering. I've called my broker and am all set for the big day.

Jerry, it has been my pleasure to work with you these past five years. I have watched your firm grow from those shakey first few months to a $33 million company just a week away from its IPO. Congratulations on this achievement and my best wishes for continued success.

Sincerely,

Lee Rodgers

MODEL LETTER 11.11

Acknowledging a Business Victory

A prompt congratulatory note is a nice gesture—and one that lets the client know you are staying current in your industry.

Dear Steve:

I was thrilled to hear of your success in winning the Jefferson account. All of us here at Focus Studio join me in congratulating you. This is a fantastic achievement, and we know that growth and continued success are bound to follow. We also know how much hard work and how many late hours went into this victory. You and everyone else at your agency must be elated.

As you prepare media plans in the months ahead, please keep Focus Studio in mind, and enjoy your hard-won victory!

Sincerely,

Michael Allen

Model Letter 11.12

Acknowledging Good Publicity

Your enthusiasm will be especially gratifying on the heels of good news.

Dear Diane:

What a thrill to be reading the morning paper and come across that great feature story about your business. It's rare that a journalistic article so strongly endorses one competitor over all the others! I know the benefits of that exposure will be far-reaching.

I look forward to hearing about all the good things that result from this great publicity. Keep me posted!

All my best,

Vicki Taylor

Model Letter 11.13

Acknowledging a Promotion

As your contacts move up the corporate ladder, remind them that you recognize their achievement and are committed to their success.

Dear Sara:

Congratulations! I understand you will be McPherson's next senior buyer. I know the promotion is well deserved. You have always been extremely dedicated, and I am glad to see your efforts recognized.

I look forward to continuing to work with you as senior buyer. Please call if I can help in any way.

Sincerely,

Robert Sampella

Acknowledging the Client's Achievement

Because so few people today bother to write to associates, your notes to clients will be distinctive reminders of your professionalism.

Dear Paul:

I am delighted that you have been chosen for the President's Club! I know that honor goes to only a select few, hard-working individuals. You have put in incredible hours—your commitment to your work has been apparent to everyone. It is great to know that your management recognizes your contribution and appreciates you.

Enjoy your trip to Hawaii. It is well deserved.

Best regards,

Ann McIntyre

MODEL LETTER 11.15

Congratulating a Client Who Is Changing Jobs

The warm relationship you establish with a customer need not end when that individual changes jobs. In fact, that contact could help you network in a completely new company.

Dear Bill:

Congratulations on your move to InvestCo, and good luck as you begin this new phase of your career. I am excited for you.

It has been my pleasure to work with you these past five years, and I hope we will not lose touch when you join InvestCo. Your insight into industry trends is always helpful, and I have enjoyed our lunches at Antoine's very much. Perhaps you will let me take you to one last lunch there next week, and you can tell me more about your plans.

Sincerely,

Renée Graham

MODEL LETTER 11.16

Congratulating a Client Who Leaves to Start a Company

This situation can make for tricky relations when the entrepreneur is leaving your current customer to become a competitor.

Dear Ken:

Let me wish you the best of luck in your exciting new venture. I know you will achieve great success.

From what you told me in our phone conversation on Wednesday, you are well capitalized and have a very viable, compelling business plan. I will pass your name along to any contacts who may have an interest in the financial services you offer.

Ken, over the past eight years it has been a pleasure to serve as your account executive. I consider you a friend and hope to stay in touch with you in the future.

Sincerely,

Terry Roberts

MODEL LETTER 11.17

Welcoming a New Mom Back to the Office

Dear Cindy:

Welcome back to the 9-to-5 routine! This must be an especially joyful time for you, Mark, and Megan, who now has that baby brother she has been wanting.

May I take you to a "welcome back" lunch next week? I'll call you on Thursday to see how your schedule looks.

Sincerely,

Becky Gordon

MODEL LETTER 11.18

Congratulating a New Dad

Dear Mark:

Congratulations on the birth of your daughter. I know that Cindy and you are delighted to be parents, and I am thrilled for you.

I'll stop by when I am in your offices for the status meeting next Wednesday. I would love to see pictures of Megan.

Sincerely,

Becky Gordon

Model Letter 11.19

Congratulating Parents on Their Student's Achievement

Use your best professional judgment to decide when it is appropriate to congratulate a client on a family member's achievement.

Dear Dianne:

How thrilled you must be about David's achievement. I still remember the National Merit Scholars from my high school class. What a tremendous honor for him!

I want to hear about his college plans on my next visit to Catalog Express. I'll call you soon.

Warm regards,

Raul Ramirez

Model Letter 11.20

Congratulating a Customer Who Is Retiring

Personal touches—such as mentioning a hobby, a relative's name, or a favorite vacation spot—demonstrate that you know your customers and are interested in them.

Dear Betty:

The next time I visit Fork Lake, I'll be looking for Joe and you. Carefree days spent fishing, boating, and relaxing at the lake are a terrific reward for your hard work at SKT Enterprises. I know you'll have an active, enjoyable retirement, and I know how much you deserve it. Please call me now and then to let me know how you are. I want to stay in touch.

Warmest regards,

Barry Ruth

Sympathizing with Customers

MODEL LETTER 11.21

Acknowledging the Loss of a Contract

Your offer to help can be a welcome gesture to a client who has just learned of a major setback.

Dear Bill:

I was sorry to hear the news that ABC canceled its contract with you. I know that company has been a significant contributor to your overall revenue, and it will be a challenge to win new contracts. I will be happy to pass on any leads that could help you generate new business.

We both know that all businesses have losses as well as successes. I wish you good luck and good fortune and will help in any way I can.

Warm regards,

Elizabeth Bridges

When Disaster Hits the Client's Company

Your response after a disaster shows the customer the true character of your relationship.

Dear Thomas:

The news about the fire in your Brooks City plant yesterday was shocking. I realize that you are still assessing losses, but let me assure you that my firm will help you recover in any way we can. In a few days—after things have settled down a bit—I will call you to discuss how we might amend your contract terms in the short term until you get past this crisis.

Sincerely,

Beth Jones

Empathizing with a Client Whose Firm's Been Sold

With rare exceptions, corporate acquisitions mean great anxiety for those in the acquired firm. A positive message from you can be reassuring to the client.

Dear Michael:

I heard the news about the sale of HiCo. I know the uncertainty is stressful, but you can take comfort in knowing that just about everyone in our industry has gone through a merger or acquisition in the past ten years. If there is anything I can do, please let me know. Also, let's get together next week to talk about the Meyers project. I have some contingency plans in mind that may be useful to you right now.

Until then,

Lisa McAfee

MODEL LETTER 11.24

Supporting the Client Through Bad Publicity

People will remember and appreciate the support you show during their trying times.

Dear Olivia:

I hope you paid no attention to that so-called industry analysis. My company is proof positive that you can live long and prosper after bad publicity. Several negative articles were published about us a few years ago, and I can relate to your experience now.

This phase may seem unending, but it won't last forever. Still, I know that in a lifetime of challenges, negative press can be the most stressful thing you endure. Remember to take care of yourself—rest and relax, or do whatever is best for you. Please call on me if there is anything I can do.

Yours sincerely,

Ann Brown

Model Letter 11.25

Offering Encouragement to a Customer After Bad Financial News

Your positive note about the future can help a client get through trying times.

Dear Ginnie:

I was sorry to read yesterday's announcement of your loss for last year. I know that this news is tough for you and everyone else at HiCo, especially considering how hard you all work. Please know that we at ABC are confident that the market will turn for you. Your strong company philosophy and product direction will withstand this temporary downturn.

Good luck this year. I anticipate good news and good fortune for you and everyone at XYZ.

Sincerely,

Bob Benzer

MODEL LETTER 11.26

Expressing Concern About the Customer's Illness

When a client is ill, send a note rather than telephoning. People often prefer not to be disturbed by numerous well-wishers, and notes provide lasting reminders that you care.

Dear Annie:

I was sorry to learn that you have been under the weather. It is not the same at your office without your enthusiasm and energy. I hope you will soon be well and back at work.

Take care and best wishes.

Sincerely,

Robin Yates

MODEL LETTER 11.27

Welcoming the Client Back
from a Lengthy Leave

Society has become more open about substance abuse, emotional conditions, and other sensitive problems. Still, in the workplace it can be awkward to acknowledge someone's leave for treatment. When a client returns from such leave, a brief, upbeat note from you can help you get past any awkward moments and reestablish your normal routine.

Dear James:

It's good to know you are back in the office. We need your expertise on the Miles project!

I missed seeing you on my last two visits to Boston, but I will be in town the week of the 1st. May I take you to lunch? I'll call next week to see how your schedule looks.

Best regards,

Kathy Mitchell

MODEL LETTER 11.28

A Note of Sympathy for the Loss
of a Family Member

It may or may not not be appropriate to send flowers to a particular client, but notes are always appreciated.

Dear Russ:

All of us on your account team at ABC extend our deepest sympathy on the loss of your mother. We are all thinking of you and look forward to seeing you when you return.

Sincerely,

Ted Loden

Model Letter 11.29

Condolences for the Loss of the Business Founder

Even if your client wasn't particularly close to his or her top executive, the loss of a corporate leader can be shocking and cause great uncertainty. The respect you show by offering your condolences will be meaningful to the client.

Dear Art:

I was saddened to hear the news about Mr. Douglas. He was an industry icon, and for decades he set the standard for warehousing automation in the Midwest. Though this is a great loss, his vision helped mold your company and the industry, and his influence will continue for years.

Warmest regards,

Michelle Michaels

Model Letter 11.30

Condolences for the Loss of a Colleague

It is always appropriate to express sympathy when a professional associate has lost a colleague.

Dear Tim:

My thoughts have been with you since I heard the news about Roger. I regret that I will not be in Phoenix for the services, and I want to extend my deepest sympathy to you and all the IncCo team. It was a delight to have been associated with Roger, and I can only imagine the loss you must feel.

If there is anything I can do at this time, please be certain to call.

Sincerely,

Mitch Wombell

Selling Outlook
The Power of Your Sincere Interest in Customers

To varying degrees, the letters in this chapter move your relationship with the client out of a strictly business context and into the personal realm. After all, customers are human, too. They have good days, bad days, ups and downs. Their families may bring them joy or sorrow; their work environments may be rewarding or abusive. Some days they feel vulnerable; other days, they feel strong.

You are just one more person competing for their time and trying to sell them something. Will you turn out to be another "snake in the grass" who says one thing to get the business, then is nowhere to be found when the product doesn't work out? Why should they see you, listen to your presentation, or buy something from you?

Well, one reason is that you seem sincere and hard-working. Your interest in them suggests that you will work to understand their situations and provide solutions to their problems.

People buy from people. They may purchase commodities, but they respond to people they like, people who are pleasant to be around, willing to work hard to get the business, and sincere in their work and personal relationships with customers.

Sincerity means doing and saying what you really think and feel. As you work to connect with people and establish relationships with them, your sincerity will distinguish you as someone wanting to provide a solution, not just sell a product. Sincerity is a first step toward trust, which is the cornerstone of an enduring client–vendor partnership.

When you have a bond with your customers, why would you not express heartfelt sympathy when one of them has lost a loved one? Why wouldn't you send a congratulatory letter after someone's hard work pays off in a promotion?

The marketplace is full of decision makers who want to buy from reliable, sincere individuals who are interested in doing a professional job. Decision makers, like most everyone else, are drawn to the people they trust, and letters are one way to help that trust flourish.

CHAPTER 12

Special Events and Customer Appreciation

The term *customer appreciation* covers a lot of territory. It can take the form of something simple, like a well-written letter of heartfelt thanks, or apply to an extravaganza of gifts, special events, and exclusive offers. The letters in this chapter offer a glimpse of the possibilities salespeople have when reaching out to say "I care" to customers new and old. Customer appreciation and special events are some of the less stressful, more lighthearted types of selling activities. They call for creativity, a bit of spontaneity, and finesse.

The letters you use to express customer appreciation and invite people to special events should be as distinguished as the events and gestures themselves. Use invitations to relate all the key information your customers need to know. For example, you'll need to handle such topics as dress code smoothly. On the one hand, no one wants to be told too much about what to wear. But on the other hand, no one wants to be embarrassed or get it wrong. Your prospects and customers will appreciate your attention to detail; they rely on your guidance in these circumstances. Another touchy subject is expenses. Some events require customers to cover some of their own expenses. Your communication needs to be clear from the beginning to prevent any misunderstanding. By putting everything in writing, you make it less likely that prospects will forget key information.

Remember that the point of customer appreciation and special events is to show your gratitude to your customers and to bring your prospects closer to you and your company. Communicate the special nature of what you are doing, and they will be delighted.

Chapter 12. Contents

Inviting Customers to Special Events

MODEL LETTER 12.1

"Come to an Exclusive Preview"

Invitations to some corporate events are highly sought-after in their respective industries.

Dear Jay:

You are invited to attend an exclusive preview of our new product at a showing scheduled for April 15 at the Grand Hotel. This invitation is reserved for our most important customers, and I think you will find the event very useful. Seating will be limited, so please let me know as soon as possible if you can join us.

The session will begin with lunch at noon, followed by a project presentation from 1:00 P.M. to 3:00 P.M. Time for questions and answers will follow.

I hope this special presentation will fit into your schedule. I will follow up with a phone call on Friday.

Best regards,

C. S. Miller

Model Letter 12.2

Come See the Future: An Invitation to
a Product Announcement

Reserve press conferences and comparable events for exceptional announcements—that will ensure high interest and maximum effectiveness.

Dear Mike:

Come see the future. On September 25, ABC Corp. will present a nationwide product announcement that will affect the future of X-ray technology. Please join us and hear the news.

Beginning at noon, we will broadcast this announcement via satellite downlink from our corporate headquarters in New York. Customers from across the country will participate simultaneously. In Chicago, we will gather at the Grand Hotel on First Avenue to hear the presentation.

Lunch will begin at 11:30 A.M. and will be followed by the downlink. After the announcement, product specialists will be available locally to answer any questions.

This announcement will change how you think about the future! Please plan to attend. Respond by filling out the enclosed card or by calling 555-555-5555. See you on the 25th!

Sincerely,

Randall Allen

MODEL LETTER 12.3

"Please Come for Cocktails"

Most customers will be happy to help you celebrate your success.

Dear Amanda:

Please come for cocktails and hors d'oeuvres at our new offices at 9131 Hallmark Way. We are having an open house January 23, from 4:00 P.M. until 7:00 P.M.

We are very excited to be in our expanded facilities. We look forward to welcoming our clients to our new space and thanking you personally for the support that helped us grow.

You are welcome to bring a guest. Please let Pat at 555-5555 know if you will attend and how many reservations you need. Hope to see you there!

Yours truly,

Marsha Miles

Announcing a User Conference

Advise clients of any contingencies that might affect flight schedules and other plans.

Dear Chuck:

This letter is to let you know that our annual User Conference will be held this year in Seattle, July 27–30. I know you have attended in the past and hope that this year's schedule will fit into yours.

I've enclosed the tentative agenda for the meeting. Please keep in mind that the schedule is subject to change. I thought several items would be of particular interest to you and have highlighted those sessions.

As you know, these conferences give you the chance to meet with a variety of users and share information. I really value that you have taken the time to attend in previous years. I will call you next week to discuss your plans.

Sincerely,

Linda Grayson

MODEL LETTER 12.5

Encouraging the Customer to Visit You During a Trade Show

Your preparation for trade meetings will help ensure a successful conference.

Dear Dick:

The fifth annual National Medical Products Show this year will be in Memphis, Tennessee, downtown at the Old Tennessee Hotel. ABC Corp. will sponsore a booth, and an ABC employee will speak at the Tuesday morning seminar. I hope you can stop by the booth and attend the seminar. We will demonstrate several new products.

We will also have a hospitality suite open for customers' convenience throughout the meeting. You are invited to stop by any time to relax and refresh.

Our booth at the show will be in the second-floor ballroom near the south entrance. Look for our blue and white signs. We'll have them displayed prominently. The seminars will run all day Tuesday, and we are scheduled to present at 10:00 A.M. Of course, these schedules may change quickly, so you might confirm them before you stop in.

I look forward to seeing you in Memphis.

Sincerely,

Paula Locke

Model Letter 12.6

"Come to Our Investment Seminar"

Educational events are appropriate in many sales situations.

Dear Mr. and Mrs. Bosley:

At Cornerstone Investments, we believe that the better informed our customers are, the more satisfied they will be with Cornerstone's investment counseling services. That is why we are continuing our Investor Education Series with a discussion this month by Don Simons, who represents the Euro Equity Builder Funds.

Please come to our investment seminar September 1 at 7:00 P.M. in the Fiesta Room of the Heights Hotel. As in the past, the seminar will be preceded by a reception with light hors d'oeuvres.

To make your reservation, leave a message with Cornerstone's voice mail. If you have any questions, please call me at 555-0878. I hope to see you on the 1st.

Sincerely,

Beth Storey

MODEL LETTER 12.7

"Come to a Reception to Meet Our New Executive"

Anyone with an interest in your firm would be flattered by an invitation to meet the new CEO.

Dear Sam:

Last week I mailed you a press release about HiCo's new CEO, Ed St. John. Now it is my privilege to invite you to a reception in his honor on August 11, from 5:00 P.M. to 7:00 P.M., in the Topaz Room of our corporate headquarters, 189 Division Drive.

I'm sure you have seen some of the broadcasts about Ed's move to HiCo. We are thrilled to have someone of his prominence join our firm. I am sending you several more articles about him, along with HiCo's most recent annual report, because I know you will want this background information if you are able to join us on the 11th.

Please call my office at 555-2231 by the 5th if you can attend.

Sincerely,

Patti Lester

MODEL LETTER 12.8

Customer Appreciation Night at the Symphony

Civic-minded corporations can combine their community-service sponsorship with customer-appreciation efforts.

Dear Mr. Howard:

It is my pleasure to invite you and a guest to TransSector's customer appreciation night at the Metro Symphony. This is TransSector's fifth consecutive year as a symphony sponsor, but it is the first year we have reserved the entire Metro Hall for a special evening with our invited guests. Please join us there on June 2 for light hors d'oeuvres at 7:00 P.M., followed by the concert at 8:15 P.M.

We have arranged for an outstanding program featuring soprano soloist Gwen McDaniels, who will be singing selections from her award-winning album, *Almost Golden.*

Please call me by Monday, May 18, to reserve your tickets.

Best regards,

Melinda Black

MODEL LETTER 12.9

"Join Our Table at the Community Gala"

Look for opportunities that arise in your company that give you the chance to honor a special client.

Dear Sarah:

First Company would like to invite you and a guest to join our table at the Community Gala, 7:00 P.M., February 8, 20XX, at Park Place Suites.

The Community Gala is a black-tie event now in its 25th year. Proceeds support the local chapter of Heart Helpers. Many celebrities from the local scene, sports, and entertainment will be present, and you'll have the opportunity to bid on fabulous prizes in the Silent Auction.

I must submit the guest list next week, so I'll call you on Monday to discuss your plans. I certainly hope you're available on the 8th because I know we'll have a wonderful time.

Best regards,

Mark Holt

MODEL LETTER 12.10

"Have Dinner with Executives from Your Company and Ours"

A meeting between the top executives from a client's firm and your own company could be the beginning of a long-term client–vendor partnership.

Dear John:

ABC Company's new CEO will be coming to Chicago May 19. I would like to invite you to meet her at a small dinner party at the Deerfield Suites. I am delighted to have this opportunity, as our chief officer rarely visits. When she does, she appreciates meeting with executives from our large accounts, such as you. As you were our first local account, she specifically asked to meet you.

I hope this date is available on your calendar. I will follow up with a phone call on Monday to discuss the details.

Sincerely,

Dan Hoy

MODEL LETTER 12.11

Clambakes, Fish Fries, and Shrimp Boils— "We're Throwing a Bash"

Attendance at your special events may be higher when you offer something for everyone—babysitters and varied events for young and old alike.

Dear Tom:

HiCo's spring fish fry has become a tradition, but it wouldn't be the same without newcomers like you. For more than ten years, we've invited customers, vendors, and friends to get to know each other a little better in a relaxed atmosphere. People tell me they look forward to it all year, and I think you'd enjoy it, too.

The dress is casual, and family members are welcome. This year's event is Saturday, April 10, from 5:00 P.M. to 10:00 P.M. at the River-walk Grounds. We'll have a Dixieland band and satellite feeds of major sporting events. There will also be activities for youngsters, including babysitters for the very young ones.

Please R.S.V.P. by April 5 by mailing or faxing the enclosed reply card. I hope you can make it!

Sincerely,

Robin Brown

MODEL LETTER 12.12

Offering Your Corporate Jet for Travel to a Special Event

Elegant events require elegant invitations.

Dear Samantha:

Our winery has chosen a select group of restaurateurs for a very special invitation. Blackburn Winery is hosting a wine tasting in our Sonoma Valley wine cellars October 16 and 17. I hope you will accept this invitation to be our guest for the occasion.

The event will begin with dinner the evening of the 16th, and it will conclude about 5:00 P.M. on the 17th. You will have the opportunity to taste Blackburn's new production and select wines for next season. As always, we'll ship your selections to your restaurant in accordance with your specifications.

To make this trip possible with minimal trouble and expense to you, I can offer you the use of our corporate jet for transport both ways. Your travel time will be reduced to two hours. We can accommodate you and up to two guests.

I am confident you will find this special event to be a convenient, enjoyable way to sample our wines and order them for La Savour.

To schedule the jet, I need confirmation by next Friday that you will attend. I will call on Monday to discuss your plans. I hope this opportunity fits into your schedule. It will be a pleasure to have you among our guests. I look forward to talking to you Monday.

Sincerely,

Marty Holmes

Model Letter 12.13

An Invitation to Visit
Our Corporate Headquarters

Extending an invitation to several guests of your client's choice allows the client to bring along influential team members.

Dear George:

I am writing to invite you and several guests of your choice from XYZ to visit ABC's corporate headquarters in New York. The purpose of the visit will be to introduce you to our executives, give you the latest product information, and offer a glimpse of what's in store with our R&D projects.

A tentative agenda is enclosed. The following dates are available for a visit to our headquarters:

    October 4
    October 20
    October 22
    November 1

To encourage you to accept this offer, ABC will cover all expenses, including airfare and hotel. I appreciate your considering this invitation and hope you will visit us in New York.

Sincerely,

Tom Tatum

MODEL LETTER 12.14

An Invitation to Tour
Our Manufacturing Plant

Renew your bond with long-time customers by inviting them to a special event or for a visit.

Dear Ted Roberts:

Several years have passed since you visited us in Cleveland, and I think you would be pleased to see the changes we've made both in processes and in our physical plant. Is there some time in the next few months you could arrange to tour our plant?

You and I have had several discussions recently about HiCo sales contracts and delivery procedures. After we talked last Wednesday, it occurred to me that both of us might benefit from a personal visit to the manufacturing site. You could see firsthand how we operate now. Plus, I would like for several HiCo managers to hear your appraisal of our performance over the past year or so.

I will follow up with a call next Monday.

Sincerely,

Pat Martin

MODEL LETTER 12.15

"Be Our Guest at the Season Opener"

Sporting events are an all-time favorite for client–vendor entertainment.

Dear Mac:

Winter's over and that can mean only one thing: it's time for base-ball. Real-Time Inc. purchased two rows of behind-the-plate seats for the season opener, and we put your name at the top of the guest list. I know how much you love the game, and I'm hoping you'll join us April 1.

I'll call you on Friday to see how your schedule looks.

Best regards,

Ted Stevens

———

MODEL LETTER 12.16

Offering Your Corporate Suite at a Pro Ball Game

Year after year, some corporations maintain an entertainment tradition with box seats, suites, or massive tents at sporting events.

Dear Mac:

I've saved this invitation for my best customer ever. Get ready for some great football, but you can put away your stadium seats and Thermos bottle. Real-Time Inc. has purchased a box at the new Pro-Ball Stadium, and we hope you will join us there for the Redskins game November 12.

I'll call you on Monday to check how your schedule looks.

Yours truly,

Greg Miles

MODEL LETTER 12.17

"Come to an Invitation-Only Pro-Am"

Golf is almost certain to improve your bottom line.

Dear Steve:

I am pleased to invite you to participate as a guest of ABC Company in the Pro-Am Tournament of the Breakaway Golf Tournament December 1 and 2 in Oklahoma City.

The Pro-Am will be December 1, preceded by dinner with all the pros November 30 at the exclusive Mayfield Club.

Steve, knowing what an incredible golfer you are, I hope this date will work for you. By the end of next week, I need to know your plans. I have sent all the necessary paperwork in hopes that you will be our guest. It's due November 15.

Let's talk about your plans this week. I'll call to follow up.

Sincerely,

Liz Carter

MODEL LETTER 12.18

"Come to Our Company-Sponsored Golf Tournament"

If capacity at your special events is limited, be sure to tell customers to sign up early and avoid disappointment.

Dear Don:

ABC Company will sponsor our Third Annual Customer Apprecia-tion Golf Tournament August 19 at the Inn on the Pacific in Car-mel, California. You are invited to attend and may bring a guest.

ABC Company will sponsor practice rounds at adjoining golf courses August 17 and 18. If you wish to play a practice round, please fill out the attached information sheet. We will make hotel reservations for you if you provide your travel schedule. ABC will provide meals in our hospitality suite throughout the event. Hotel and transportation will not be provided by ABC.

This year's event promises to be even more exciting than the one last year. Pro Danny Shore will attend. I hope this works into your schedule, and I look forward to joining you for golf overlooking the Pacific.

We expect this spectacular location to attract an overwhelming crowd, so please register early by sending us your paperwork. Call me with any questions you may have. I can be reached at 555-7000.

Sincerely,

Susan Trent

Model Letter 12.19

"Participate in Our Industry Forum"

You can honor important clients and gain valuable industry information by hosting a forum.

Dear Mrs. Adamson:

I feel very privileged to invite you to HiCo's first-ever Industry Forum, October 10–11, in Aspen, Colorado. We're inviting 100 very special customers to spend a weekend in the Rockies, hear distinguished guest speakers, and talk about the challenges new technology and rising costs mean for our industry.

HiCo will cover the cost of lodging at Aspen's Chalet Azure and catered meals throughout the weekend. Although we will not cover airfare, the company has arranged convention rates on In the Sky Airlines (code 567).

This promises to be a very exciting weekend that could change the way you think about our business. I am enclosing a complete agenda and will call you on Tuesday to discuss your plans.

Sincerely,

Taylor Harris

Model Letter 12.20

An Invitation to Participate in a Prestigious Study

Customers are often willing to contribute financially to an effort that advances their industry.

Dear Mr. Vincent:

At the Trade Review Conference in Aspen, you indicated that you would be interested in participating in a study being sponsored by the Accounting Institute (AI), the Research Group (RG), RHMC, and two other firms. This letter will give you background on the study.

In 20XX, AI issued a practices and techniques statement entitled "The Accounting Classifications of Real Estate Occupancy Costs," which provided guidelines for capturing and classifying these costs. The focus of the study is to develop a new chart of accounts that redefines traditional occupancy costs in a broader perspective to reflect the changing nature of work settings for office space, technology, real estate and facilities, and other support services.

RHMC is conducting interviews this month and next month with a select group of corporations to receive their input on the new proposed chart of accounts. We request that corporations schedule a 1½-to-2-hour meeting with a representative from the corporate real estate facilities, accounting, and information technology. The meeting agenda includes three items:

- Discussion of Davenport's general philosophy and approach to providing office space for employees
- Organizational structure for providing services relating to corporate real estate and facilities
- Obtaining input from Davenport's representatives in completing a questionnaire.

The results of the surveys conducted will be analyzed as a group (that is, no results from an individual corporation will be made public) to produce findings and conclusions regarding the appropriateness of the proposed chart of accounts and associated implementation issues. A white paper will be drafted for submission to the AI for review as step I in the process of AI's issuing a new statement to replace the 1991 publications referenced above. Further, preliminary results will be presented at the fall Trade Review meeting in Atlanta.

The sponsors of the study feel the initiative is very timely and reflects the tremendous interest by corporate real estate professionals in the development of unifying principles to benchmark and analyze occupancy costs. In this regard, our probable primary question is, What are the benefits to Davenport for participating in this study?

The primary benefits to Davenport are the opportunity to take a leadership position in influencing the development of a new set of standards for occupancy costs and to be acknowledged for the contribution, and to gain insight into the thinking of other major corporations on this issue.

To help defray the costs of conducting the survey, we are requesting a contribution of $7,500 from the participating corporations. This is not a precondition for Davenport's participation, but simply a request.

I look forward to your participation in this cutting-edge initiative. I will call you next week to answer any questions and schedule a time in September for the interview.

Thanks for your participation.

Sincerely,

Thomas H. Wenkstern

(Courtesy of Thomas H. Wenkstern, Plano, Texas.)

Twenty Ways to Express Customer Appreciation

MODEL LETTER 12.21

"Thank You for Your Order"

Show customers you notice their patronage. Send them a timely thank you.

Dear Hank:

Thank you for reordering Bristol Pet Supplies. I'm glad your trial with Tiger Treats was so successful.

As I told you during my sales call in June, I am impressed by your store and your efficient use of space—you have a huge number of SKUs, yet the store looks neat and organized. I'm sure customers can find the products they need with minimal fuss.

I look forward to our next visit. It's customers like you who have made the first six months in my new sales territory truly delightful. Please know that I sincerely appreciate your business.

Best regards,

Katie Biggs

MODEL LETTER 12.22

Thank Customers with a Reminder of Your Work on Their Behalf

Don't be shy about reminding customers of the favors you've done for them.

Dear Michelle,

We don't often have an opportunity to say "thanks for the business" to individual clients. Recently, your agency bought several additional spots for your client's second-quarter schedule, and we were able to add these two no-charge spots:

Thursday, 12:30 P.M. to 3:00 P.M.   Soaps
Sunday, 11:30 A.M. to 2:30 P.M.   *Zoo Time/Real Stories*

Thanks again. KOOO-TV appreciates your business.

Regards,

Sally Lombard

MODEL LETTER 12.23

Presenting an Industry Calendar

Something you produce anyway—like a calendar of industry events—can become your signature giveaway.

Dear Mark:

It can be a real challenge to keep up with all the trade shows, sales meetings, product announcements, and other events in this industry. That's why TransSector prepared a calendar of industry events for our special customers. This is one small way we can express our appreciation for the support you give us all year.

I've added your name to the mail list to receive quarterly updates. The calendar is also posted on our Web site, www.notreally.com, along with links to other sites of interest.

Since this is the first time we've distributed a calendar like this one, I am eager to know what you think of it. I'll be in Denver the week of April 5, and I hope we can meet then. I'll call you soon to see how your schedule looks.

Sincerely,

Tricia Roberts

MODEL LETTER 12.24

Offering Coupons as a Token of Appreciation

Coupons are a great way to thank your most active customers. They also work wonders when you need to gently prod someone who hasn't ordered in a while.

Dear Mrs. Walker:

You have been one of my most loyal customers for some time now, and I want to express my thanks by sending you these dollars-off coupons for our hypoallergenic cosmetics.

I'm also sending you our new catalog. See all our beautiful new spring colors on page 24. I'm sure you'll find something you like, but don't worry. If you decide not to order at this time, the coupons have no expiration date.

Please know how much I appreciate your business and how much I enjoy our visits when I deliver your products. I hope to hear from you again soon.

Yours truly,

Martha Morgan

MODEL LETTER 12.25

Offering a Volume Discount

Special incentives can be particularly helpful if competitors are courting your best customers.

Dear Ted:

HiCo is making a special offer to show how much we appreciate high-volume customers like Sure Freight.

In the coming year, your company can receive a volume discount for all the business you give us in excess of last year's invoices. What this means is once you pass the dollar amount we billed you last year, the discount kicks in and you save on every new order. Even better, the more you order, the more you save. Here's how it works:

Amount of increase in your orders over last year	10%	15%	20%
Amount of discount off each order	10%	15%	20%

As you can see, this offer could mean thousands of dollars to your company. Of course, HiCo benefits from your increased orders, so neither of us loses.

I am available to make a presentation on this incentive plan to your management if you desire. We at HiCo are very excited to be making this offer, and we look forward to saving you money in the months ahead.

Sincerely,

Tom Rogers

MODEL LETTER 12.26

"I Thought You'd Like to Know About These IPOs"

Even a brief note lets customers know you are paying attention to their needs.

Dear Mr. and Mrs. Williams:

I thought you would like to know about some very interesting initial public offerings from the technology sector. I am sending you prospectuses from three highly rated software makers whose IPOs are scheduled to take place in the next two months.

These are not the kinds of companies that make a splash in international news one week, then fizzle out a month or two later. These companies have outstanding growth potential for the next one, five, . . . ten years. I highly recommend that you look at each prospectus, then talk to me for an update.

I'll follow up with a call next week.

Sincerely,

Miles Lewis

Model Letter 12.27

To-the-Trade Travel Incentives

Keep your clients interested in working with you by adding an extra incentive for them.

Dear Sue:

It's hard to impress a seasoned travel agent, but I'm betting that you haven't been here and you haven't done this. In the Sky Airlines is offering a special incentive to qualifying travel agencies.

Book ten groups of twenty or more in the next three months, and we'll double your comp tickets for the rest of the year. That means that after your 10th booking, you get two—rather than one—comp for each group of twenty.

This offer expires December 31, so start booking now and get a bonus the rest of the year!

Best regards,

Lee Rogers

MODEL LETTER 12.28

Announcing Courtesy Shopping Days

Give customers a reason to develop loyalty to your store, your products, and you.

Dear Mrs. Brown:

We're only telling our best customers. May 1 and 2 are our Courtesy Shopping Days before we advertise our biggest sale of the season.

We have great savings in every department—and especially good values in menswear, ladies shoes, and the toy store. Cooking demonstrations will start on the hour from 10:00 A.M. through 2:00 P.M. on both days, and there will be an after-school teen fashion show at 4:00 P.M. on May 2.

Please stop by and partake of the values and enjoy the entertainment.

Best regards,

Maureen Miller

MODEL LETTER 12.29

Season's Greetings: Thanks for Making Us a Success

Forget the fruitcake. Send a gracious message to bid your customers season's greetings.

Dear Dr. Farmer:

All of us here at B&C Inc. wish you and yours a joyous holiday and a prosperous new year. Thank you for the success you helped us achieve in the past year and for the opportunity to serve you in the new year.

Best wishes for a joyous holiday and prosperous new year,

The B&C Staff

MODEL LETTER 12.30

Season's Greetings: A Note to Accompany a Gift

To the extent possible, personalize the gifts you give customers. A handwritten note is a great way to convey your sincere appreciation for the customer's support.

Dear Tom Parks:

Season's Greetings from everyone at HiCo. Please accept this gift as an expression of our gratitude. Your support helped make this year the best ever for our company. Our goal for the new year is to keep making the products you rely on even better.

Wishing you the best,

Betsy Robbins

MODEL LETTER 12.31

A Gift for the New Year (Discount)

A discount extended to your best customers expresses appreciation while bolstering your bottom line.

Dear Donna Brown:

All of us here at Office Suppliers wish you and yours a happy, prosperous new year.

Your business helped make Office Suppliers' first year a smashing success, and we want to express our appreciation by inviting you to visit our showroom and receive a 15 percent discount on purchases of $1,000 or more. We have stocked several new lines of executive furniture to complement the selections in our catalog. Of course, we also offer a full range of office supplies.

Please stop in soon. We look forward to your visit.

Sincerely,

Tom Green

MODEL LETTER 12.32

Good Luck in the New Year

In states that have lotteries, scratch-off cards can be a fun way to brighten your customer's day. You could drop off a scratch-off card enclosed in a New Year's greeting with a message that says . . .

Dear Laura:

Wishing you luck in the new year. Not to worry if you don't win the lottery. Our spring line will keep your sales high and inventories low. I can't wait to show it to you.

Best regards,

Tom Lee

MODEL LETTER 12.33

"Here's a Housewarming Gift"

A housewarming gift need not be elaborate. Something home-baked, a gardening book, or a plant are all excellent choices.

Dear Joan:

Here's a housewarming gift to help make your moving day even more special. I am so happy you found the Logan property and were able to close the sale. It was a pleasure helping you find your ideal home. Our treks around the countryside were an adventure I won't soon forget. You've even got me daydreaming about leaving the city for a pastoral home.

You know I live off referrals, so please keep me in mind if any of your new neighbors want to make a change. And please keep in touch. The most fun part of my job is meeting interesting people like you.

Yours truly,

Cynthia Thomas

MODEL LETTER 12.34

"Can You Keep a Secret?"

Special promotions make your customers feel valued.

Dear Beth:

Can you keep a secret? I know you can when it involves a deal this great. I've been authorized to tell a select list of my most prized customers about our one-day customer appreciation sale, April 9. This sale will not be advertised and is not available to the general public.

Only customers who present this special invitation are eligible to save 25 percent on the items of your choice—all day at our Town North location! The only restrictions are on designer leather goods and cosmetics, which are not on sale.

Of course, as your personal shopper, I would be happy to put aside any items of special interest now so you they will be available on the 9th. Call me at 555-9991 to let me know.

I look forward to seeing you on the 9th. Happy shopping!

Yours truly,

Kelly Wynne

MODEL LETTER 12.35

Presenting Premiums—Calculators, Mouse Pads, Key Chains, and More

Product promotions can be a form of customer appreciation. You give customers something useful that becomes a constant reminder of your product. Of course, the supply of tokens, knickknacks, and other promotional items seems endless, probably because, despite their sometimes corny tie-in, they build customer awareness and goodwill. In this example, a card bearing this message accompanies a spray bottle of window cleaner to use on computer screens.

Dear Tom:

At TranSector, we do Windows. That's because the DataKeeper software you've been using on your mainframe now works equally well in the PC environment.

I'm sending product information (along with this handy spray for your monitor). The brochures describes DataKeeper's archiving features, which I know is an application you use a lot in your business.

Of course, you told me you plan to stay with the mainframe a while longer. Just keep me in mind when you are ready for a transition.

Sincerely,

Ben Coleman

MODEL LETTER 12.36

"You're Among the First to Know"

Private sales can make customers—as well as your vendors and employees—feel like part of the corporate family. They can also save you thousands in advertising costs.

Dear Elizabeth:

As one of my most valued customers, you're among the first to know about an opportunity HiCo is offering on a first-come, first-served basis. Our success over the past two years has forced us to expand to larger quarters. Rather than move the furniture and equipment we have now into the new offices, we plan to liquidate everything and replace it in the new facility.

On Tuesday, June 4, at 10:00 A.M., HiCo will auction all our current office furniture and equipment, including computers. But we're giving our friends first choice on everything. We are accepting bids through May 31. If the office manager accepts your offer, it's yours.

You may be able to get a great deal on some of that office equipment you've been needing. Call me, and we'll plan a time for you to visit. You can place your bid anytime between now and the 31st, and take delivery anytime between the 31st and the 3rd.

Best regards,

Tom Bridges

Model Letter 12.37

"Please Accept This Thank You for the Great Referrals"

Keep valuable referrals coming by showing that you appreciate the support.

Dear Kathleen:

You must have the most fascinating friends, because I've enjoyed meeting every one of the people you've referred to me. You know that my real estate business depends on satisfied customers like you and the home-buying and -selling prospects you refer to me.

You've been a tremendous help to me in the past two years. So please accept this gift certificate to the Très Chic Restaurant as a thank you for all those great referrals.

Best regards,

Michelle Trent

Model Letter 12.38

"Thanks for Helping Me Make My Quota"

When you have a close relationship with customers, they like hearing how you are doing.

Dear Linda:

It's customers like you who have helped me get where I am today—Maui! That is why I'm sending you these macadamia nuts as a token of my appreciation. Thanks to terrific customers like you, I surpassed my quota last year and won a Hawaiian vacation. I also continued to be part of my firm's Super Achievers Club for top performers. I could not have made either accomplishment without your loyalty and support.

It is always a pleasure to call on you, and I look forward to our visit May 25.

Sincerely,

Tom Beasley

Asking a Valued Customer to Move with You

Depending on your product or service, your customers may feel a much stronger bond with you than with your firm.

Dear Larry:

I have valued your business greatly over the past five years and can truly say it was a pleasure working with you. As I mentioned during my visit last month, I am venturing out on my own. My insurance office opens in two weeks, and I would like you to consider making the move with me.

I will be able to offer some attractive alternatives to your current life and automobile coverage. I'll call next week to make an appointment.

Sincerely,

Linda Selph

MODEL LETTER 12.40

Expressing Appreciation to Participants in Your Customer Survey

Companies have learned the importance of maintaining an ongoing dialogue with customers. Your involvement in surveys and other marketing endeavors helps you stay in touch with them, too.

Dear Ms. Hart:

Your participation in our customer survey was an important step in helping my company provide the best products and services possible, and I am taking a moment to express my personal appreciation for your effort.

As we have discussed, my company aggressively seeks information about our industry and our firm's standing with customers and noncustomers alike. Much of the nonproprietary information we have gathered is reported in *Industry Overview.* My company produces this publication each year for customers like you. You took time to express your thoughts and views, and we want to thank you by sharing the important information you helped us uncover.

I plan to be in your city March 19 and 20 and would like to visit with you to check your satisfaction with our A Model. I'll call you next week to see how your schedule looks.

Sincerely,

Mike Allen

Selling Outlook
Strengthening the Client–Vendor Bond Through Special Events and Customer Appreciation Initiatives

It's easy to come home tired after a day of playing caddie at the customer appreciation golf tournament, fall into your favorite armchair, and moan, "Why?" But you know the answer.

As a salesperson, you want your customers to know that you realize they are the cornerstone of your career. It's important that they be happy with you and your company, and you want them to know how much they matter to you. That's why you give up a Saturday once or twice a year to work the company golf tournament. And that's why you spend an extra hour after making calls all day to send a thank you for each and every order.

Special events take you out of the usual sales call context and put you into situations that can bring your customers closer to your company, your product, and you. Special events broaden customers' view of your company to include your company executives. The net effect should be to increase the customers' comfort level in doing business with you and your organization. The key is to offer customers and prospects well-orchestrated events that create favorable impressions and enhance your marketing efforts. Pulling off these events requires incredible attention to detail, and something inevitably goes wrong. But despite the disappointments, special events are well worth the effort. When your customers attend a well-executed special event, the marketing process magically moves forward.

Not all forms of customer appreciation occur on a specified day at a specified time. Expressions of customer appreciation can be as individual and diverse as the people who make them. It's easy to trivialize the concept of customer appreciation as nothing more than the calendar you receive from your insurance rep every January. But decision makers' bond with companies, products, and sales representatives is an important influence, that builds success year after year.

CHAPTER 13

References and Recognition

If sales had to be summed up in one word, that word would be *persuasion.* Customers must decide that your product, your services, and you are the best choices. Within your organization, your sales and support team must be motivated to deliver top performances day in and day out. Your persuasive ability has a tremendous influence on what customers choose and how your organization performs. Two powerful tools to help persuade customers to buy and support teams to stay sharp are references and recognition.

References from satisfied people outside your organization are more compelling than anything you or others in your company could say. References lend credibility to your sales message by demonstrating that your product works for another customer. (And there's an added bonus: while selling something to a new customer, you compliment a current one. Your request implies that the customer's product choices and business practices are exemplary.)

Recognition today can be persuasive in the future. By calling attention to someone's special efforts and expressing heartfelt gratitude, we say, "I value you and your work." And when colleagues know you've recognized their past efforts, they will be that much more motivated to excel on your next project.

CHAPTER 13. CONTENTS

References and Recognition that Involve Customers

Recognizing Your Team Members

References and Recognition That Involve Customers

MODEL LETTER 13.1

Asking a Client to Provide a Reference

Although it is scary to ask someone to give you a reference, people who like you will probably be flattered by your request.

Dear Ann:

Thank you for the trust you place in me as your investment advisor. I appreciate and enjoy working for you.

I am trying to expand my client base and would like to ask for your help. As I talk with prospective clients, they frequently ask to speak with a current client. Would you be willing to talk to several prospects?

Please give this some thought. I will follow up next week.

Sincerely,

Tom Hannah

MODEL LETTER 13.2

Thanking the Client for Being Your Reference

Share your success with the people who helped you achieve it.

Dear Liz:

Thanks for talking to the Murphys.

You must have been very complimentary, as they called back ready to open an account. I have been talking with them off and on for over six months. Although I thought I did a good job for them, they continued to hesitate. Talking with you made all the difference.

Thank you very much. I really appreciate your help.

Best regards,

Laura Smith

MODEL LETTER 13.3

Replying to the Customer's Request for a Reference

If a prospect asks for a reference, provide all the relevant information in writing. That way, the prospect can initiate contact at his or her convenience.

Dear Chuck:

Last Friday you requested the name of a customer who has relied on my firm's 1-800 help desk for a service request. I am pleased to refer you to Jim Mitchell, manager of data operations, Hi-Tech, Inc., 543-555-2626.

Jim assures me he would be happy to answer your questions or discuss any concerns you may have about my firm's products and service. Thank you for your interest in Meadows and Company.

Sincerely,

Eileen Wynne

MODEL LETTER 13.4

Recognizing Your Customer's Teamwork

Sometimes a letter needs to communicate two messages, the first being, "We as a company have a problem"; the second, "Certain people within the company have developed solutions." Good salespeople know when and how to communicate problems to management. They also know that identifying the solutions and recognizing the problem solvers pave the way for a smoother sales cycle the next time around.

Dear Todd:

I want you to know how much I appreciate the efforts of your team. They were instrumental in closing the $1.2 million sale to Heartland Bank this quarter. Heartland was one of the first customers to buy our Modular Open Unit Systems Equalizer ("MOUSE"). When I began collecting the information and resources to propose a MOUSE solution to Heartland, I found myself in a wilderness. Our internal collateral support was scattered. In particular, we had no sample system proposals and no clear method of determining specific system size and configuration, and technical sales support was not focused on the product. Thanks to the efforts of your colleagues, we overcame these problems, made the sale, and identified our internal weaknesses so that they could be addressed systematically in the future.

First of all, Tom Phillips, from corporate, went out of his way to participate in teleconferences, both internally and with the customer. The questions seemed endless, and Tom energetically chased down answers from within corporate and from a variety of outside vendors. He played a key role in getting the story straight and helping us commit to realistic timeframes and expectations.

Marcie Marberry, from the Cleveland office, participated in one of the few previous MOUSE installations. She shared her time and her insights generously throughout the sales cycle. Please pass on to her manager how much her efforts are appreciated.

Finally, David Young became our de facto district specialist on MOUSE during the six-month sales cycle. He gave many hours to the project and ultimately developed a general system-sizing model that can be used to generate specific configuration proposals for future customer installations. Furthermore, David's energy and enthusiasm helped maintain my confidence in the MOUSE solution in my moments of doubt.

My experience convinces me that MOUSE is a viable customer solution, and if we continue to improve collateral support, we will be able to close more business in this category. Please join me in recognizing Tom, Marcie, and David as valuable resources and in thanking them for their assistance in whatever way you think appropriate. Thanks for your support.

Sincerely,

Colin Hubbard

Model Letter 13.5

Asking a Customer for a Product Testimonial

Customers will appreciate the effort it takes to write, rather than telephone, your request for a product testimonial.

Dear Ed:

Online Investments, Inc., is looking at a large power generator system like the one you bought from me. Online's decision makers have expressed interest in talking to someone who owns this type of system.

Would you be willing to talk to them? The person you would be talking to has responsibilities much like yours, and I thought you might be interested in meeting him, in addition to helping me.

I know you are very busy, but if you could work this in, I would really appreciate it.

Sincerely,

Fran Carter

MODEL LETTER 13.6

Thanking a Customer for Providing a Product Reference

This note would be appropriate typewritten or handwritten.

Dear Ed:

Thank you for talking with the Online Investments decision makers. They were very excited about your report of our projects' reliability and our performance as a vendor. I am drawing up purchase contracts for them today!

I appreciate your help. Thanks for being a good customer and a great reference.

Sincerely,

Fran Carter

MODEL LETTER 13.7

Asking for Names of Prospects

If you are reluctant to ask for help in person, send a note with your request.

Dear Susan:

I am launching a marketing campaign for In the Sky Airlines and am writing to ask for your help. Because you used to work there, I wonder if you remember the purchasing agents who handle travel services. Their names would help me get started, and I promise not to reveal you as the source of the referral.

I appreciate any help you can offer. I'll call next week to discuss my request.

Yours truly,

Linda Rogers

Model Letter 13.8

Asking for Leads About Potential Customers

Even though you intend to talk over lunch, this letter tastefully and professionally explains your interest.

Dear Jennifer:

I am trying to expand my client base and am writing to ask you for some help. I know you have a wide circle of friends and acquaintances, and I wonder if you would share with me the names of people who might be seeking investment advice.

Your assistance to me would be completely confidential, unless you wanted me to indicate your referral. I know you value your contacts, and I respect the need for confidentiality.

Jen, I appreciate any assistance you can give. I know you understand the challenges of building a business, and I am glad to have people like you to call on for help.

I'll call next week to see if you are free for lunch. It would be good to talk to you about this in person.

Best regards,

Cindy McDonald

MODEL LETTER 13.9

When Your Firm's Advertising
Will Involve Your Customer

Companies occasionally call on satisfied customers for advertising testimonials. These projects tend to involve several departments, including sales, marketing, and legal. Even so, plans that involve your customer at some point will involve you, too.

Dear Elizabeth:

Success stories similar to yours have inspired our advertising department's plans. Our creative director wants to feature satisfied customers such as you in print and televised ads next year to promote home use of our copier/fax/printer combinations.

I cannot think of a more compelling example of how to build a profitable business at home than the one you set over the past two years. An ad featuring you would bolster use of our products while giving you a fortune in free promotion. With your permission, I will give your name to our advertising staff and encourage them to feature you and your business prominently in their next ad campaign.

Elizabeth, I will call you next week to discuss this idea. I am excited about the possibilities.

Best regards,

Melissa Meyerson

MODEL LETTER 13.10

Asking to Include the Customer
on Your Client List

Most customers will be complimented by your request to add them to a client list.

Dear Roger:

As you know, my company has been fortunate to experience rapid growth during the past two years. To extend our growth trend over the next twelve months and beyond, we have launched an aggressive marketing effort in six states where we previously had no representation.

As part of this effort, we would like to include your company's name on the client list that representatives show prospective new clients. A brief note from you will suffice to indicate that permission is granted. If I need to refer this request to someone else, please let me know.

I will call you on Tuesday to follow up.

Sincerely,

Brenda Goodman

Model Letter 13.11

Recognizing the Customer's Employee

When your customer's staff contributes to your success, let the customer's management know.

Dear Jack:

I want to compliment the outstanding effort of your staff member Brian Dowdy. Brian's cooperation with my technical staff was an important factor in the success of the installation.

Brian's efforts began when my company initiated our feasibility study of our messaging system in your organization. He provided insight into your requirements that contributed significantly to our effectiveness.

As project leader for the implementation, Brian demonstrated outstanding organizational skills and attention to detail. His efforts ensured that all went smoothly, and his enthusiastic attitude encouraged everyone to cooperate.

Thank you for assigning Brian to our project. We sincerely appreciate his contribution and look forward to working with him again.

Best regards,

Tom Marks

MODEL LETTER 13.12

Recognizing the Customer's Teamwork

Customers enjoy having a vendor tell them their employees' work is exemplary.

Dear Beth Simpson:

This letter is to recognize the successful teamwork between your staff and ours on our recent project with you.

Our success depends on the level of teamwork and cooperation we establish with our customers. Your staff graciously helped us with whatever needed to be done, including working extra hours. Without your support, we would not have accomplished our goals.

On behalf of everyone at ABC Corp., thanks to you and all your staff for hard work and enthusiastic support.

Sincerely,

Matt Williams

Model Letter 13.13

Recognizing a Successful Joint Effort

Successful joint efforts are the cornerstone of long-term client–vendor relationships.

Dear Bill:

On behalf of the entire MegaDisk implementation team, congratulations on your achievements in orchestrating the Briggs project. It is a rare manager who can coordinate the work of two consulting firms and an in-house staff and deliver a complex project on time, on budget, and on target with productivity goals. We commend you.

Bill, I am elated that the Briggs project went so smoothly. My only regret is that the successful conclusion means I won't be working as closely with you. I know, though, that your firm will likely continue automation in other parts of the company. When you do, I hope you will keep us in mind.

Sincerely,

David Reagan

Model Letter 13.14

When Your Project Wins Recognition
for the Customer

When your product or service is strongly linked to an award or other recognition for clients, a letter from you serves two purposes: congratulating the clients and reminding them that your work contributed to their achievement.

Dear Ted:

It was great news about your Editor's Annual award for the Big River photography section we did last year. Not only was that series a pleasure to shoot, it apparently outshone anything the competition could muster. Congratulations on the recognition from your peers in the industry. It is well deserved.

Best wishes for continued success.

Tim Gibbs

MODEL LETTER 13.15

Recognizing Your Product's Contribution to the Customer's Productivity Gain

Several months after a successful product implementation, you may be able to document an improvement that the client anticipated at the time of purchase. Use this achievement to your advantage by sending a letter of congratulations that reinforces the validity of your sales message.

Dear Ed:

Tuesday, during my sales call in your data center, I was pleased to read your first-quarter post-implementation report. Although I am not surprised to see MegaDisk drives performing as promised, it is gratifying to know that their implementation helped your firm achieve the 3.4 percent productivity gain in just three months. That is quite an achievement, but you can expect even more in the future.

Thank you for supporting MegaDisk, and congratulations on this achievement.

Sincerely,

Mary Baxter

MODEL LETTER 13.16

Recognizing Your Customer's Innovative Use of Your Product

Customers delight in hearing that you think their approach is innovative.

Dear Lee:

As I mentioned during our meeting today, your configuration of the new MegaDisk drives is an exciting innovation. I have sent a summary of our discussion to my R&D manager.

Lee, I commend you on your creativity and tenacity in finding new ways to make use of MD products to solve client-server needs. This is a significant accomplishment.

Sincerely,

Paul Patterson

MODEL LETTER 13.17

Recognizing the Customer's Contribution to Your Success

Letters that tell customers about your professional achievements remind them of your professionalism and demonstrate that you appreciate them.

Dear Elaine:

This week my company honored me with membership in the President's Circle, a distinction reserved for associates with sales in the top 10 percent. I am writing to thank you for helping make this achievement possible.

I rely on customers like you who have shown consistent loyalty to my products and me. I look forward to continuing to work with you. Thanks for your support.

Warm regards,

Conor Hubbard

Recognizing Your Team Members

Model Letter 13.18

Recognizing Administrative Support

If you don't tell managers their staff is providing outstanding administrative support, how will they know?

Dear Claire:

Heidi Montrose has provided excellent administrative support for me throughout 20XX. She is diligent, hard working, thoughtful, and very quick in learning anything new.

Additionally, Heidi is a real boost to office morale. Her personality and leadership provide great examples for others.

I am delighted Heidi came to work at ABC Company, and I look forward to her enthusiastic contributions in 20XX.

Sincerely,

Roger Myers

MODEL LETTER 13.19

Recognizing Helpful People—
A Note to the Employee

Special events mean long hours and increased responsibility for someone. Express your gratitude in a personal note.

Dear Myra:

Your help throughout the recent Customer Recognition Golf Tournament made the event a great success. You were willing to take on any task; your energy was boundless, despite the long hours; and you were courteous with everyone involved.

Thank you for your help. I hope we can count on you next year as well.

Sincerely,

Frank Jones

MODEL LETTER 13.20

Recognizing Helpful People—
A Note to the Manager

Even if management changes, the letters of praise you write for a helpful coworker can influence that person's promotions, bonuses, and raises as long as the letters remain in personnel files.

Dear Tim:

I think it is important to recognize and thank Felicity Jones for her boundless energy in solving problems and her excellent interpersonal skills in dealing with our clients. As a salesperson, it is a great comfort to know that if the client has a question or billing concern, I can turn the situation over to Felicity. I am confident she will conscientiously pursue details and answers and will always be courteous and patient with our clients.

I am both thankful and appreciative of Felicity's hard work and "can do" attitude.

Sincerely,

Tina Priest

MODEL LETTER 13.21

Passing Along a Compliment

Whether a compliment is written or oral, pass it along to the employees and managers involved.

Dear Hugh:

I thought the attached note would be of great interest to you. Our customers at Alpha Omega, Inc., could not be happier with the annual report your designers and writers produced for them. The response to the report has been all positive, and AOI wants to meet next week to talk about more projects.

Thanks for all your effort.

Best regards,

Marsha Mobley

Model Letter 13.22

"Thanks for Helping Me
Land the New Account"

Letters make lasting records of your recognition of colleagues. To create lasting memories, you may want to combine recognition letters with victory celebrations.

Dear Ted:

After six months of lengthy RFIs, demonstrations, and sometimes stressful negotiations, I learned today that we have won the ABS account.

Your efforts and the contributions of your staff were essential elements in ABS's decision. I think you know the significance of this new business to the company. ABS is an emerging leader in the industry with a growth trend that outpaces the competition two to one.

In honor of the occasion and to say thanks for helping me land the new account, I invite you, your staff, and your guests to Leo's for cocktails and hors d'oeuvres on Friday, May 15. Please call me at 555-6262 to let me know it that works for you.

Sincerely,

Carole Roberts

MODEL LETTER 13.23

Telling Management about a Coworker's Dedication

Reliable, dependable coworkers depend on you to inform their management of their contribution to your success.

Dear Harry:

The purpose of this letter is to let you know what an asset Mike Hogan has been during our recent product installation at XYZ Corp.

Mike is not only reliable and dependable, but he can also be counted on for consistent professionalism and cooperation with all coworkers. I am very pleased that Mike has been involved at XYZ, and I look forward to working with him again soon.

Sincerely,

Michelle Porter

Model Letter 13.24

Recognizing Outstanding Project Management

Don't overlook mid- to upper-level employees. Everyone appreciates recognition for a job well done.

Dear Al:

Rodney Peterson provided outstanding project management at High-Tech Corp. throughout 20XX. His service was especially noteworthy during the conversion project, which was very critical to the customer.

With fewer than thirty days between the customer's decision to proceed with the conversion until the actual conversion, Rodney did an excellent job of coordinating the project. The customer's expectations, the manpower shortage, and hardware management were just a few of the challenges he faced. I attribute the successful completion of the conversion in less than twelve hours to Rodney's hard work, tenacity, and leadership.

I greatly appreciate having Rodney as our service manager at High-Tech. I know he will continue to be an asset to our marketing efforts in 20XX.

Sincerely,

Fred Mann

MODEL LETTER 13.25

Recognizing a Special Team Effort

Maintaining a list of contributors as a project progresses is one way to avoid omissions when it is time to thank your team.

Dear Bob:

I want to recognize the outstanding teamwork that went into the successful implementation at ABC Corp.

The team leader, Charlie Jones, gave the project 150 percent of his energy from the time we announced the sale until "go live" day. He managed our special project without sacrificing his attention to other responsibilities—quite an accomplishment! Charlie kept the project and all the players on course by paying attention to detail yet never losing sight of the big picture.

The technical support of both Tommy Lee and Bobby Hounds could not have been surpassed. They are dedicated, hard-working individuals who have earned the respect of our customers at ABC Corp. Without their long hours of work and their expertise, the team could not have accomplished its goal.

Finally, the installers themselves, David Scott, Angie Myer, Colin Hubbard, Marie Ackerman, Preston Bateman, Tim Baker, Howard Frankel, Peter Bond, and John Howarth, worked incredible hours under stressful circumstances. They worked well with each other and with the customer's staff. They accomplished their goal ahead of schedule and did so with courteous, professional attitudes. We should all be proud of their work and pleased to have them working for us.

I am proud to be associated with such an outstanding group of professionals.

Sincerely,

Chris Simms

Recognizing a Valuable Team Member

Don't assume that managers realize what someone has done for you. You must communicate!

Dear Betty:

George Brown has been a valuable asset to the marketing team at XYZ Corp. this year.

George was the driving force behind our recent sale to LWB. He developed the solution to the customer's needs and very skillfully presented it to upper management. XYZ managers are very aware of George's contribution and have praised him to me on several occasions.

George has also been extremely willing to support the customer. He has come in early and stayed late to help solve problems and is always willing to answer the customer's questions and address any special needs that may arise.

In addition, George is delightful to work with and a cooperative team member.

Sincerely,

John Biggs

Model Letter 13.27

Recognizing Outstanding Performance

Dedication to customer satisfaction is always noteworthy.

Dear Barry:

I want to let you know what an outstanding job Joe Townsend did at a recent installation at Alpen Inc.

Joe put in extraordinary hours. The hardware was a new product and the customer was a new account. Between those two factors it took many hours of very frustrating work to get the equipment running and make the customer happy.

Joe persevered with patience and professionalism, proving an excellent example of our quality program and our dedication to customer satisfaction. The customer even commented that, through all the problems with the hardware, Joe's outstanding technical expertise was apparent.

I am thankful to Joe, and I know you will acknowledge his efforts appropriately.

Should you wish to discuss Joe's performance further or need additional details, please contact me.

Sincerely,

Trish Nelson

MODEL LETTER 13.28

Recognizing Outstanding Technical Support

As much as possible, mention specific contributions that distinguish individuals.

Dear Ted Brown:

All year, Darryl Davidson has been providing excellent technical support to a variety of demanding customers. Our customers respect and admire him. He is an invaluable resource for our organization, and I appreciate having the opportunity to work closely with him.

Sincerely,

Jan Rogers

MODEL LETTER 13.29

Recognizing a Helpful Associate

Team sales efforts warrant recognition of everyone involved.

Dear Sam:

Lisa Sutton continues to be an extremely important asset to me in managing my sales territory. Lisa is conscientious and thorough in her approach to customer-needs studies and technical projects. Her thoroughness has earned her great respect from our customers. Lisa helps us gain their confidence, which in turn helps us attain our sales goals.

Lisa also has an astute marketing sense. She is skillful in choosing the right approach and strategy for each customer, and she is tolerant during the long, challenging sales cycle.

I am delighted to work with Lisa and look forward to our continuing together as a team.

Sincerely,

Roger Briggs

MODEL LETTER 13.30

Recognizing Outstanding Marketing Support

This letter recognizes an individual and compliments a manager.

Dear Gus:

My customers at Adams Enterprises are delighted with our products and service, and I'm writing to let you know that Janet Majors is a major reason we've been this successful. Janet provides outstanding marketing support to me on this and other accounts.

She brings a special combination of desirable traits to the selling process: a high level of technical expertise, poise, and flexibility in dealing with the most challenging situations. She is detail-oriented yet capable of offering insightful strategic vision.

I am proud to have Janet as a colleague. You are building a spectacular marketing support team, and I am most appreciative.

Sincerely,

Bob Carter

MODEL LETTER 13.31

Recognizing Emergency Support— A Note to Management

Immediate follow-up is important after someone helps you resolve a tough situation.

Dear Theresa:

Thank you for allowing me to borrow Steve Cramer last week. Steve flew to Chicago on very short notice to help with the Fountain Head account. He provided excellent technical support at a near marathon pace for about seventy-two hours.

The situation was a tough one technically and emotionally. The customer was highly frustrated by the time Steve arrived. Steve skillfully handled both aspects of the situation and was a tremendous asset to our team.

Thanks again for making Steve available to us during the crisis. Please pass on to Steve how thankful we are for his assistance.

Sincerely,

Dick Armstrong

MODEL LETTER 13.32

Recognizing Emergency Support—
A Note to the Specialist

Of course, it's important to let management know about someone's special effort, but don't forget to thank the employee. Here's a note you might send along with a copy of the note to the boss.

Dear Steve:

I hope you know how much everyone at Fountain Head appreciates the technical support you provided last week.

You truly were grace under pressure. You flew to Chicago on short notice, kept grueling hours, and helped defuse an emotionally charged situation. It was obvious to everyone there that your technical expertise is second to none.

It is reassuring to know people like you are on our team.

Sincerely,

Dick Armstrong

Model Letter 13.33

Recommending a Colleague for a Promotion

The team your company organizes to support the sales effort is critical to your success. That is why you need to call attention to the best efforts of your coworkers when it is time to fill key positions.

Dear Art:

I was surprised to hear that Niles Green is leaving the customer service department. I enjoyed working with him for many years.

Naturally, the news of Niles's departure raises the question of a successor. You face a critical decision in choosing a new customer service manager. The job calls for a very special combination of people and organizational skills. That is why I am recommending Becky Hendriks as our new customer service manager.

Over the past five years, I have come to rely on Becky a great deal. She has made important contributions to my success by helping me resolve numerous difficult situations—remember the Bradley crisis and "D-Day" in Vancouver? As manager of the customer service department, Becky could infuse her staff with her positive outlook and convey that attitude to our customers.

Please give the idea some thought and call me if you want to discuss it.

Sincerely,

Bill Sammons

MODEL LETTER 13.34

Providing a Reference for a Former Colleague

Unfortunately, when one company fails to recognize good employees, they often end up working for competitors. After employees sever ties to your company, you can still show your gratitude in letters of recommendation.

Dear Prospective Employer:

I highly recommend Becky Hendriks as a customer service manager.

From 20XX through 20XX, I relied heavily on Becky's ability to solve problems. She helped save more than one sale and was instrumental in keeping customers satisfied. Becky demonstrated considerable skill at clarifying issues, negotiating with customers to resolve conflicts, and training new personnel. What's more, her positive outlook seemed contagious among her coworkers.

These qualities would make Becky an ideal customer service manager.

Sincerely,

Bill Sammons

Selling Outlook

No Rep Is an Island: Thanking and Recognizing Your Support Organization

We all want to be recognized and appreciated for our contributions—at work and in our personal lives. Knowing that we have performed well and gotten the job done isn't enough; we like the people we respect to tell us they acknowledge our efforts and our good work. Knowing we are appreciated and seeing some reward for our efforts inspires us to give our personal best in future endeavors.

In sales, it is easy to feel alone, to feel as if you bear sole responsibility for accomplishing a sale. Although you bear bottom-line responsibility, in most organizations, many people contribute to a successful partnership with a customer. The list of contributors includes support personnel who help close the sale, administrative staff who help take orders, warehouse workers who ship the product, technicians who install the product, accounting staff who process invoices, and managers who help mitigate problems.

How can you tell these people how much their support means to the organization and to you? Of all the possible ways to express appreciation, letters of recognition to employees and their management can have the most long-lasting benefits. Letters from a satisfied team member can be saved in personnel files as evidence that someone deserves a great evaluation, bonus, or promotion.

These letters also yield benefits to the people who write them. They show you are a team player who can share success with others; they acknowledge the efforts of others in a way that encourages employees to do their best and fosters a healthy work environment in which individual efforts are recognized, appreciated, and rewarded.

Words that Sell

Frequently Asked Questions

Q: When is a sentence too long?
A: Your letters will be more interesting when you vary sentence length. A good average is 20 to 25 words.

Q: Is there an ideal paragraph length?
A: In school, you probably learned to write a topic sentence and continue all related sentences in the same paragraph, regardless of length. In business, you will have a more appealing page if you keep paragraphs between two and seven sentences.

Q: What does *reading* mean?
A: Reading level indices vary in the exact measurements they produce, but the general idea is to relate the number of syllables and words to the number of sentences in your writing. The index number indicates how easy or difficult the work is to read. Many word processing packages have readability index features, and it is a good practice to use them. Try to keep your work at the 11th-grade reading level or less—that's higher than the level of most business magazines.

Q: It's perfectly all right to use quotations in sales letters, isn't it?
A: Not necessarily. Be very careful when quoting someone for commercial purposes. Always ask permission to quote a person in your sales letter or advertising.

Q: Writers today say he, his or her, he/she, or alternate between he and she. What's the best approach to take in a sales letter?
A: Styles vary. We prefer to say he or she, or better yet, to avoid sentence constructions that force you to choose.

Q: Which is correct, *toward* or *towards*?
A: *Toward* is the preferred American spelling. The same is true of *forward* and *backward*.

Q: Which is correct, *helped* close the sale or *helped to* close the sale?
A: Either is acceptable. *Helped to* is the British standard, and *helped* is more common in American English.

Q: Should you say *between you and I* or *between you and me*?
A: Me. Between is a preposition—like for, to, among, before, after—and prepositions always take me (not I), him (not he), her (not she), or us (not we).

Q: When should you use *who,* and when should you use *whom?*
A: The answer is complicated, but briefly, use *who* when someone is doing the action and *whom* when something is done to them. *Who* is coming to the sales presentation? *To whom* did you address the memo?

Q: Which is correct: If I *were* in Memphis, or if I *was* in Memphis?
A: Either. *Were,* in this case, is the subjunctive mood, something that is disappearing from modern English.

Q: Are split infinitives still taboo?
A: No. Many people learned in school that split infinitives, such as *Star Trek*'s famous line "to boldly go," were forbidden in correct English. That view has largely changed, but many former students still look upon the construction as a mistake. For that reason, it's a good idea to use them sparingly.

Q: Which is correct: We *shall* being the meeting at 8:00 A.M., or we *will* begin the meeting at 8:00 A.M.?
A: Most people today would say *will,* and that once-forbidden usage is becoming the norm.

Q: Should you say *a* historical or *an* historical?
A: *A.* When the first syllable of a word sounds like a consonant, use *a.* When the first syllable of a word sounds like a vowel, even if it is a consonant, use *an.*

Q: How can I format letters to look more professional?
A: Technology has given us the ability to change typefaces or add graphics with the click of a mouse. Your sales letters, however, are no place to experiment. Keep them neat by using one primary typeface and size of type, and by limiting the graphics you add to them. A letter should look like a letter. Save the special effects for brochures and advertising.

PART 4
Letters in Cyberspace

Customers Are Just an E-mail Away

To millions of Internet users, a stamped letter entrusted to the post office is snail mail, something slightly more advanced than hieroglyphics and smoke signals but vastly inferior to electronic mail. Internet access and e-mail have become as essential to corporate life as fax machines, PCs, and cell phones for millions of people. And it's easy to understand why.

An e-mail message can traverse continents with the ease of a crosstown phone call. With the click of a mouse, you can announce product news and sales promotions to hundreds of customers. You can attach a proposal to a brief message and collaborate with a project team scattered across the country—and beyond.

A home page on the World Wide Web lets you add graphics, audio, and video files to your message—and potential customers around the globe can access it twenty-four hours a day. The Web lets you save time, money, and grief looking up information about your industry. In fact, letter-writing entrepreneurs on the World Wide Web will write your sales letters, identify lists of qualified prospects, mail the letters, and resolve any disputes or collection problems that result from your mailing. Every day, more companies purchase digital cameras and telecommunications technology to "post" e-mail that includes audio and video messages—just like the Jetsons.

But while many people are perfectly content to communicate online, e-mail and the Internet may take a while to catch on in some industries, and some customers may never feel at ease communicating when a computer is involved. As with so many situations, the sales professional must judge the customer and the circumstances to decide what's appropriate.

For those willing to try the new media, this chapter presents ideas and examples to get you started.

CHAPTER 14 CONTENTS

Finding Profit in Cyberspace

Internet pioneers of the 1970s may lament the commercialization of the World Wide Web, but just about everyone else is celebrating the explosion of opportunity that has followed the Web's debut in the mid-1990s. For some, the Web offers the chance to put up a home page and do business online. For millions more, however, the Web is a communications tool that augments the office; it enables companies to post corporate communications worldwide on private intranets. It lets companies save thousands of dollars on travel expense with videoconferencing instead of face-to-face meetings.

In *The Road Ahead,* Microsoft founder Bill Gates wrote:

> For a large company, the biggest benefit of personal computers comes from improving the sharing of information. PCs do away with the huge overhead large businesses incur staying coordinated through meetings, policies, and internal processes. Electronic mail has done more for big companies than for small companies.

One small company that became a much larger one using e-mail each step of the way is America Online. As AOL's membership rose to 1 million and then far beyond, Chairman and CEO Steve Case used monthly e-mail letters to every member to keep them informed about improvements, milestones, problems, and their solutions, as an extracted example from April 3, 1995, illustrates:

MODEL LETTER 14.1

A Letter from Steve Case, Chairman of the Board, America Online

Dear Members:

I want to start out this month's letter by updating you on some of the progress we've made since my March letter.

As I said last month, providing you with a World Wide Web connection has been one of our top development priorities. We're readying Web browsers for both Windows and Mac. . . .

We continue to invest heavily in increasing network capacity and high-speed access to America Online. Our new AOLnet network is now available in more than fifty cities—and more cities are being added each month. . . .

AOL is now growing by leaps and bounds, so new services are being added every day. To keep up, I recommend that you go to key words NEW and WHATS HOT frequently to stay current on the latest additions. And I'll of course continue to tell you about a handful of services in my monthly letter.

Warm regards,

Steve Case

(Courtesy of America Online. Reprinted with permission.)

Electronic mail and the Internet have the potential to dramatically change many types of selling. In real estate, for instance, computer-savvy agents have learned to draw prospective homebuyers and sellers into their home pages. Homebuyers can enter the area, price range, and amenities they seek and preview as many listings as they care to see. In the travel industry, travelers can make flight arrangements on airline home pages, and several major airlines send weekly e-mail to subscribers interested in last-minute bargains on flights that have not sold out.

Whether or not you are interested in a home page of your own, chances are your company has its own home page, and directly or indirectly through a Web master, customers and prospects can reach you via e-mail. What's more, they can access your name and number, product information, client lists, and much more if you care to cultivate this potential source of leads.

If you haven't already discovered the advantages of e-mail and the Web, consider these examples from one small-business man.

Secrets of Online Sales

Letters 14.2 to 14.16 are from the collection of a Dallas-based sole proprietor who built himself a home page and watched his profits take off. Ron Campbell began collecting e-mail addresses in 1993 when he started posting ads on America Online. That was long before he heard of the World Wide Web—before there even was a Web. By the time he debuted his home page in 1996, he had compiled a long list of customers and prospects. The letters that follow are adaptations of e-mail messages sent from Campbell's new sales office in Cyberspace.

(The following letters are courtesy of Ron Campbell, Dallas, Texas.)

MODEL LETTER 14.2

Announcing That
You're Open for Business Online

Staying in touch with customers online is easy and inexpensive.

Hello again! As promised, we now have Artcraft's Web page up and running. Now you can review our catalogs online, ask questions, check prices, and quickly locate specific label sizes.

Artcraft offers a broad assortment of papers and labels for your needs year-round. Visit our Home Page at http://www.CompuForms.com.

We always look forward to supporting our many friends on AOL.

Regards,

Ron Campbell

MODEL LETTER 14.3

Prospecting Online—
A Sample Online Bulletin Board Posting

One way to approach customers is to offer ideas for using your products.

Create your own custom-designed business cards. It's fun and easy! Just e-mail me a request for "Detailed Business Card Instructions." I'll send you a step-by-step guide for formatting attractive business cards in any of these popular software programs:

Ami Pro™
Word™ for Windows
WordPerfect™
Microsoft Publisher™
PageMaker™

Most other software uses commands similar to those for these programs.

Artcraft offers over 30 different colorful background designs for business cards and matching stationery. We've priced our business cards at $X.XX for 25 sheets (250 cards). Ask for a free catalog.

Artcraft specializes in all standard and unique paper products for use in all types of computer printers. Please give us a call if you need custom forms or have special requirements.

Model Letter 14.4

Responding to an E-mail Inquiry with Samples

E-mail can help you cut your response time.

> Thank you for your interest in our labels. Today I am sending you samples of VHS Tape Labels (Spine, Face, and Sets) for evaluation in your printer. These labels are $XX.XX for 100 sheets or $XX.XX for 250 sheets.
>
> We offer larger price discounts for larger quantities.
>
> You will soon be receiving the catalog you requested on e-mail. The catalog shows hundreds of unique and standard items, all of them 100 percent guaranteed.
>
> Contact us with any questions you may have. We'll respond promptly by e-mail or fax.

Model Letter 14.5

Thanks for Your Prompt Payment

Customers appreciate a thank you, and with e-mail, sending one promptly is almost effortless.

> Thanks for your recent order and prompt payment. We have added many new laser and pinfeed labels and cards and a selection of ink-jet labels. You'll find a complete catalog and price list on our home page, or call us at 972-555-7292.

MODEL LETTER 14.6

Confirmation of Your Order and E-mail Attachment

Thanks to your e-mail messages, customers can know the status of their orders at any given time.

Your label order will ship Monday morning, and you should have it in hand by Wednesday.

A few days after you receive the labels, you will receive an invoice by mail for payment and recordkeeping. I have attached a file that almost any word processor can read. The file lists our large selection of laser and inkjet labels, cards, and unique stationery. Prices listed are good through 20XX.

Visit Artcraft online at http://www.CompuForms.com.

Thank you for your order and for using e-mail.

MODEL LETTER 14.7

A Christmastime Promotion on an AOL Bulletin Board

Ron Campbell includes a tip for online viewing: Try expanding the screen or print the file for easy viewing.

Beautiful, colorful Christmas paper and labels for your Christmas For INKJET, PINFEED & LASER Printers

Artcraft's high-quality stationery is available in both religious and secular designs—thirty in all—to delight everyone on your list. Select a pattern and add your season's greeting.

Your holiday greetings and packages will be even more attractive with our labels. Choose one of our vivid designs, then simply add your addresses and print on your own laser, pinfeed, or inkjet printer.

Order a free catalog now, and be ready for the holidays.

Artcraft offers a broad assortment of papers and labels for your needs year-round. Our products are guaranteed, and we deliver almost anywhere in the United States in approximately three days.

We accept e-mail orders and mail invoices for payment and recordkeeping.

Ron Campbell,

Online to answer your questions

MODEL LETTER 14.8

Faxing a Thank You That Confirms the Order

Messages can be warm and personal—even on the Internet.

Fax to: The Wireless Ones
Attn: Jill Mann
From: ARTCRAFT COMPUTER FORMS, Dallas, Texas
Name: Ron Campbell
Date: Tuesday, December 03, 20XX
Total Pages: 1

Good morning, Jill.

The phone company changed our area code, so we are now using
972-555-9377 for both phone and fax.

Your label order (6 boxes M2–xyz) will ship first thing Wednesday
morning. You should have them by Thursday.

Visit us on the Web at http://www.CompuForms.com.

Thanks for your order.

Regards,

Ron Campbell

Thanks for Your Interest in Our Company

Immediate follow-up can turn casual Web surfers into loyal customers.

Brad,

Thank you very much for your interest in Artcraft Computer Forms Corp. Artcraft is a sales company that specializes in all paper products that feed through computer printers. We buy our inventory from manufacturers and sell it nationwide. Our specialty is being able to keep up with new products. We sell the entire range of paper products for laser, pinfeed, thermal, and inkjet printers. You'll find a catalog and price list on our home page, http.www.CompuForms.com.

Updating a Customer about Your Products

Customers who enjoy your products will appreciate news about upgrades.

Dear RKH@xxxx:

Recently you inquired about our products for computer printers. Since my last message to you, we have added inkjet labels and many new laser items. Many of the items in our line can be hard to find locally.

I have attached a text file that lists a large selection of products, along with our 19XX prices.

To access our catalog listing, simply press "Download File" and select the directory where you wish to store the file. The directory C:\aol30\Download is often preferred. The download time is less than ten seconds (only 13,021 bytes). It is very easy.

Thank you for using e-mail. Visit Artcraft often on the World Wide Web.

Thank You for Your Interest

The response you send one customer provides the basis of a new e-mail message to adapt for the next customer.

Thank you for your interest in our laser labels.

I have attached a text file that lists the labels and cards we offer. Artcraft ships your order on the first business day after we receive it.

When ordering, please specify your name, street address, quantity, description, phone or fax number, e-mail address, and purchase order number.

All correspondence with Artcraft can be expedited by using fax or e-mail. We also accept verbal orders on messages and orders by mail.

New orders are confirmed by return fax, e-mail, or phone message.

A few days after you receive your order, you will receive an invoice by mail for payment and recordkeeping. Payment is to be by check only. We do not ship COD or accept credit cards at this time.

Please contact me if you have any questions. I look forward to working with you.

Model Letter 14.12

"Personal Achievement Is In"

Give customers ideas for using your products—people love to *experiment*.

Personal achievement is in, and our impressive award certificates are the perfect way to recognize accomplishments, boost morale, and encourage effort. And they're affordable.

Quality paper, intricate detail, and attractive accessories result in a look and feel as outstanding as the performance they recognize. These patterns are widely used by offices, schools, social organizations, and corporations.

You can make them even more distinctive with our crowning touches—frames, foil seals, and colorful ribbons.

Make a lasting impression with these high-quality certificates!

Subtle and appealing, certificates will make a positive statement about your teams, students, employees, company, or product warranties!

Contact me by e-mail, and I will send you a full-color catalog and price list.

Regards,

Ron Campbell

MODEL LETTER 14.13

"What Do You Think of Our Samples?"

Be careful about offering samples on the Internet—you may not be prepared for the response!

Dear Geoff@xxxx:

Thank you for your interest in our checks. Today I am sending you samples of check forms (in blue, three up) to test in your printer. These checks are: $XX.XX for 300 and $XX.XX for 600. Many other sizes and formats are also available.

You will soon be receiving the catalog you requested on e-mail. It shows hundreds of unique and standard items.

Send me any questions you may have when you receive this material. I'll respond promptly by e-mail or fax.

MODEL LETTER 14.14

Answering a Technical Question

One typical feature of Internet sites is a "frequently asked questions" category. The same concept works for electronically generated letters and messages. If you receive this sort of technical question once, you would certainly want to save the answer and use it again when the opportunity arose.

Q. What is the difference between laser and inkjet labels?

A. The major difference between laser and inkjet labels is a coating that is applied to the inkjet labels to keep the ink from wicking into the paper. (The present coating cannot be applied to laser labels because it interferes with the toner bonding). If it wicks, it can cause the graphics or words to be slightly rough along the edge. Of course, nothing is simple concerning this subject, and precise answers are difficult because the roughness also depends on the type of ink, amount of ink, and make of the printer.

There are only a few sizes available in the inkjet labels; most folks use laser labels. There are a few who tell me they absolutely must have inkjet. Others say laser labels work great. Who knows?

Soon there will be coatings that work both for laser and inkjet. Artcraft's unique papers and cards work well in both types of printers.

I hope this answers some of your questions.

Model Letter 14.15

E-mail Instructions for Using a Product

Customers appreciate the rapid responses that e-mail makes possible.

Making labels using word processing software is easy. For instance, in MS Word™ simply select "tools" on the tool bar, "envelopes & labels," then "labels tab." You can then select the specific label template for the size you need.

Word™ lists the Avery™ part numbers (visit our home page for label sizes and prices) for most laser labels. You can view the label sizes in the right-hand corner of the screen. You can also make custom sizes if you wish.

Next click OK to return to the "envelope and labels" window. Select "new document," and the label template for the label you selected will appear. Then simply type in your text using normal Word™ procedures. You can add graphics, change fonts, bold, underline, etc., after you finish the first label layout. You can copy and paste to the rest of the label positions. You can also import mailing lists, etc. To print, follow regular print procedures. Save just as you normally would. Have fun!

Model Letter 14.16

Getting Past the First Order
for Repeat Business

Cyberspace may seem impersonal to some, but it is possible to build a huge following of loyal online customers.

By now you should have received the catalogs and samples you requested recently. What do you think of our selection and prices?

Artcraft offers many unique products that are not included in our catalog, and the samples we sent you are a small representation of our product line.

In general, our prices are lower than our competition, and we don't pad the shipping bill with handling charges—you pay exactly what we're billed for freight.

We can answer your questions quickly using e-mail, so please send me any questions you might have concerning our products.

Visit us again soon on the World Wide Web.

Selling Outlook
Letter-Writing Resources
on the World Wide Web

The Internet puts more resources at your fingertips than would have filled city libraries only a decade or two ago. Reference books, grammar hotlines, professional organizations—the world—are just a few keystrokes away. The trick is to learn how to use this tool efficiently to enhance your selling and writing abilities.

For instance, a fear of making a grammatical mistake inhibits many otherwise prolific letter writers. On the Internet, however, you can type a specific question into a search engine and search the world for an answer. Chances are, though, you won't need to venture far. Newsgroups and university faculties have been piling up answers for years—just hoping you would ask.

But perhaps you're weary of writing you own letters. Search engines on the World Wide Web will lead you to professionals who will do the writing for you. You'll find everything from Mom & Pop shops to full-service public relations agencies.

Some search engines to get you started:

- www.webmaster.com
- www.infoseek.com
- www.yahoo.com

And some key words to start your search:

- sales letters
- professional selling
- letter writing

Although offerings on the Web change every day, these are some examples of what you could find a short time ago:

- "How to write letters the easy way . . . 25 proven, do-it-yourself marketing letters"
  — http://www.netm.com/mall/infoprod/jojarra/jojarra/1.htm
- "Never again waste valuable time creating business letters from scratch"
  — http://www.letterworks.com/BusinessLetterWorks.html
- "Differences between literary and business English"
  — http://www.smartbizaa.com/sbs/arts/pbw2.htm

Or maybe the whole sales process has you wiped out and inspiration is what you need. Visit "the man they call Mister Fire!"—Joe Vitale—at http://www.speaking.com/vitale.html.

Improving Internal Communication with the New Media

The same technology that has ignited so much enthusiasm for home pages and Web-surfing has found its way into the workplace in the form of intranets and e-mail systems. E-mail has been available in many firms for years, and it enables workers to communicate easily and rapidly with one another and with the outside world. It provides a quick way to get information to one or a number of people at one time, regardless of location. It bridges time zones with near instantaneous timing. E-mail is especially appropriate in team selling, when a number of people need to be in the loop about account activities and strategies. In the event of a conflict, or differing point of view, e-mail eliminates emotions and keeps issues focused on facts and events.

A much more recent development are intranets, limited-access versions of a home page that are typically designed for the employees of a large company. They require effort and maintenance from a corporate standpoint but, if utilized, can be an online library of information about products, competitors, employees, and the organization. Intranets that are strictly internal to the company, and this can provide forums for the sharing of problems and competitive strategies—safe from public scrutiny. This chapter explores how sales representatives can use e-mail for productivity-enhancing communication. The "Selling Outlook" presents ideas for using an intranet to enhance communication among the sales and force and various departments of an organization.

CHAPTER 15. CONTENTS

Messages to Support Teamwork

MODEL LETTER 15.1

Thanking Your Team for Helping You
Win the Account

Whether your sales support team includes three members, thirty, or more, e-mail software lets you create a distribution list so that addressing messages to each person takes no more than a second. Messages that list everyone's name at the top help recipients see themselves as a team, too.

> To: The #1 Team
> From: Pat Meyers
> Subject: We Got the Phoenix Account!
> Date: 1/15/XX
>
> I want you to be the first to know: we just signed contracts in Phoenix for this agency's biggest new account in two years. It was thrilling to hear Joe Biggs say yes, but I know it wouldn't have happened without contributions from each of you. The client repeatedly mentioned the quality of our mockups, written documents, presentations, and people skills. Thank you so much for your support. It's great to work in such a class organization.

MODEL LETTER 15.2

"We'll Do Better Next Time—
I Appreciate Your Efforts"

The recognition you give for one effort can be the catalyst for your next success.

To: The #1 Team
From: Pat Meyers
Subject: I Appreciate Your Efforts
Date: 1/15/XX

The Tucson prospect looks like a "no-go" for now. I am disappointed, as I know you all will be. Everyone worked hard for this business, and I appreciate your efforts. The client was impressed with our proposal, but Software, Inc., won the day with more attractive price points. I will distribute a report on SI's approach when I get back to the office. I know we can beat these guys if we put our heads together to improve our strategy.

MODEL LETTER 15.3

A Plan to Move Forward During the Sale

The energy you convey in messages can be catching.

To: [Distribution List A]
From: Pat Meyers
Subject: Two More Requests from Corporation Z
Date: 3/5/XX

The folks at Corporation Z are very interested in the package we put together. In our meeting this morning, they asked to see mock-ups for point-of-purchase displays. They also asked for new pricing based on volume twice the amounts we proposed.

I know Cynthia and Larry can take care of these requests with no problem. Would you all get to work on them right away? I'll call you tomorrow.

Let's plan to meet when I'm back in the office Friday. I appreciate the hard work of everyone on this team. We can't slack off now because I know we can get this business with a little extra effort.

MODEL LETTER 15.4

Moving Forward After the Sale

E-mail helps you keep your team focused, even when you are miles from the office.

> To: [Distribution Lists A & B]
> From: Pat Meyers
> Subject: Work on the Corporation Z Account
> Date: 4/5/XX
>
> We did it! We beat TOG Corp. and won the Corporation Z account. Now the real work begins.
>
> We have several items to discuss that will require coordination of the entire team. Is everyone available for a video conference on the 15th? Denise, please make the arrangements. I need at least one representative from Marketing, Sales Support, Distribution, and Purchasing. Let Denise know if the 15th works.
>
> Corporation Z has asked us to put together an aggressive marketing plan that will require good communication and organization from all of us. I'll send you the details before the 15th.

MODEL LETTER 15.5

Recovering from a Setback

Your efforts to keep everyone informed help unify people in different departments.

> To: [Distribution List A]
> From: Pat Meyers
> Subject: Need Revisions on Tyler Proposal?
> Date: 4/4/XX
>
> I need all of you to put your heads together to help solve a problem on the Tyler proposal. The client has changed the specifications to move the delivery date up six weeks. This is a challenging request, but one I think we can accommodate if we approach it creatively. What do you think?
>
> I return to the office in a week, and I will need to give the client our response the following Wednesday. In the meantime, please keep me posted on your progress in revising our proposal.
>
> This account will mean a lot to our company, so I'm counting on each of you!

MODEL LETTER 15.6

Passing Along a Compliment from a Client

Don't let your colleagues hear good news second-hand! Send an e-mail that keeps everyone in the loop.

> To: The Best Sales Support Team Ever
> From: Pat Meyers
> Subject: A Happy Client in Tyler
> Date: 5/5/XX
>
> Congratulations! You all really came through for the client, our company, and me. The Tyler product managers were elated with your work and more than happy to sign a five-year contract with us. As one of them put it, "We've been marketing this product for fifteen years and never had half the ideas your company has given us in just three months. You have to be our partner now—you know too much about us!"

MODEL LETTER 15.7

Thanking Colleagues for Their Work on Your Behalf

Your constant positive reinforcement can keep your team motivated.

> To: [Distribution List B]
> From: Pat Meyers
> Subject: Thank You
> Date: 5/6/XX
>
> In just one more week, we will make the proposal to the Game Time Company. Don't think I haven't noticed your long hours and hard work to get the job done.
>
> Over the years, you have proved I can count on efforts like this one. Just know that I don't take it for granted. You are a team of dedicated, committed individuals who give this firm a tremendous competitive edge. Thank you.

Model Letter 15.8

Expressing Concern and Encouraging
Greater Progress

Coworkers will be more receptive to bad news when you have established open communication that includes good—as well as occasional bad—news.

> To: [Distribution List C]
> From: Pat Meyers
> Subject: Progress on the Game Time Company Account
> Date: 6/2/XX
>
> In just one more week we will make the proposal to the Game Time Company. I am concerned about our progress. Let's meet Tuesday morning for a status report from each department.
>
> You know how much I count on each of you to give 100 percent to help us win and keep accounts. We still have time to put together a winning proposal for Game Time, but it will take focus and commitment from everyone. I know you'll come through for me.

Reporting Milestone Events to Team Members

Printouts of your messages help coworkers document their contributions and can mean better performance appraisals for your team.

To: [Distribution Lists A & B]
From: Pat Meyers
Subject: We Made the Cut at Game Time
Date: 4/30/XX

Just a brief update on the Game Time proposal: we made the first cut! Of ten competitors vying for the account, three will continue as candidates for the business. In addition to us, the two other firms still in the running are TOG, Inc., and Mayberry Associates. We beat out Big League Advertising, XYZ, and five other agencies. Keep up the good work!

Soliciting Feedback After Project Completion

It is important to ask your team for ideas.

To: [Distribution Lists A & B]
From: Pat Meyers
Subject: We Can Do Better
Date: 5/15/XX

We did it. We got the Game Time business. But you and I know it wasn't exactly smooth sailing to a happy close. In the interest of refining our approach to developing sales proposals, I would like your views about how we contact prospects, our distribution of work, and any processes that need attention.

I know we accomplish great things here, and if we put our heads together we can do even more.

Reminders for
Sales Support Departments

Many messages you send by e-mail could be handled by phone. The advantage of e-mail in many sales situations is the precise, written record the software automatically generates.

MODEL LETTER 15.11

"Is It All Systems Go?"

To: T. J. Turner, Technical Support Manager
From: Tom Love, Sales Representative
Subject: Is It All Systems Go on the Bloomington Account?
Date: 7/8/XX

Just three more days until we meet in Bloomington for the installation. How does everything look? If there are any problems, such as any deliveries yet to come in, I'd like a heads-up. I will be talking to the client tomorrow and would like to give my assurances that everything is in place.

MODEL LETTER 15.12

Asking for a Copy of the Service Report on Your Account

Faxing may be helpful, but you could also attach a document to your e-mail and eliminate the need for a fax.

To: T. J. Turner, Technical Support Manager
From: Tom Love, Sales Representative
Subject: Bloomington Service Call
Date: 7/8/02

T. J.:

In case any questions come up later, would you fax me a copy of the Service Call Report from your department's June 30 call in Bloomington? I stay in close contact with several managers there and need as much information as possible about how the operation is running and how our products are performing.

Thanks for your help.

Tom

MODEL LETTER 15.13

Confirming a Meeting with the Client

Even people who avoid your phone calls will have a hard time escaping e-mail.

To: T. J. Turner, Technical Support Manager
From: Tom Love, Sales Representative
Subject: July 15 Meeting
Date: 7/13/XX

Please confirm that you will be present for the July 15 meeting at the Bloomington account. I've attached an agenda. As you can see, several service and performance issues will be on the table, and your attendance is crucial.

MODEL LETTER 15.14

Reporting a Problem to the Service Department

E-mail can help you resolve your customers' problems without delays.

To: T. J. Turner, Technical Support Manager
From: Tom Love, Sales Representative
Subject: Bloomington Is Still Having Product Failures
Date: 7/1/02

Mike Campbell called me last week to express his frustration with our efforts to correct the timing problem they are experiencing with our equipment. Generally, Mike likes our system and wants to continue with it, but that could change if we do not resolve his problems soon. Are we doing everything we can? What about calling in a specialist? Our ability to respond quickly could mean the future of our business.

MODEL LETTER 15.15

Complaining to the Service Manager

As problems become more pressing, you would probably follow up this e-mail message with a phone call.

> To: T. J. Turner, Technical Support Manager
> From: Tom Love, Sales Representative
> Subject: Problems on the Bloomington Account
> Date: 7/30/02
>
> T. J.:
>
> We must overcome the problems at Bloomington immediately. The account records reflect six service calls in the past nine months, yet the client still is not satisfied with our product service and performance. Bloomington has requested a meeting to discuss these problems with our top management, you, and me. I know this seems like we're on the hot seat, but we can solve these problems if we muster the resources available to us. Let's talk in person before the end of the day.
>
> Tom

MODEL LETTER 15.16

Passing Along the Client's Feedback

It is especially important to pass along good news when there have been problems in the past.

> To: T. J. Turner, Technical Support Manager
> From: Tom Love, Sales Representative
> Subject: Brittany Manager Pleased with Our Service
> Date: 7/30/02
>
> T. J.:
>
> I want to pass along some feedback from Brittany, Inc. Marcy Taylor, a manager there, said your service technicians have shown noticeable improvement over the past eighteen months. She is very pleased with our service and said it will weigh heavily in her recommendation to renew our contract next month. Keep up the good work!
>
> Tom

———————

MODEL LETTER 15.17

Asking for a Meeting During
Your Next Visit to the Home Office

E-mail helps you manage time and work efficiently.

> To: T. J. Turner, Technical Support Manager
> From: Tom Love, Sales Representative
> Subject: Request to Meet During the Week of 4/6/XX
> Date: 3/30/XX
>
> Let's meet when I'm in the home office the week of April 6. Your department has made several important improvements over the past few months, and I want to make sure I understand them thoroughly so I can use them to our advantage with clients. I look forward to seeing you.

MODEL LETTER 15.18

"My Travel Arrangements for the January Sales Meeting Are . . ."

If the printed version of an important e-mail is lost, it can be printed again—unlike faxes or posted letters.

To: Julia Cox
From: Elizabeth Brown
Subject: January Sales Meeting
Date: 12/6/XX

My travel arrangements for the January sales meeting are as follows:

Arrive In the Sky Flight 250, 9:00 A.M., 1/3/2000.
Depart In the Sky Flight 251, 11:00 A.M., 1/8/2000.

I can't wait to see everyone from the head office. Have a great holiday!

MODEL LETTER 15.19

Verifying Your Commission

Because e-mail is fast, responses to your questions may be fast as well.

To: Steve Blair, Commission Accounting
From: Elizabeth Brown
Subject: December Commission Check
Date: 12/6/XX

Steve:

Would you verify my December commission? Something seems amiss. I was expecting the check to include my commission for the Chenango account. My records confirm that I submitted all necessary paperwork by the November 1 deadline. Please let me know what happened.

Elizabeth

Model Letter 15.20

Reporting a Change in a Client's Profile

Chances of mistakes are minimized when someone copies account information from your e-mail rather than rekeying it.

> To: Lee Rogers
> From: Elizabeth Brown
> Subject: Revised Client Profile at Chili to Go
> Date: 12/6/XX
>
> Please update the client profile files at corporate to reflect a new product manager at Chili to Go. Bryan Simms replaces Rick Thomas. Bryan's phone number is 404-555-6677. Thanks!

Model Letter 15.21

Ordering Supplies by E-mail

E-mail helps you take care of routine tasks without procrastination.

> To: Lee Rogers
> From: Elizabeth Brown
> Subject: Supplies
> Date: 8/9/XX
>
> Please send me five additional sample kits A & B. The kits may be billed to Department 543. My inventory is rapidly getting depleted!

MODEL LETTER 15.22

Thanking the Staff for Their Help

Immediate follow-up with a warm message can add to your colleagues' enjoyment of a special achievement.

To: Julia, Steve, and Lee
From: Elizabeth Brown
Subject: The January Sales Meeting
Date: 1/9/XX

The January sales meeting was the best ever, and I know it was because of the work each of you contributed. Your creativity, organization, and attention to the smallest detail helped make the meeting more useful for everyone on the sales team. Thank you!

MODEL LETTER 15.23

Sending Files to Update the Intranet

The "Selling Outlook" at the end of this chapter presents ideas for using the company intranet to the sales staff's advantage. As this message implies, an intranet site is a good place to give reps recognition by allowing them to post tips and tales about their experiences.

To: Bob, the Web Master
From: Elizabeth Brown
Subject: Intranet Update
Date: 5/6/XX

Bob:

My sales manager told me last week that you wanted "war stories" from the field to add to the intranet sales home page. Well, here's one for you. I've attached a file explaining how my manager and I pulled an almost-lost account back into the fold after several setbacks that, at least in hindsight, are a bit humorous. Hope you can use it.

Elizabeth

Using E-mail on the Road

It's 2:00 A.M. and you can't asleep. You're in a hotel room 250 miles from home, nervous about your first call in the morning. Is there something you forgot? Did something happen since you left town? Put your mind at ease by sending an e-mail to someone in the home office. Depending on the time zones involved, you may have your answer by the time you wake up.

MODEL LETTER 15.24

Verifying the Feasibility of the Client's Technical Request

Because e-mail is written, it may help prevent confusion about highly technical points that can be misunderstood in a phone call.

> To: T. J. Turner, Technical Support Manager
> From: Tom Love, Sales Representative
> Subject: Request from Atlanta, Inc., to Integrate Systems A and D
> Date: 7/30/02
>
> T. J.:
>
> A team of engineers here at Atlanta, Inc., is interested in integrating our Systems A and D in a client-server configuration. I am not aware of any installation that uses this combination. Is it feasible?
>
> I will visit this account again tomorrow and could pass along any information you have. Thanks for your help.
>
> Tom

MODEL LETTER 15.25

Verifying Product Availability

E-mail helps you stay productive after regular business hours.

> To: Dan Merk
> From: Pat Meyers
> Subject: Availability of 250 Cases of Unit B
> Date: 1/9/XX
>
> My contacts at Georgia Enterprises want to take delivery of 250
> cases of Unit B no later than March 1. How does your inventory
> look? Will this request be a problem? I would appreciate receiving
> your answer before my 2:00 P.M. appointment with Georgia Enter-
> prises tomorrow. Thanks.

MODEL LETTER 15.26

Asking for the Latest Product Release Date

By helping you stay in touch with the home office, e-mail helps you give better
information to customers.

> To: Lynn Roberts, Marketing Manager
> From: Pat Meyers, Sales Representative
> Subject: What's the Latest Product Release Date on Unit C?
> Date: 5/6/XX
>
> Lynn:
>
> Before I call on my Boston accounts next Wednesday, I need to
> verify that nothing has changed on the product release date for Unit
> C. We are still set for June 1, right? I'll be hard to catch by phone,
> so please reply by e-mail as soon as you can. Thanks.
>
> Pat

MODEL LETTER 15.27

Getting an Updated Status Report
on Your Customer's Project

You don't want surprises when you walk into a customer's office. Use e-mail to stay informed.

> To: Michael Allen
> From: Lee McKnight
> Subject: Request for an Update on the Vickers Account
> Date: 2/14/XX
>
> Has anything changed on the Vickers account since I left the office Friday? At 9:00 A.M. (Central time), I will call on several Vickers managers, and I am sure they will ask about the Sunshine Project. Please check with Larry in Marketing and Lynn in Service, then send me a message. I'll check my e-mail at 8:30 A.M.
>
> Thanks for your help.

MODEL LETTER 15.28

Asking Legal to Send a New Contract
Based on the Client's Changes

Sometimes a handwritten modification is all you need to give a client the desired contract terms and close a sale. Other situations may require approval from your corporate legal experts, and that's where e-mail can help.

Contracts can be ready to sign almost immediately when you and the legal staff exchange e-mail messages with revised contracts attached. Of course, phone calls work in some situations, but with e-mail you can exchange document files and print them as necessary. It beats waiting for snail mail, overnight delivery services, and even faxes.

To: Laura Mills
From: Michael Allen
Subject: Davis Contract Terms
Date: 5/5/XX

I hope to close the Davis sale this afternoon, but first I need Legal's approval of the revised contract terms the client is requesting. Please look at the Product Specification and Configuration sections of the attached contract. I have modified the terms to comply with the wishes of Davis's project manager, L. P. Roberts. I explained to the client that these terms were subject to your review, and I have made no verbal assurances of any kind.

Please leave me a phone message when you have reached a decision about these terms. If you have any questions, you can reach me at 972-555-3030.

MODEL LETTER 15.29

Confirming Technical Support for a Sales Presentation

An e-mail message from you can help ensure that all the elements come together for a successful meeting.

> To: Pat Lee, Manager, Sales Support
>   Brad Wyatt, Technical Specialist
> From: Linda Simms
> Subject: Request for Confirmation of Technical Support for the
>   May 8 Brinkley Meeting
> Date: April 25, 19XX

Please confirm Brad's availability for the Brinkley meeting May 8. The meeting will begin at 8:30 A.M. in San Diego's Park City Plaza. Brinkley has requested a review of our System 707 model and the service options available with it.

MODEL LETTER 15.30

Staying in Touch with Reps in Another City During Joint Projects

As cross-country sales efforts become more complex and involve growing numbers of people, e-mail becomes essential to keeping things organized.

To: Pat Meyers
From: Mike Thomas, Oklahoma Sales Representative
Subject: Georgia Enterprises' Oklahoma Affiliate
Date: 3/15/XX

Pat:

I learned from one of my accounts that you are working with Georgia Enterprises on their possible installation of System 515. You may not be aware that Georgia's Oklahoma affiliate, OK Enterprises, is also looking at the system. Perhaps we can coordinate our efforts and come up with a more attractive proposal. Let me know what you think. Thanks.

Mike

MODEL LETTER 15.31

Explaining Where to Forward Your E-mail

The forward and reply features in e-mail software are making the term "duplicate copies" obsolete. When necessary, someone in the home office can forward a sales rep's messages to a city halfway around the world, and the rep can reply with equal ease. (Not that you want to spend your vacation answering e-mail!)

> To: Barry Long, Sales Assistant
> From: Elizabeth Brown
> Subject: Please Forward My E-mail Next Week
> Date: April 9, 19XX

> I'll be on vacation next week, but I want to receive my e-mail messages on my home computer. Please check my e-mail every afternoon and forward everything to elizabeth@not.really.

MODEL LETTER 15.32

An E-mail Model for Your Monthly Mileage Report

The more routine tasks you automate, the more time you can devote to selling. This message shows a simple model for a routine report. For more complex reports, templates from a spreadsheet or word processing package can be attached to an e-mail message and submitted electronically to the home office.

> To: Ed Reeves, Sales Manager
> From: Pat Meyers, Sales Representative
> Subject: Monthly Mileage Report
> Date: June 30, 19XX

> *Start, June 1, 19XX:* 27, 543 miles
> *End, June 1, 19XX:* 30,005 miles
> *Gasoline purchased:* 60 gallons @ $72.56
> (See corporate card expenses for June for receipts on 6/1, 6/7, 6/11, 6/15, 6/19, and 6/28.)

MODEL LETTER 15.33

E-mailing Your Weekly Expense Report

Depending on company policy, you may need to back up the computerized reports with receipts or other documentation.

> To: Ed Reeves, Sales Manager
> From: Pat Meyers, Sales Representative
> Subject: Expense Report for Week of April 1 Attached
> Date: 4/7/XX
>
> My April 1–7, 19XX, expense report is attached. I'm mailing hotel and dinner receipts to Steve Blair for his files.

MODEL LETTER 15.34

Filing the Sales Call Report

Information you learn on a sales call may have immediate importance for others in your organization. By writing your call reports on a modem-equipped laptop, you can distribute them quickly and as widely as necessary.

> To: Ed Reeves, Sales Manager
> Mike Thomas, Oklahoma Sales Representative
> Laura Rogers, Marketing Manager
> From: Pat Meyers, Sales Representative
> Subject: Call Report, Georgia Enterprises, 4/6/XX
> Date: 4/7/XX
>
> Please see the attached call report from my visit yesterday to Georgia Enterprises. Mike and Laura need to be aware of the changes in promotion points and coordination with Georgia's Oklahoma affiliate. Let me know what you think. Thanks.

MODEL LETTER 15.35

Using E-mail for a Memo of Record

Information a rep gathers that is valuable but not immediately useful can be filed as a memo of record. In the e-mail example below, the rep instructs a sales assistant to add the information to the client's file at the home office.

> To: Barry Long
> From: Pat Meyers
> Subject: Memo of Record for Atlanta, Inc.
> Date: 6/5/XX
>
> Please add a hard copy of this message to the Atlanta, Inc., file.
>
> The president of Atlanta, Inc., announced June 1 that she will be retiring in two years. The company is forming a search committee to recommend a replacement.
>
> This announcement will have no immediate impact on the projects we have under way. But the change in leadership could affect the account as the time for the transition nears.
>
> If we know of any candidates for this position, we should find a way to make that introduction at the appropriate level.

Selling Outlook
Using an Intranet to Build Rapport and Enhance Productivity

Both e-mail and internal home pages can facilitate rapid, effective communication among employees, and they present a challenge of their own. "Communicating via computer forces us all to be better writers. We really have to be careful to be clear because words and documents that appear on a screen are subject to misinterpretation. Don't just assume that by posting a document everyone will interpret it the same way you do," cautions June Ramos, a management training consultant from Colorado Springs–based Zoe, Inc.

E-mail creates an emotional distance, which can help defuse tension when problems arise. Written messages remove the emotion our voices sometimes convey in conversations, plus printed messages serve as permanent records of events.

And e-mail can be especially effective in reducing phone tag that occurs in large organizations when numerous people across multiple time zones need to communicate information quickly.

Intranets, the employee-only version of a company's home page, can be a convenient place to post information needed quickly or that can serve as a reference for an extended period. For example, reps may find it helpful to have 24-hour access to this information:

- A "whom to call" list for the home office
- Detailed information about the company, its products, manufacturing facilities—anything that could provide the rep useful information about the company and its products with clients
- Names, phone numbers, and e-mail addresses for the sales staff
- A catalog of sales incentive premiums for the year
- Online information about the commission and bonus structures
- Complete, downloadable files for all routine sales communication forms
- Online copies of company newsletters

Words That Sell
Tips for Computerized Correspondence

Anyone who has slumped over a manual typewriter, bottle of Liquid Paper™ in hand, trying to perfect an important document, can appreciate a good computer. In the past fifteen years, many executive assistant jobs have given way to office-suite software, leaving most of us to navigate spreadsheets, presentations graphics, and word processing packages on our own.

Technology has relieved the tedium of typesetting, writing, and calculating, only to replace it with new challenges. The tips that follow present some ideas for coping with technological innovation.

Know the limits of the technology. Spell checkers are wonderful but not fool-proof. You still need to proofread your work.

Not too fast. Computers make it easy to zip off letters and e-mail messages quickly, but we are as error-prone as ever. Don't get in too big a hurry.

Remember typesetters. The vanishing craftsmen who for years—before word processing software and scanners—rekeyed newspaper articles, books, and all things printed can teach a valuable lesson. Typesetters paired up to find typos. They read articles aloud to one another and sought out "new pairs of eyes" to help make copy as error-free as possible. Their legacy is one of teamwork. The more we share with one another, the better our individual efforts can be. We all benefit from feedback from our peers.

Develop computer skills. We each have our own comfort level with technology, although just being in an office today requires a degree of computer skills. Still, some of us will stretch far beyond the basics. Others will find an intermediate level of competence, and still others will stay in the hunt-and-peck ranks. We don't all aspire to be Thunder Lizards, but we can all benefit from digital correspondence.

Tidy up now and then. Try to have no more than one copy of a file on your hard drive. Back it up on another drive or floppy disk.

Archive big projects. Keep copies of major proposals or presentations. It makes life easier the next time around.

Index

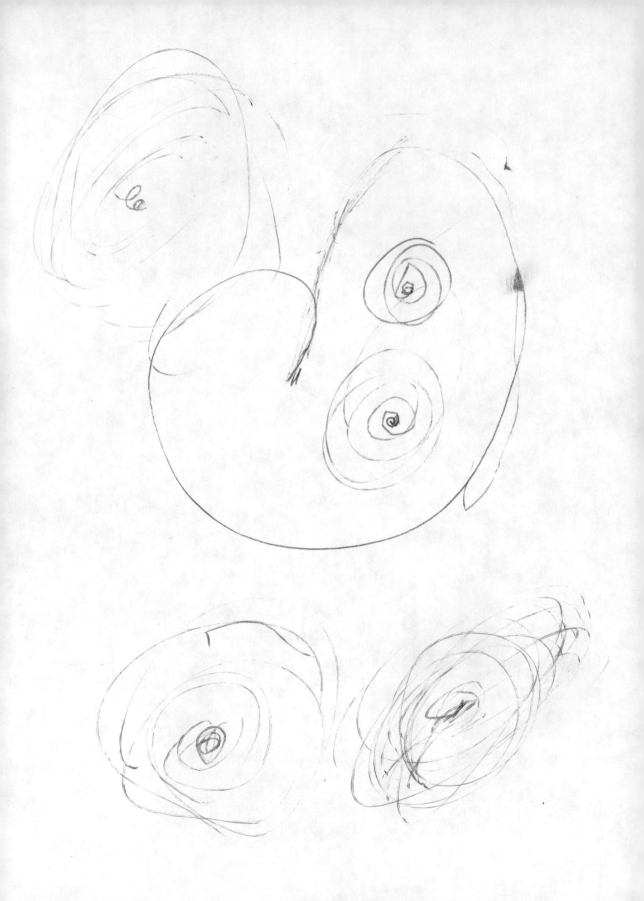